FLY FISHING
THE FLORIDA KEYS
THE GUIDES' GUIDE

"The Florida Keys . . .
a good place to fish for any fisherman with enough sense to hire a guide."

President Herbert Hoover ~ 1960

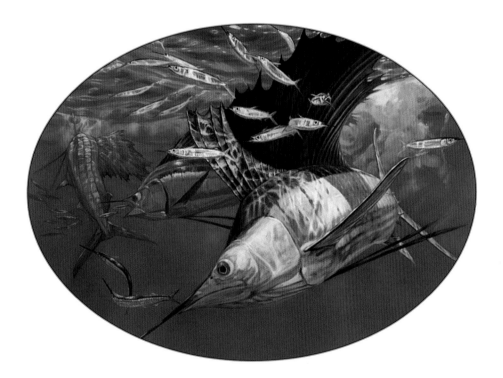

Skip Clement &
Andrew Derr

Foreword by Steve J. Kantner

Frank Amato
PORTLAND

SKIP CLEMENT

Skip grew up on Long Island, NY, starring in all the major sports at Westbury High School. He was offered several athletic scholarships in several sports. He chose the University of North Carolina where he starred in both football and track. In his senior year, he was drafted by the NFL Steelers and the, then, AFL Chargers. He chose Pittsburgh. It would be home for the next 30 years, and it would also be where he was introduced to fly fishing.

"I learned fly casting in my backyard, and fly tying and knot making in the cold winter months. The first few years of my fly fishing experiences were limited to the local streams and rivers of western PA. However, in the spring of 1970, a friend asked me to help him ready his summer cottage on Michigan's Lake Superior. Serendipitously, I brought along my fly rod and a few trout flies. My friend, a non-fisherman, said that there were trout in nearby Lake Superior feeder streams. With a few flies and a 6-weight I ventured off one afternoon to investigate a nearby stream. The trout looked awfully big—they were steelhead! That afternoon, and way undergunned, I fought and landed 3 double-digit fish. I had fished into darkness, and I was wet head to toe and nearly frozen. That one experience transformed me from a casual seasonal fisherman to a fanatic."

In the early 1970's, a local Pittsburgh dentist, Mike Fitzgerald, and his wife, Suzie, started a small outdoor travel company, Frontiers International. Skip and several friends engaged Frontiers to help them expand the scope of their fly fishing pursuits. For the next 20 or so years Skip and his friends would fish some of the world's richest fisheries: Iceland, New Zealand, most of South America and Latin America, the American west, Canada, Alaska, Caribbean, and the Florida Keys.

In the late 1990's, several years after Skip had retired to Ft. Lauderdale, FL, Andrew Derr, his stepson, became a Captain and guide in the Keys. It was there in the Keys that Andrew and Skip decided to chronicle the collective views of the guides and offshore captains about their fishery and how they fished for each species, then build it into a book about the Keys as a whole. Skip and Andrew resisted all temptations to write yet another misleading "X" marks the spot book.

Today, Skip, when he's not on the tennis court, fishes the Everglades with his friend, writer and guide, Steve Kantner.

Skip and Andrew's new book, *Fly Fishing The Everglades*, will be out in 2006.

ANDREW DERR

Andrew first fell in love with the sport while fly fishing in the Adirondack Mountains where he has summered since birth. It was there that he began tying flies and daydreaming of far-away tropical destinations where strong fish roam in shallow waters. He first bonefished while on a family vacation in the British West Indies and became enamored with the puzzles that flats fishing presents. Soon after graduating from the University of Vermont, where he majored in English, he moved to the Florida Keys, bought a flats boat and began fishing with locals in the northern Keys each year from November through May. He is an innovative fly tyer, USCG licensed captain and enthusiastic instructor. Andrew now resides in New York City fishing regularly for striped bass in the waters between there and the eastern end of Long Island. He still enjoys regular trips to the High Peaks region of the Adirondacks to fish the hallowed waters of the Ausable River system, as well as hundreds of small tributaries in search of brilliantly speckled brook trout.

Published in 2005 by
Frank Amato Publications, Inc.
PO Box 82112
Portland, Oregon 97282
(503) 653-8108
www.amatobooks.com

Softbound ISBN: 1-57188-342-8 • Softbound UPC: 0-81127-00176-7
Hardbound ISBN: 1-57188-343-6 • Hardbound UPC: 0-81127-00177-4

All photographs taken by the author unless otherwise noted.
Cover Art: Don Ray
Book Design: Tony Amato

Printed in Singapore

1 3 5 7 9 10 8 6 4 2

CONTENTS

FOREWORD

Fly-fishing the Florida Keys has become all the rage. With the amount of verbiage that's already been written about it, it's a wonder anyone finds something new to say. Nevertheless, I discovered that Skip Clement and Andrew Derr have done just that, and without degrading the resource or exploiting the captains who work the area professionally.

What they have accomplished (and I believe they have done a good job of it) is incorporate each aspect of Keys fishing into an updated compendium. At the same time, they maintain a historical perspective. As for the actual fishery, they treat it from a point of view of a guide, which makes uncommon sense.

Don't look for marked charts or GPS coordinates. Instead, consider the time Skip and Andrew spent fishing and interviewing guides (interspersed with frequent bouts of check writing), and how that qualifies them as navigators capable of steering us through murky waters without reading a map.

Top-notch captains provide verbal channel markers. Yet it's equally apparent the authors have both fished well and listened hard. In the process, they manage to boat enough information meat to satisfy beginning and expert anglers alike.

"*Fly Fishing The Florida Keys: The Guides Guide*"does not purport to be a fly-fishing text. However, read it with interest and you'll end-up tying knots that the top guides prefer, learn what "arriving prepared" really means, and that all guides are not created equal. Want more information? Look for pages full of strategic material and anecdotes galore. While they treat definitive subjects like how to choose a fly pattern or the biology of Keys game fish with the scrutiny they deserve, they never lose their laid-back style. I like that.

"*Fly Fishing The Florida Keys: The Guides Guide*" will serve you well as a handy reference manual for anyone interested in doing what the title suggests. I look forward to unearthing its treasures time and again.

Steve J. Kantner is Regional Editor of Florida Sportsman *Magazine. He's also a regular contributor to* Saltwater Flyfishing, Flyfishing in Saltwaters, Fly Rod & Reel, *and* Salt Water Sportsman *magazines. Steve is also the proprietor of Landcaptain, Inc., a South Florida-based, walk-in guide service. Currently, he teaches flycasting and lectures on fly-fishing-related subjects. Steve has appeared on TV several times, most notably with Andy Mill on OLN's "Sportsman's Journal."*

—*Steve J. Kantner*

INTRODUCTION

This book is about three elements that define the Keys: its bountiful fishery, singular history, and the rich, compound other-worldliness of its environment.

The fishing coverage in this book is not the narrower story of a single messenger, but the broader chronicle of many. For the first time, expert fly fishing captains, from Biscayne Bay to Key West, share their knowledge of the Florida Keys fishery. They explain how they find each species of game fish, approach them, tease them into a biting mood, and also define what fly pattern types are best in a variety of situations. They make clear how to cast for each species, how to manipulate the fly, and when and how to set the hook, as well as how to land them. Refreshingly, your mentor captains put into perspective just what arriving in the Keys ready to go fly fishing really means. They also make familiar the generally unfamiliar need-to-know details that spell the difference between catching and losing fish, and pull no punches when it comes to telling just what fly fishermen are up against in the complex fishery of the Florida Keys.

The history chapter puts the reader in touch with where he is, connects him to the past, and provides an insiders' view of today's still singular end-of-the-road place that is very much about a fishery, and an environment of extraordinary importance.

The environment chapter invites discovery of the unseen, reexamines the easily seen, and sheds light on the delicate ecological balance of one of the world's most unusual coordinates.

The practical information coverage is about need-to-know information for the sport fisherman. It also looks at some of the best sites to visit on the rare rainy day, reviews a few of the historically exceptional accommodations, and a handful of the outstanding dining opportunities found in the Keys.

Anyone who visits the Florida Keys can only have visceral memories that replay in color. This book expresses the remarkable phenomena of colors found in the Keys through the incredible art work of Don Ray, Diane Rome Peebles, Klaus Schuler, Frank Zorman, and the photography of Stephen Frink.

ACKNOWLEDGEMENTS

Authors of non-fiction books must accept the fact that they will be defeated in any attempt to thank, appropriately, all those who helped along the way. We are not an exception.

Our first thanks is clearly due those that helped us the most, the expert fly fishing captains of the Florida Keys. They, thankfully, delivered a real-time picture of the entire Keys fishery, and how they go about the business of catching each of the game fish species found in their waters. A true first.

Without any hesitation we also thank your most certain hosts when in the Keys, the five legitimate fly fishing outfitters, fly shops, and charter marinas in the Keys: The Florida Keys Outfitters in Islamorada, World Wide Sportsman in Islamorada, Seaboots Charters & Outfitters on Big Pine Key, Bud n' Mary's Marina in Islamorada, and The Saltwater Angler in Key West.

The individuals that helped us produce a fly fishing picture of the Keys fishery for you are: Sandy Moret, Tim Borski, Christina Sharpe, Sue Moret, and captains: Gary Ellis, Doug Berry, Skip Nielsen, Bob "RT" Trosset, Paul Dixon, Allan Finkelman, Tim Carlile, Tom Rowland, Duane Baker, Paul Dixon, Lenny Moffo, Bill Curtis, Jim Sharpe, Richard Stanczyk, George Hommell, Jr., Dustin Huff, Jeffrey Cardenas and many, many more.

With special mention we thank Captain Lenny Moffo. He tied dozens of flies for us, and then, tirelessly pho-

tographed all of them. Also, Captain Paul Dixon who, with a great sense of humour and enthusiasm, piloted us into seldom seen waters to pursue seldom found species.

When we began writing our book, we were very much less than credentialed, and as such, not always greeted openly. That was not the case with the International Game Fish Association. The I. G. F. A's fish biologist, Glenda Kelley, and librarian, Gail Morchow, treated us royally from the get-go. They gave us their valuable time, pointed us in the right direction, loaned us some wonderful archive photos, and granted us unrestricted access to the fabulous E. K. Harry Library of Fishes. We also want to thank The Billfish Foundation for providing staff time, and sharing research findings, papers and publications.

We can not thank our neighbor, Captain Steve Kantner (The Land Captain), enough. Steve always, and willingly, took time from his own writing schedule, guiding commitments, video shoots and fishing show obligations to advise us, and edit many of the technical aspects of our book.

We are without words when it comes to thanking artists Don Ray, and Diane Rome Peebles. Their respective art and illustrations are flawless references of the game fish found in the Keys fishery. Their collective work contributes enormously to our book.

With the help of Key Largo photographer Stephen Frink, the most well known underwater photographer in the world, and his assistant, Liz Johnson, we are able to share with you a fraction of Stephen's spectacular photographic collection on the Keys.

It would be hard to thank South Florida's premier watercolorist, Klaus Schuler, enough for his contributions. Klaus' now famous, *On The Water's Edge Series*, captures the very essence of the Keys through its landmarks. His work adds immeasurably to enlivening the history chapter.

We were extremely fortunate to get South Florida's top illustrator, Frank Zorman, to help with the gritty task of drawing knots illustrations, flies and maps. Frank may have drawn the best knot tying instructions yet put to paper, and his loose watercolor interpretation of the Keys geography provides readers with a totally uncluttered look at the whole landscape. His fly illustrations of Captain Lenny Moffo's flies are worthy of a separate book.

No book that included a reference to the Keys history could approach relevant without the input of Jerry Wilkinson, overview of Tom Hambright or a referring to John Viele's books. Jerry is president of the Upper Keys Historical Society, Tom Hambright is the head of the Monroe County Library's (Key West) historical section, and John Viele is the author of three volumes of works on Keys history. We thank them for all for their contributions to our history chapter, and for contributing private and public domain photos.

We were very fortunate to be able to share just a miniscule portion of Seth Bramson's coveted photo and memorabilia collection. He, and his wife Myrna, have the world's largest collection of photos, and memorabilia, on the Florida East Coast Railroad.

Special thanks goes to Julie Olsen, Director of Public Relations for Cheeca Lodge. She shared her authored paper on the historic property, took time to escort us around the property, and put a perspective on the lodge's long association with sport fishing in the Keys: tournaments, celebrity fishermen, Sandy Moret's fly fishing school, Curt Gowdy Lounge, and home to Gary Ellis' radio show. We also thank Chris Everhart, CCM and GM of KLAC. Chris, in true Keys style, loaned us his own copy of *Key Largo Anglers Club History* (Roger Williams, III and Sue Poyntz Williams), and entrusted us with rare club photos, as well as let us tour the hallowed old-club grounds and main lodge.

A very warm thanks to the friendliest couple in the Florida Keys, Lloyd and Miriam Good, owners of the Sugar Loaf Lodge, Sugarloaf Key, FL. Miriam took time out of her hectic schedule to escort us around their historic 400 acre lodge property, and Lloyd was our willing commentator on all manner of Florida Keys subjects. Too, we thank the Good's friends, Herb and Kitty Herbert, for their input on Lower Keys historical facts and for sharing their knowledge of the Keys.

We also thank the Florida Keys National Marine Sanctuary's, Lt. Commander Dave Savage. He provided us with sanctuary documents, photos, and a real overview of what lies ahead for both the sanctuary, the Everglades, Florida Bay, and the Florida Keys.

Additionally, we thank the following for their interview time, publications, and papers: The University of Miami's RSMAS (Marine Biology and Fisheries group), Florida Institute of Technology (Harbor Branch Oceanographic Institution), Florida Marine Research Institute, the University of South Florida, Florida State University (FSU Marine Lab), and Karen Burns (Mote Marine Laboratory) for her many references, and referrals. Also, the National Marine Fisheries Service, Florida Fish and Wildlife, Gulf Coast University, South Florida Water Management, Gulf of Mexico Fishery Management Council, South Atlantic and the Fishery Management Council.

We especially thank Al Adams, Angler Outreach, Florida Fish and Wildlife Conservation Commission, Tallahassee, FL, for his enthusiasm, tireless cooperation and shared knowledge of sport fishing.

A very special thank you goes to Dr. Bob Halley, and Dr. Eugene Shinn (USGS), for providing their respective and brilliant papers on the geologic history of the Keys, geologic history and current benthic characteristics of Florida Bay.

Many thanks to Keys engineer, John Larkin, Environmental Tactics, Inc., Big Pine Key, for his insights into the Keys' past waste water treatment problems, overview on waste management and for providing access to water quality test reports. The latter, a rare and eye-opening view of the politics of the environment.

We are, and will forever be, in the debt of our editor, Joanne Everett. She came to the edit rescue just when we were dealt the worst of hands. Joanne skillfully took over the story, edited it, masterfully coached us to a better story, and encouraged us to stay the intended course. Her efforts, and endless enthusiasm pushed us, and this book over the top and into print.

THE FLORIDA KEYS

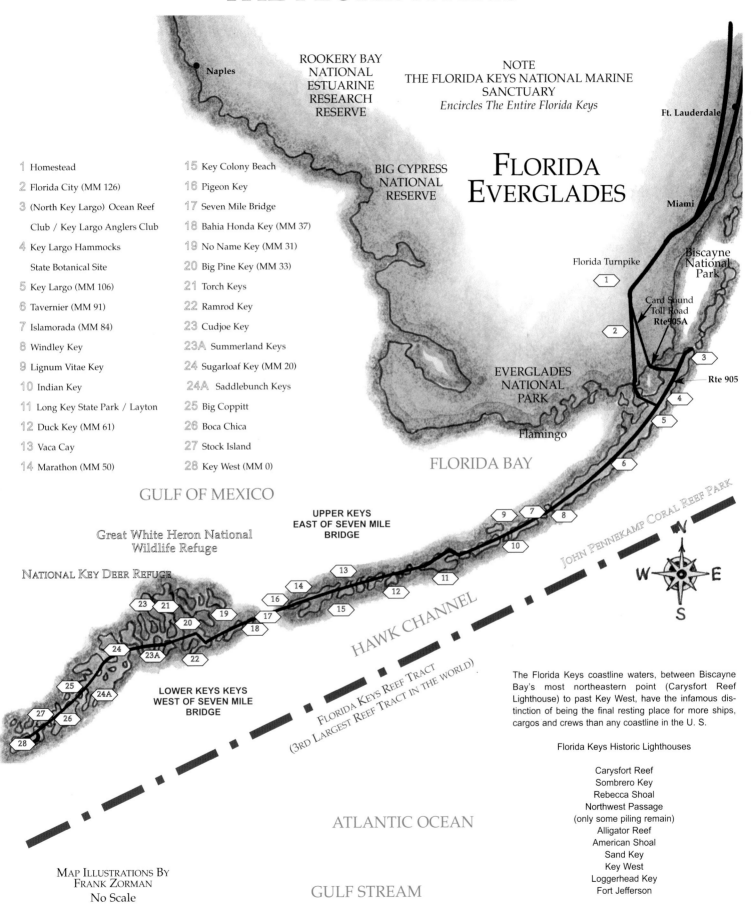

Naples

ROOKERY BAY
NATIONAL
ESTUARINE
RESEARCH
RESERVE

NOTE
THE FLORIDA KEYS NATIONAL MARINE
SANCTUARY
Encircles The Entire Florida Keys

Ft. Lauderdale

BIG CYPRESS
NATIONAL
RESERVE

FLORIDA
EVERGLADES

Miami

1 Homestead

2 Florida City (MM 126)

3 (North Key Largo) Ocean Reef
Club / Key Largo Anglers Club

4 Key Largo Hammocks
State Botanical Site

5 Key Largo (MM 106)

6 Tavernier (MM 91)

7 Islamorada (MM 84)

8 Windley Key

9 Lignum Vitae Key

10 Indian Key

11 Long Key State Park / Layton

12 Duck Key (MM 61)

13 Vaca Cay

14 Marathon (MM 50)

15 Key Colony Beach

16 Pigeon Key

17 Seven Mile Bridge

18 Bahia Honda Key (MM 37)

19 No Name Key (MM 31)

20 Big Pine Key (MM 33)

21 Torch Keys

22 Ramrod Key

23 Cudjoe Key

23A Summerland Keys

24 Sugarloaf Key (MM 20)

24A Saddlebunch Keys

25 Big Coppitt

26 Boca Chica

27 Stock Island

28 Key West (MM 0)

Florida Turnpike

Biscayne
National
Park

Card Sound
Toll Road
Rte 905A

Rte 905

EVERGLADES
NATIONAL
PARK

Flamingo

FLORIDA BAY

GULF OF MEXICO

UPPER KEYS
EAST OF SEVEN MILE
BRIDGE

Great White Heron National
Wildlife Refuge

John Pennekamp Coral Reef Park

National Key Deer Refuge

HAWK CHANNEL

LOWER KEYS KEYS
WEST OF SEVEN MILE
BRIDGE

Florida Keys Reef Tract
(3rd Largest Reef Tract In The World)

The Florida Keys coastline waters, between Biscayne
Bay's most northeastern point (Carysfort Reef
Lighthouse) to past Key West, have the infamous distinction of being the final resting place for more ships,
cargos and crews than any coastline in the U. S.

Florida Keys Historic Lighthouses

Carysfort Reef
Sombrero Key
Rebecca Shoal
Northwest Passage
(only some piling remain)
Alligator Reef
American Shoal
Sand Key
Key West
Loggerhead Key
Fort Jefferson

ATLANTIC OCEAN

MAP ILLUSTRATIONS BY
FRANK ZORMAN
No Scale

GULF STREAM

CHAPTER I

A BRIEF HISTORY OF THE FLORIDA KEYS
People, Places And Events That Shaped A Fisherman's Paradise.

SOUTH AMERICAN VISITORS

There are many theories, along with well established facts, about aboriginal peoples in the Florida Keys. One theory is that the Calusa and Tequesta tribes used the Keys for fishing (and hunting), populating the Keys with small tribal sub-groups that stayed for only brief periods of time to advantage fish and game migrations. There are many known Indian midden / settlements on the Keys with some evidence to support other aboriginal groups having used the Keys as well. One major site is on the upper tip of Upper Matecumbe Key and another on the lower tip of Upper Matecumbe Key. However, the preponderance of archeological evidence has long since been buried by a rising sea.

It is roundly believed the Calusa were distinguished from other Indian groups, and tribes, by their organizational skills. They had very elaborate political, social and trade networks, produced highly stylized carvings, and their maize horticulture was singular to them. The latter is strikingly similar to that developed on the savannahs of northern South America by indigenous Indians there. The suggestion is strong that Calusa migrated north to Florida. The only South American peoples theorized to have done so.

THE FIRST LIGHT-TACKLE FISHERMEN

Much of our ballyhooed modern fishing techniques and inventions were just every day stuff for the Calusa Indians, whom many historians believe were much advanced in their fish catching skills. The Calusa had specialized fishermen whose job it was to provide that staple. Fish and shellfish were true staples for all the coastal Florida Indians.

An archaeological dig in the Pacific Northwest unearthed a man buried with his afterlife needs, including his tackle box, which had 82 items. Included were 30 hooks (circular hooks and composite hooks plus barbs), drills, knives, fish scaler, flake tools for cutting and scraping, abrader for sharpening hooks and a natural gum-like substance used to attach hooks and sinkers to fishing line. Sinkers were elongated, made of stone and carved to look like fish. Some sinkers had holes in them, others grooves where line was kept in place by the gum material. Carbon dating put the dig elements in use around 10,000 years ago.

Florida's own archaeological digs confirm evidence of sophisticated fishing by its indigenous peoples as well dating back to over 10,000 years ago. Common to all the advanced aboriginal maritime cultures, as first reported

Carved wooden eagle circa 2,000 years ago. Made by burning then carving with a cutting tool made from shark teeth. Fish catching and hunting were believed to have been assigned tasks in this structured Calusa Indian culture. The Calusa, along with Tequestas, (Miami and just north of it), according to scholars, probably made seasonal visits to the Keys and suggest there were fixed camps there that enabled them to secure fish and game. It is not understood how, if at all, game and fish were preserved. Some scholars theorize that small bands or even the entire tribe went along with the fishing and hunting specialists.

in the 1700's, were 3 types of hooks: gorges, composite hooks and one-piece hooks. Gorges were bait-holding mechanisms that allowed the fish to swallow. When tugged on, the gorge got stuck in the fish's throat. Composite hooks were forked tree branches of springy wood with barbed points from a deer bone attached to the short fork by a gum-like material. Hook shanks showed evidence of line attached, suggesting deep-water fishing. One-piece hooks, carved of animal bone, are strikingly resemblant of today's modern designs. Also found (Marco Island) were items that suggest artificial lures were used along with reels made of columellae (spiralled center of a large conch shell). There is also strong evidence to suggest trolling mechanisms were employed. The three common hooks were used on trot lines or handlines.

Spears, however, were the most common method of fish catching in the Keys as the fish were quite abundant. Spears were also the earliest used tool for fish harvesting. There were 3 types of spears: simple spear, harpoon and leister. A spear was wood shafted with a sharpened point of the same wood, or with an attached stone or bone as point (billfish bill or stingray spine). Harpoons had a point made of animal bone (deer or alligator). The harpoon was attached to the thrower by line that served as a retrieving device. A leister was a combination harpoon and spear with 3 or more prongs. The center prong was a spear and penetrated. The other prongs were flexible and held the fish for retrieving. Florida Indians also mastered the use of a weir and fish traps, but evidence of this is only well north of the Keys. There is no evidence that Calusa or other indigenous Indians anywhere used a pole for fishing (Egyptians had fishing poles 4,000 years ago).

DEATH OF A CULTURE

The Calusa, and other tribes, all but disappeared soon after contact with Europeans. By the 1700's, they were all but gone. They were either overtaken by influenza, smallpox, measles, the common cold, enslaved or mixed with other aboriginal Indian tribes and later became Seminoles.

UNDEFEATED

There were many aboriginal tribes in Florida (see map), but Seminoles were not, originally, one of them. Seminoles are a mix of Creek Indians from Georgia and Alabama forced south to seek new lands because of internal Indian conflicts and because of confrontations with white settlers. When they moved into Florida, escaped slaves, indigenous Yuchis & Yamasses and other aboriginal remnants attached themselves and were, collectively, called Seminoles by whites. The name Seminole, like most Indian tribal designations, are not names Indians ever called themselves. A $20,000,000 bankroll, a nation behind the U. S. army, and our best generals on the mound were never able to defeat the Seminole Nation. The war's end: unaccounted for dead, 50 Seminoles captured and 20 canoes confiscated. Oceola, unfairly imprisoned, died a captive, but became a legend and martyr, as well as an example of just how unreliable a forked tongue can be.

UPPER KEYS

North Key Largo (Ocean Reef Club), Key Largo (John Pennekamp Coral Reef Park), Tavenier, Plantation Key, Upper Matecumbe Key, Islamorada, Lignum Vitae Key, Indian Key, Lower Matecumbe Key.

"CHEESEBURGERS IN PARADISE"

Each year over 2,500,000 people come to visit the 79,589 (2000 census) inhabitants of the Florida Keys. That all works out to 70.4 house guests per year for every (2.24 avg./census) household in the Florida Keys! Their house guest-visitors collectively spend $2.1 billion each year.

People come from around the world to take in the 1,700 Caribbean-like islands (only 822 islands have names that appear on nautical charts) that make up the Florida Keys and to stay on one or more of the 32 inhabited islands during their visit.

The Florida Keys span around 220 miles in an arc (northeast to southwest) between the southern tip of Key Biscayne (south of Miami) to the Dry Tortugas Islands, west of Key West. One hundred and twenty six (126) miles is the paved Overseas Highway with 42 bridges connecting its land falls, and another 70 water miles make up the distance from Key West to the Dry Tortugas. The most northeastern extreme of the Florida Keys: Old Rhodes Key, Elliott Key, Sands Keys and into Biscayne Bay are not accessible by road.

The Florida Keys are totally bounded by water and its history written around it. To the north, the Gulf of Mexico, Florida Bay, and the Everglades. The latter of collection land hammocks and slough-like rivers (Taylor and Shark) that sift through a unique plain of grasses and drain into Florida Bay. In practical Keys-speak locator terminology, any place north of the Overseas Highway is called bayside and its waters referred to as backcountry. To the south, the Atlantic and Straits of Florida side are called oceanside. The oceanside from land to the coral reefs is Hawk Channel, which runs the length of the Keys. Beyond Hawk Channel are the coral reefs and beyond them the sharply color contrasted blue water of the tropical Gulf Stream, which Hemingway dubbed, " . . . *the great, blue river* . . .". The 40-or-so-mile-wide Gulf Stream current influences the greatness of deep-sea fishing and the magnificence of Keys fishing in general, as well as the weather of two continents.

NORTH KEY LARGO

The early history of North Key Largo is much like the rest of the Keys, except Key West. Pioneer homesteaders attempted to make a living at farming, fishing and wrecking. Flagler's railroad extension did not much influence North Key Largo. The Ocean Reef Club, a rather impressive imposition on the nature of things, is about the only land-use change that has significantly impacted North Key Largo in over a century. A dozen or so hurricanes have, of course, done a fair bit of landscaping. To get to North Key Largo choose Card Sound Road at Florida City just after the FL Turnpike ends. At the Card Sound Road

(Rte. 905A) terminus you can only choose to go left or right on 905. Left to the Ocean Reef Club or right, which will deposit you in Key Largo. Check out the botanical park on 905 (oceanside) a few miles from Key Largo. Stopping is a truly worthwhile investment of time.

KEY LARGO ANGLERS CLUB . . . STILL TICKING

The Key Largo Anglers Club is located in North Key Largo. It is the oldest surviving fishing club in the Florida Keys and one of the oldest in the world. The KLAC is a private club with a history that dates back to 1885. It matured into a traditional fishing club along the way and is now a valuable part of Florida Keys history. The club remains dedicated to sport fishing. Its past fishermen (and women) membership roster is filled with names that colored the future of the nation: Hoover, Eisenhower, Nixon, Ford (as in cars) and another Hoover (as in vacuums). There were many other early and mid-century industrialist family names, principally Midwestern socially elect. KLAC, as a matter of note, has outlasted almost everything on the Keys except for a few lighthouses and Whitehead's platting of Key West's Old Town. The club remains unknown to even long-time Conch residents. Its three hundred or so members are well practiced at keeping it that way. Today, the club's greatest charm is manifested in its management; self effacing in a way that does not suggest the opposite. A true reflection of its members.

Individual members, member teams and the club itself have not been insulated from the rigors of fishing tournament circles in the Keys or the Caribbean. Most members are serious fishermen and some have held world-record catches for periods of time. The clubs internal tournament records suggest it could best most saltwater fishing clubs in the world. Local guides provide the best possible compliment, *"The (Key Largo Anglers Club) members have the right stuff; all damn good revelers and tellers of tall fishing tales."* Unquestionable proof of the clubs authenticity.

In the 1980's, the KLAC faced a life-threatening survival test when its principal benefactress died. A power take-over from the Ocean Reef Club was launched. Loyalties were tested, and an end to the storied fishing-

Jewfish Creek.

club lifestyle that members had for so many years managed to create and nurture was in danger of social reengineering. *Nouveau* would replace ancient rites, events that honored the clubs ancestors would be replaced with posturing, and most assuredly, an all-too-small, funky bar with walls that knew the tales of many old men and the sea would have to go. Fortunately, the bar still serves, and rites have been preserved.

After a few years of tumult and tension, the cavalry finally arrived and a Grand Dame of fishing clubs was saved from extinction, history preserved . . . still ticking.

KEY LARGO - MM 106 TO 95

Key Largo, for all practical purposes, is embarkation point to the Florida Keys. Its physical appearance may greatly diminish expectations for visitors looking for idyllic Caribbean settings, not strip malls. Not to worry, the Keys are very democratic and cinderblock architecture and tacky strip malls go all the way to Key West. Hidden behind the gaudy strip malls along the way are the panoramas of Florida Bay, an ethereal backcountry, a surreal-like Everglades, never-ending grand-slam flats, the gamefish highway of the Gulf Stream and magnificent coral reefs. There are also some marvelous restaurants, tasteful and pleasant accommodations, fitting Keys architecture, but always the laid back and accommodating Keys inhabitants. The endemic beauty of the Florida Keys has not been spoiled and you will not be disappointed. For pure anomaly to all this drunken planning committee development one faces along the Overseas Highway, there are postcard-like visceral interruptions to it all awaiting anyone who cares to take in the dramatic horizon while crossing any of the over-the-sea bridges. Forty-two bridges stitch the Keys together and make up 15% of the entire road length of the Overseas Highway.

Today, Key Largo is probably best known as the dive capital of the Keys. It is generally overlooked by serious fly-fishing visitors in favor of points westerly. A great mistake. Key Largo has prolific gamefish waters and passing them up is like skipping eastern Idaho in favor of Montana. Key Largo's focal point remains, however, diving and John Pennekamp Coral Reef State Park. A park that extends to a 3-mile limit (21 miles - from Carysfort Reef to Molasses Reef and inshore to the coastline) with the Key Largo National Marine Sanctuary extending it to a 6-mile limit.

John Pennekamp, an outspoken Miami newspaper editor, was an advocate for the preservation of the coral reefs and the Everglades, and is credited with being the prime mover and shaker in the establishment of both John Pennekamp Coral Reef State Park (1960) and the Everglades National Park (1947). Marjory Stoneman Douglas made the latter famous by taking the word swamp out of the Everglades in her world-famous book, *The Everglades: River Of Grass*.

TAVENIER - MM 94 TO 91

Tavenier was first a wreckers colony utilizing the protective anchorage of Tavenier Key. It was settled as Lowesport in 1864 and then it became Planter, a homestead that laid claim to having the only post office between Miami and Key West. Mr. Flagler's railroad

President Hoover, KLAC Commodore past, sits in front of the club's fishing tournament catch results tote board while preparing for a CBS interview. Hoover was an avid and accomplished sport fisherman of many a venue, but never fished without a guide, according to memoirs (Hoover Library).

claimed a different piece of real estate near Planter property and called it Tavenier, leaving Planter for history buffs and an obscure neighborhood park site (Harry Harris Park). Several railroad-era historic homes remain. One slightly post-era house is that of Robert Porter Allen, author of *Roseate Spoonbill* (1942). He purchased the house in the 40's. A true surviving era piece of real estate is the more visible Tavenier Hotel (MM 91.8 oceanside), which was under construction when the '35 hurricane hit. It was designed to be a theater, but served as a hospital after the '35 hurricane and is now a motel.

UPPER MATECUMBE KEY

Upper Matecumbe was the signature site of the infamous 1935 Labor Day hurricane. By mid-afternoon that Labor Day, stranded Keys RR personnel (Depression-era government workers), and Islamorada inhabitants finally made contact with FECRR offices in Miami. According to Miami newspaper reports, J. J. Haycroft, the train's engineer, was dispatched for a rescue mission a short time after 3:10PM with eleven rail cars. At Homestead, Mr. Haycroft reversed the position of the locomotive and tender so he could use lights on the return. By the time the rescue train reached the Upper Keys in the early evening, the storm had already slowed progress, considerably. One delay, 3 miles from Islamorada, accounted for a lost hour because of a sagging gravel pit boom line. Rain water, Mr. Haycroft stated, had already covered most of the rail line and debris littered the tracks. By late evening (no time mentioned in several reportages), the hurricane had reached full force and the much delayed rescue train finally made it to Islamorada. According to survivors, the

Photographer G. W. Roemer captures the social implications of the Key Largo Anglers Club in 1932, well before it became a true members-only club. For this posed shot, models were imported from Miami, as were many of the guests. The shot delivers the desired beautiful people image. This Sunday edition photo was followed by a ta-ta story.

Henry Flagler (top hat center) meets with staff in Key Largo at a place called Railroad Flats on December 17, 1906.

Florida Keys Fishing Guides Association and Sandy Moret's Florida Keys Outfitters. More charter captains make Islamorada home port than any single place known to man. At any sit-down establishment in town, without eavesdropping, you can overhear more opinions about fly fishing and fly patterns than there are books written on the subjects.

THE ISLAMORADA FISHING CLUB
Thanks to a very few, the founders of The Islamorada Fishing Club, millions get to enjoy great fishing in the backcountry of Florida Bay and the Everglades Park. Back in 1950, a small group of professional guides and dedicated sport fishermen, and women, put their earned respect on-the-line as hard currency. They put together a then controversial plan to restrict their own

train, on its return, initially missed the stop at Upper Matecumbe because of storm blindness. When it maneuvered back to pick up its screaming and desperate human cargo, an 18-foot tidal wave struck. It destroyed everything standing between Long Key and Tavenier. Amazingly, there were survivors to tell the story.

The much debated count of those who perished in the '35 hurricane ranges from 408 (NOAA) to the actual coroner's report of 423. The latter stating 164 civilians and 259 veterans. Veterans were employed during the Depression to build the Overseas Highway, which would replace the ferry system.

ISLAMORADA - MM 85 TO 66
Sport fishing gets noticed here, evidenced by Islamorada's proclaiming itself the "Sportfishing Capital Of The World" as you enter its domain. The proclamation is worthy as fly fishing celebrities seem to congregate here. Sandy Moret's Florida Fly Fishing School, probably the best saltwater fly casting & fishing school in the world, is here along with its frequenters: Chico Fernandez, Flip Pallot (ESPN's Walker Cay Chronicles), Stu Apte, Steve Huff, Rick Ruoff, Jose Wejebe and Steve Rajeff (world distance fly-casting champion) and many others. It is also home to the

Bogart & Bacall in a scene from the 1948 movie, *Key Largo*. Neither actor ever set foot in the Keys. In 1952, Rock Harbor was renamed Key Largo. The movie made famous the Caribbean Club, which is still in operation.

Aftermath of the '35 hurricane left tons and tons of Pittsburgh rail car steel and iron flipped like duck pins, and 40 miles of tracks were twisted like pretzels. Not much remained standing in the aftermath except the locomotive, tender car, the badly damaged house of Leo Johnson (the house still exists) and a grave marker of a 15-year-old child, Dolores Pinder (the stone angel sits, today, in Pioneer Cemetery next to Checca Lodge at MM #81.5). The bridges withstood the test, but the embankments for the rail-line dammed water and became, eventually, the lead battering ram of built-up debris when the 18-foot tidal wave retreated back to the Atlantic Ocean. Both photos show the aftermath evidence of the 1935 Labor Day hurricane. The unnamed hurricane registered the lowest barometric pressure ever recorded in the northern hemisphere, at that time, 26.36.

Counting and dealing with too many dead. Bodies had to be cremated on common funeral pyres. Remains and bodies were found months, even years later in Florida Bay.

William Krome, a Cornell University schooled engineer, became the hands-on man that would finish the RR extension. J. C. Meredith, Flagler's chief engineer, died in 1909, leaving many to believe the RR extension would never get finished. Krome, literally, stepped up to the plate and finished the project a year to the day ahead of schedule. The project, in the minds of many, compared as a feat to that of the Panama Canal project. In any event, it was a marvel of human effort, engineering, ingenuity, dogged determination and aspects of character fast fading from the American Pie in us all.

J. C. MEREDITH

WILLIAM KROME

Keys neighbors from commercially harvesting the Florida Bay. Their plan would, forever, favorably impact the future of the Everglades Park. Their call to arms was out of concern for the future of a fishery they understood could not tolerate plundering harvests of shrimp and fish stocks, or be sustained as an environmental treasure, if development of any kind were allowed a foothold. They articulately delivered a message that was accepted, in its first and essentially only draft, by commercial fishing interests, Everglades Park management and the U. S. Department of Agriculture. Can anyone imagine what the Florida Bay would have become if it had been plundered of its bounty by commercial fishing interests or the southern tier of the Everglades had been developed like the Keys?

The Islamorada Fishing Club's past and present membership roles are impressive. The member list reads like a Who's Who of fly fishing salt water, a Hall of Fame kind of place that nobody really knows much about. Its members are not at all impressed with themselves and about as far from having celebrity neuroses as any on earth. The highly principled men and women who are today's members are just as dedicated to the club's venerable creed as its founders. The Islamorada Fishing Club creed reads: *"Believing as we do, that fishing is one of the greatest and most beneficial sports on earth, we mutually resolve and steadfastly swear to do everything in our power to help protect, preserve and guard the various game fishes we go for, wherever they may be and wherever we may fish."* No fishing club in the Keys, probably the U. S. and quite possibly world, has done more to keep fishing property environmentally safe, and out of the wrong hands than the Islamorada Fishing Club. Thanks! IFC, MM 82.5 Bayside, 305/664 4735 or on-line at www.islamoradafishingclub.com.

LIGNUM VITAE KEY

Lignum Vitae is an island that has survived man's interventions to be a biologist's and botanist's treasury. Despite many abuses suffered, it is the only true remaining link to what the Florida Keys was 500 years ago. At 18 feet or so above sea level, it is one of the highest pieces of real estate on the Keys (Windley Key boasts 17 feet, and property just about where the Monroe County Library sits in Key West is 18 feet above sea level). Originally, Lignum Vitae was a thick hardwood hammock and even though timbered by the Spanish in the 1700's it still is considered virgin forest. Lignum Vitae is a dense, resin-rich wood with 30% by volume of *guaiac gum*, coveted by boat builders due to its almost permanent resistance to rot and worms. The Nature Conservancy bought Lignum Vitae from its private owners, two Miami dentists and a Homestead farmer, in 1970 and turned it over to the state. You can visit by boat, daily.

INDIAN KEY

Indian Key is also uninhabited and visitable daily. Indian Key has produced more fables than told by Aesop and certainly remains the most historically storied of the Upper Keys. The Key got its name from its tragic past. Some accounts state that 400 shipwrecked French soldiers were slaughtered there by Calusa Indians in the late 1700's (a 1775 account by Bernard Romans states, however, only that the assailants were men and there was no mention of a slaughter). Around 1831, much of the 11-acre island was purchased by Jacob Housman, a wrecker who reconnoitered there to evade Key West's new salvage laws. One of several homes there was occupied by Dr. Henry Perrine, a medical doctor posthumously recognized as a world-class botanist.

In the 1840's, Housman's wrecker colony was overrun by Seminoles who were at war with the U. S. Some accounts suggest as many as 55 inhabitants were killed, others say 5. Amongst the dead was, however, Dr. Henry Perrine. Paradoxically, Housman, who wanted to impose a bounty on Indians, as opposed to Perrine who often treated and respected Indians, escaped back into the Key West salvage business only to die in a ship's accident less than a year later. Another settlement was established in the 1870's to build ships. Its craftsman, however, were only noted for constructing the Alligator Reef Lighthouse.

In the 1930's and 40's, after years of abandonment, treasure hunters plundered Indian Key for its wealth of colonial artifacts and left the place deflowered of everything but its brutal history.

LONG KEY - HALF WAY

The Florida East Coast Railroad made a fixed camp here by 1906 to build the first of three long, over-the-sea crossings. The Long Key Viaduct would connect today's Upper Keys to the Middle Keys. Railroad housing was established in cottages with additional quarters set up on barges called quarterboats. The latter provided sleeping quarters, offices built atop and dining as well as kitchen facilities in the hull below. After the viaduct was finished, the campsite (a coconut grove since 1880) was upscaled with a deluxe lodge called, Long Key Fishing Camp. The lodge, designed to meet the needs of rich and famous rail passengers of the day, even had its own narrow gage railine (shuttle). The fishing camp soon evolved into a club (Long Key Fishing Club), and thanks to Zane Grey's writing about it, the world would come to know the Florida Keys as a bountiful sportfishing destination.

LONG KEY FISHING CLUB

Zane Grey, a dentist from Zanesville, Ohio, and granddaddy of the western novel, was a frequenter at the Long Key Fishing Club after he and his brother, RC

Indian Key. Photo taken in the 1950's.

FROM THE COLLECTION OF JERRY WILKINSON WWW.KEYSHISTORY.ORG

TIDBITS
THERE ARE 42 BRIDGES IN THE
FLORIDA KEYS THAT CONNECT 100 ISLANDS

Mile Marker	Bridge Name	Span Feet
106	1. Jewfish Creek Drawbridge	223'
103.5	2. Key Largo Cut	360'
91	3. Tavenier Creek	133'
86	4. Snake Creek	192'
84	5. Whale Harbor	616'
80	6. Tea Table Relief	22'
79	7. Tea Table	614'
78	8. Indian Key	2,004'
77.8	9. Lignum Vitae	790'
73	10. Channel 2	1,720'
71	11. Channel 5	4,516'
65	12. Long Key	11,960'
61	13. Tom's Harbor 3	1,209'
60	14. Tom's Harbor 4	1,395'
53	15. Vaca Cut	120'
47	16. 7 Mile	35,716'
39.5	17. Little Duck Missouri	800'
39	18. Missouri - Ohio	1,394'
38	19. Ohio - Bahia Honda	1,005'
36	20. Bahia Honda	5,356'
33.5	21. Spanish Harbor	3,311'
29.5	22. North Pine	620'
28.5	23. South Pine	806'
28	24. Torch Key Viaduct	779'
27.5	25. Torch - Ramrod	615'
26	26. Niles Channel	4,433'
23.5	27. Kemp's Channel	992'
20	28. Bow Channel	1,302'
18.5	29. Park	779'
18	30. North Harris	390'
17.5	31. Harris Gap	37'
16	32. Harris	390'
15.5	33. Lower Sugarloaf	1,210'
14.5	34. Saddle Bunch 2	554'
14	35. Saddle Bunch 3	656'
13	36. Saddle Bunch 4	800'
12.5	37. Saddle Bunch 5	800'
11.8	38. Shark Channel	1,989'
10	39. Rockland Channel	1,230'
6	40. Boca Chica	2,573'
5	41. Stock Island	360'
4	42. Key West	159'

• Three bridges are National Historic Sites: Old Seven Mile Bridge, Bahia Honda Key and Long Key.

• 18.8 miles of the 126 miles of Overseas Highway are on bridges, about 15% of total travel is spent on bridges.

FLY-FISHING THE FLORIDA KEYS: THE GUIDES' GUIDE

Top: Islamorada s Bud n Mary s.
2nd: Papa Joe s, another famous Islamorada stop.
3rd: The epicenter of fishing speak is Islamorada s famous Lorelei s Bar & Restaurant. A top hangout for a cold one after work and home port for several Keys fly fishing guides. It is a real Keys kind of place and a great bayside spot. It is also next door to the Islamorada Fishing Club.
Bottom: Islamorada Fish Company, an institution known for having the best fish sandwich in the Upper Keys.

(Roemer) discovered it quite by chance. In 1910, the Grey's, on their way to Mexico for a fishing trip, learned of an epidemic there, and made their way back through Cuba to Florida. On a hunch about great fishing in the Keys, they made their way to Long Key via Flagler's new rail line. Zane Grey would soon bring international fishing prowess to the Long Key Fishing Club and the Keys. It is here at the LKFC that he would introduce light-tackle fishing, make proper the sport of bone fishing, sail fishing and tarpon fishing, as well as others, then thought to be nuisance catches.

Grey's accomplishments as a fisherman set the bar so high that celebrity fisherman of the day measured themselves against his feats; including Hemingway. Zane Grey was one of the first to promote the release of catches not scheduled for table, a radical thought in the early 1900's and even until a decade ago. Today, there are still several remaining Neanderthals, bent on killing fish, and game, just for the boast of it, unfortunately.

Zane Grey was also a naturalist, easily swayed from a day with rod and reel " . . . *So much beauty and wildlife, so wild that it was tame, seemed a rare and marvelous fact of nature. The great spirit of creation was brooding here.*" Zane Grey and his brother were also the first to go after sailfish, tarpon and bonefish as a sport fish. *"I believe I have proved to myself - that the sailfish is the gamest, the most beautiful and the hardest fish to catch on light tackle."* King mackerel would no longer be the only sport fish of the day nor would the rod, line or rigging be the same. Zane Grey helped define a new sport, light-tackle fishing, with the help of LKFC's most knowledgeable guide, Captain W. D. (Bill) Hatch. In many ways Zane Grey, perhaps with the help of his brother, was the Babe Ruth of sport fishing for the common man. Zane Grey made the Long Key Fishing Club famous and Presidents Hoover and Roosevelt, as well as other notables of their day, would be visitors between 1910 and its last season in 1934. The LKFC would never recover from the 1935 Labor Day Hurricane.

The Long Key Fishing Club was revitalized in the late 60's with charter members of note: Ted Williams, Arthur Godfrey, Jackie Gleason, Mike Douglas and Jimmy Carter (before he was president). The club never really got going because the state eminent-domained the property of Long Key and turned it into a park.

LONG KEY FISHING CLUB - 1910 TO 1934

- Zane Grey's 10lb. 5oz. bonefish was the LKFC and world record for many years.
- Zane Grey's 130lb. tarpon was then a world record.
- Zane Grey introduced sailfish fishing.
- Zane Grey probably introduced the world to the 'teaser' and, essentially, bait-and-switch when he began his love of sailfish fishing and then billfish fishing.
- Zane Grey proposed to all he met and fished with that it would be a good practice to throw back the fish you did not intend to eat.
- Zane Grey rarely fished without a guide or offshore captain.
- Zane Grey and his brother, Roemer (RC), were keen naturalists and accomplished photographers.
- Zane Grey established bonefish as a target species at the LKFC, and it attracted a new cult of believers called the "Bonefish Brigade."

The brigade fished for the silver ghost a little differently than we do today. Try this today and see if you get a dozen or so bones, every day! The Brigade fished for bones from a chair set at shoreline. It was fashionable to catch your own bait, so sweating a bit was not out of the question. A bait with hook and sinker were cast out as far as possible in more or less a foot of water. One sat with his finger on the line waiting to feel the tug, which rarely, according to accounts, took long to happen.

MIDDLE KEYS

Conch Key, Duck Key, Grassy Key, Crawl Key, Key Colony Beach, Key Vaca, Marathon, Pigeon Key and the Seven Mile Bridge

Passport to the Middle Keys begins with the Long Key Viaduct at MM65, an impressive expanse that treats the visual senses. At midday, water and sky blend here to create an occasional visual phenomena; a seamless connection. The Long Key viaduct also puts the first real historical perspective on Flagler's

Above: The Long Key Fishing Club. Date photo taken unknown. The LKFC had 14 cottages, narrow gage railroad, post office, general store, entertainment center, and the main lodge's dining offerings were considered gourmet.
Middle: Locomotive 431 pulls into the Long Key Depot. The Long Key Fishing Club is out of sight to the right (oceanside). Date photo taken unknown.
Below: Era Postcard - Late teens or early 1920's. Long Key depot looking towards Miami, ocean right and Florida Bay left.

Zane Grey, 1930's Bimini. Note reel. It was the largest ever built, at the time (20.0). Grey heralded the Keys as a world-class sport fishery. He also served as president of the LKFC, and it is from that Keys association that he made popular light-tackle fishing, as well as, sport fishing for sailfish, bonefish, tarpon and several other Keys species.

Above: Quarter boats provided office space, dining, sleeping quarters and mobility. However, during a 1906 hurricane, 175 workers went out to sea when Quarter Boat #4 broke from its moorings. One hundred and three died at sea, but 72 men were rescued by passing vessels. Some were taken to Key West, others to ports along the East Coast, and some as far away as Liverpool, England. Quarter boats were done away with and fixed land camps were used after the tragedy.

Long Key, before it was transformed into a fishing camp, was significant because the RR, at Long Key, replaced quarter boats due to losses during hurricanes. The new fixed camp, or staging area, concept readied the RR for its first big over-the-sea engineering hurdle (Long Key Viaduct).

Also, by the time the RR reached Long Key it began implementing a reconfigured bridge-building design, which accommodated the receding-water phenomena from tropical storms. Local homesteaders had impressed on Krome, Chief Engineer, that receding water was far more devastating than initial storm surge.

1917-1918

LONG KEY
FISHING CLUB
LONG KEY, FLORIDA

TO DEVELOP THE BEST AND FINEST TRAITS OF SPORT, TO RESTRICT THE KILLING OF FISH, TO EDUCATE THE INEXPERIENCED ANGLER BY HELPING HIM, AND TO PROMOTE GOOD FELLOWSHIP

Bottom right:
Hey days for the LKFC (1917-1918).
In 1925, LKFC sailfish tournament records show Capt. W.D. (Bill) Hatch's boat, *Patsy*, caught 113 sails while 12 other captains caught only 106. Hatch had, by accounts of the day, figured out sail fishing and was known as the sailfish guru. He closely guarded his (bait & switch) knowledge. Sails then were much larger, and more plentiful, than they are today.

Above: The end of a beautiful thing. Long Key Fishing Club just after the 1935 Labor Day hurricane. The camp, and the railroad, were finished forever. The only building that appears to be partially standing is the post office. The depot, telegraph lines, rails, 14 cottages, general store and main lodge were all completely destroyed or rendered irreparable. The land was reconfigured by the storm and where the lodge once stood became permanent watery turf.

LONG KEY FISHING CAMP
LONG KEY, FLORIDA

On the Key West extension of the Florida East Coast Railway, 457 miles south of Jacksonville. Through trains and Pullmans to and from New York stop here daily during the entire year.

RATES
AMERICAN PLAN
1 Person $6.00 up
2 Persons $11.00 up

WITH BATH
1 Person $7.00 up

In the heart of the Florida Fishing area. Easy of access. Comfortable accommodations, guides, boats, tackle, everything you need.

Above Left: An ad/postcard for the LKFC circa early 1920's. NOTE: Current rates in the Keys for accommodations and guiding have moved up, slightly.

Above Right: The logistics of building an over-the-sea RR were well beyond any planners' or engineers' understanding. Amazingly, Flagler pressed on, and spent far more millions of dollars than budgeted.

Marathon around 1950.

MARATHON - MM 65 TO 40

By 1906, eighty-six miles of track had been completed and that brought Flagler's RR traveling show to Key Vaca (Marathon). The RR put Marathon on the map as a legal entity in 1908. The next over-the-sea engineering hurdle was but a stone's throw away.

Knight's Key Dock (Marathon) became the first commercial link for the railroad extension in the Keys. The first regular through passenger train service between New York and Knight's Key was in January, 1909; a milestone for the project. Imported pineapples and other fruits from Cuba could now be hauled back by train to the mainland. When the Seven Mile Bridge was completed. Marathon was left with its open town personality, which remains its signature even today. NOTE: By 1926, Marathon's population, in an unofficial census, reported only 17 people lived there. Marathon's modern airport, bayside, was the site of the B-17 Flying Fortress training grounds (WW II). A semblance of a town took shape during the war years, and its vacating war-time residents helped Marathon's image with leaked reports about fabulous fishing.

PIGEON KEY RESERVE

Pigeon Key, all by itself, a few miles out into the water beyond Marathon, still has remnants of the railroad maintenance crew housing, which would later become housing for the automobile toll bridge personnel. During WW II, Pigeon Key served as a military training facility and was followed by a University of Miami research project with sewage-eating African fish, talapia. The replants were to help reduce pollution, but they only pushed out indigenous fish and the project was abandoned. Today, it serves as headquarters for the Pigeon Key Foundation, a restoration organization with camp-out environmental workshops, field trips and a visitors center very much worth the walk or shuttle to it. No cars allowed.

Florida East Coast Railroad Extension with substantial vestiges of its skeleton paralleling the present 2.5-mile-long Overseas Highway bridge.

KEY COLONY BEACH

Key Colony is a development delivered to the Keys in the 50's by a prophesier from Detroit who understood what would sell real estate in Florida. Today, it is a picture-perfect postcard of itself frozen in time. It still has every mainland suburban signature: retirees, driveways filled with cadillacs and early-bird specials at local eateries.

KEY VACA

In the 1800's Key Vaca was a settlement of Bahamian and Yankee (Connecticut) fishing families. By the 1820's a few wreckers called it home and it became one of three Keys settlements along with Key West and Indian Key. Farming was soon producing considerable crops of limes, guava, avocados, sugar apples and other cash crops that could be schoonered to Key West. The Indian Key massacre of 1840, during the Second Seminole War, chased all but nine citizens away. In 1860, there were 26 people, and after the Civil War only two farmers remained. By 1910, Key Vaca was a staging area for the RR. Six hundred workers quickly made it a boom town that would soon be renamed Marathon.

TIDBITS

PARTIAL MATERIAL CONSUMPTION RR EXTENSION

Pittsburgh structural steel - 19 million tons
Concrete - 461,000 cu. yds.
Gravel - 96,000 tons of rock (combined 377,927 cu. yds.)
Pittsburgh steel reinforcing rods - 2,000 tons
Pine piles - 70,000
Sand - 25,000 yds.
Trestle piles - 78,000
Catamarans - 1
Dravo steel barges - 151 plus 25 launches.
NOTE: All 'floating' equipment had dynamos (generators).

LOWER KEYS

Bahia Honda Key, Spanish Harbor Key, No Name Key, Big Pine Key, Torch Keys, Ramrod Key, Summerland Key, Cudjoe Key, Sugarloaf Key, Saddlebunch Keys, Big Coppitt Key and Boca Chica Key.

The Seven Mile Bridge is 35,716 feet long with a 65-foot maximum mast clearance. It begins at MM #47 and deposits you on Little Duck Key. Plants and trees indigenous only to the Caribbean start to appear here in the Lower Keys, no doubt the inspiration of a break in the reef system allowing seeds a landfall entry with wind and fowl as players in the process. The Lower Keys are osprey turf and home of the Great Heron National Wildlife Refuge, 264 square miles and 7,500 water acres in the Florida Bay designated in 1938 as protected habitat. North America's largest such enterprise for wading birds.

BAHIA HONDA KEY

Bahia Honda Key has the best beach of the entire Keys (MM37). It has every element to complement its magnificence. It is, however, a do-it-yourself camping plan. From here you can fish at the Bahia Honda Bridge, buy your needs at a general store, enjoy its well-kept picnic

Faro Blanco is a Marathon landmark.

Captain Harry Snow was one of the early Marathon guides of note. An expert at bonefishing, with evidence as proof. Photo believed to be taken in the early 40's.

area, walk a short, but good nature trail, and get a real sense of what kicking back just might be all about. You will, however, be sharing the space. The park is an all seasons favorite for Conchs and mainlanders.

BIG PINE KEY - MM 39 TO 9

Big Pine Key is home to the key deer, and the original "make my day" man, Mr. Watson. Most of Big Pine Key, and several smaller keys, make up an 8,000 acre refuge that protects the key deer. When your are in Big Pine you've entered a new climate zone, which is considered frost free. Its being frost free is due to the Gulf Stream, more than a connection to coordinates. Also, its geological formation is different from the Upper Keys. Big Pine Key is second only to Key Largo in land size, with 5,816 acres. It is, essentially, made up of Ramrod Key, Summerland Key, Big and Little Torch Keys, No Name Key and Newfound Harbor Keys. The first U. S. government survey (1873) reported finding abundant wildlife, big stands of pine, hardwoods, evidence of prior settlement attempts, and clear evidence that indigenous peoples had lived there before the Spaniards arrived. The Indians, more than likely, were Calusa or Tequesta.

TIDBITS

In 1906, John Gifford of National Geographic made these observations in an article about the Keys and Key West; ". . . enormous quantities of pineapple, limes, bananas, vegetables and fruit grow in abundance. . . ."

The copy went on to tell of an abundance of natural resources. Wharfside Key West photos supported his claims, depicting a flotilla of commercial vessels, ponderous catches of fish, mountains of sponges and many, many turtles. Mr. Gifford further describes seeing huge hammocks of hardwood in the Keys; ". . . cocobola, pigeon plumb, torchwood, ironwood, lancewood, stopperwoods, lignum-vitae, mahogany . . ." He describes other indigenous flora that are less abundant in today's Keys environment. The copy also sells the frontier possibilities that Flagler's rail line offers all comers.

ART PROVIDED COURTESY OF KLAUS SCHULER

Old and new Seven Mile Bridges.

Homesteaders were deeded property on Big Pine starting around 1870. A small traceable and hardy band of both black and white families came here by sea from Key West to work at farming onions, tomatoes, guava, limes, and charcoal making, as well as fishing, sponging and gathering conch. Principal among those who came were the Watsons from Watson St. in Key West. In 1905, Robert, Jr. came to Big Pine with his wife and seven children, and in 1907, Robert Sr. came to Big Torch Key.

A condensed version of an article written by Mizpah Watson Saunders, *The History of Our Homestead on Big Pine as I Remember It*, appearing in The *Monroe County Environmental Story,* contains a window into the life and times of homesteading in the Keys. Note: Originally, it was Jack Watson (no relation to the National Key Deer Wildlife Refuge Watson) who settled the area. Throughout the entire article of her early 1900's remembrances, Mizpah does not even hint at complaining about her obviously hard life. Oddly, she shares only great memories: discovery and adventure, lots of deer, laughter, wonderful black neighbor families (their only neighbors), but there are accounts of frightening schooner treks to and from Key West. The Big Pine homesteaders, like other Keys homesteaders, were all extended communities, fraternal and almost tribal because they were close to Mother Earth's rhythms and unified by common risk. The entrepreneurial efforts these pioneers endured to survive and earn cash was Herculean.

Big Pine was essentially isolated and unto itself until the FECRR Extension made it there in 1912. Even then there was no rush to populate Big Pine. Robert Watson, Jr. built a rock dock on No Name Key (remnants of which can still be seen), from which, according to Mizpah, her father used to sail their own and neighboring black families' goods to market in Key West. Eventually, a ferry system from Marathon would deposit travelers on No Name Key. That ferry, essentially, was out of business after the RR extension made it to Key West, but revitalized after the RR went out of business following the 1935 hurricane. It died for good when the Overseas Highway finally connected the Keys all the way to Key West.

Big Pine and its contiguous Keys are unique real estate. Its pinelands, natural aquifers, key deer and hardwood hammocks are singular in the U. S., and as such, they have been the focus of several environmental groups as well as state, county, local and wildlife agency officials. Land-use issues are always at the top of the list of concerns.

Brothers by the name of Johnson built a fishing camp east of Big Pine that was short lived, late 1920's until the early 1930's. Many fishing camps sprung up during those years and they were no doubt inspired by what Zane Grey and the Long Key Fishing Camp did to popularize sport fishing in the Florida Keys.

In 1923 a company called Hydenoil (hides and oil) went into the shark catching business and flourished until 1931.

One landmark is sadly missing, Big Pine Inn, which was built in the early 1900's and burned to the ground in 1978. It was one of the earliest attempts to introduce the Keys romantic lifestyle to visitors. The history of Big Pine Inn included a real connection with rum running during Prohibition, gambling, and some old-timers suggest other pleasures could be bought there. Most Keys eateries and bars were never much influenced by Prohibition. Drinking, or obtaining a brand in the Keys, especially the Lower Keys and Key West, remained pretty much wide open. Many a federal man was runoff as a trespasser by the local sheriff. Prohibition did, however, provide for lots of outside income for many Conchs, and the unexplained disappearances of a few.

PHOTO COURTESY OF BILL OLIPHANT

Munson Island, just South of Little Torch Key, was bought by Ada Munson in the 1920's. Ada Munson's secretary, Ruth Ellison, was given the property and she turned it into a fishing camp (1930's). Portions of the movie, "P. T. 109", were filmed here. The property, at the time of the filming, was owned by Senator John Spottswood (FL). Munson Island was sold in 1972, and is now called, Little Palm Island, a very 'posh' resort.

In 1945, there were but 7 permanent residents on Big Pine Key. By the 1950's, water and electric were available, and a surge of development started, but that all slowed due to the destruction caused by hurricane Donna in 1960. Developers, however, pressed on, and by the end of the 1960's Big Pine Key real estate development topped the charts for such undertakings in the Florida Keys. Today, however, land-use arguments have slowed growth significantly and the endemic beauty of Big Pine Key looks as though it will stay in intact. See Watson Trial, No Name Pub and Blue Hole in the Practical Information Chapter.

ABOUT JACK WATSON

Jack Watson's legend, not to be confused with Peter Mathiessen's Mr. Watson in *Killing Mister Watson*, lends credence to calling him the original "make-my-day" man. Big Pine Key's Mr. Watson of 1960's fame dedicated himself to protecting the all but then extinct key deer. At the time of his enlightenment there were only 50 or so deer. Now there are over 1,000, but still considered endangered by authorities. It became Mr. Watson's personal business to see that poachers, of which he was reported to have been the best, would have no further say in the extinction of key deer. As a conservation convert he assumed the zeal that goes with it. Mr. Watson's distinction, however, was his adopted Sicilian-like penchant for vendetta. Any who boasted of a key deer kill, or hung around after their indiscretion, was tracked down with inquisition fervor. He converted many to his way of seeing things. Big Pine's Mr. Watson, like Mister Watson in Mathiessen's book, was not at all a shy man when it came to seeing things his way. Legend goes that a former compatriot, recently having sacrificed one of the two-foot, seventy-pound anomalies for table fare, was repairing his roof when Mr. Watson called on him to discuss the issue of an illegal kill. The poacher's confession was not at all contrite, and the sinner stated he had no intention of repenting and would, in fact, be indulging again. Just admission usually meant a thrashing, but it was the lack of contrition that got him shotgunned off his roof and Mr. Watson, a true crusader, into the news. The exorcism was not fatal. A point, though, was made. Poaching seemed to trail off quite a bit thereafter. As serendipity would have it, a national movement was already underfoot to alarm the American public that the dread pox of extinction was afoot. Key deer had a platform and "make-my-day" Watson became an unlikely poster child.

Today, there is a hardwood forest named Watson's Hammock and a Watson Boulevard, but they are named after the homesteaders who settled the hammock. It is only Jack Watson Nature Trail that is named after the original "make-my-day" Jack Watson.

THE TORCH KEYS

Torchwood is a resinous wood that was used by early settlers because it burned well even when green. Today, area hardwood trees have been thinned out or disappeared as everything indigenous was cut to fuel Key West years

Perky's Bat Tower today, still batless. You can visit the bat tower at Sugar Loaf Lodge. Sugarloaf Key, FL.

FLORIDA STATE ARCHIVES

Englishman, Charles Chase bought this Sugarloaf Key property from Dr. J. V. Harris in 1909. Chase renamed the property and it became a small community. His plans to mine sponge by a unique forced farming scheme went awry. The tower (R) guarded the sponge beds from poachers.

ago, including the once abundant charcoal-making buttonwood tree. Key limes can still be found in spotty supply, the residual of attempts to farm them.

Little Palm Island is a nearby island accessible only by boat. It is the many times bought and sold millionaires' resort, which is financially manageable with huge amounts of cash. Panache, truly getting away and top-notch cuisine reign supreme here.

NOTE: When you are in the Torches or Lower Keys the whole Keys fly-fishing experience is available and best advantaged through Sea Boots Outfitters in Big Pine Key. They can put you in touch with excellent inshore or offshore captains that will take you to the promised land 12 months a year.

RAMROD KEY

The Looe Key Reef, just off Ramrod, is part of the National Marine Sanctuary and worth every effort to explore. It is the real coral reef thing and your authors' favorite. The reef is named after the English warship that ran afoul of its water in the 1770's. The scars of recent commercial ship collisions (1989 and 1990) with the reef are quite evident. The latter events (3) were responsible for national and state legislation that expanded the authority of Florida Keys National Marine Sanctuary. The FKNMS is now is responsible for the waters surrounding the entire land masses of the Florida Keys.

SUGARLOAF KEY

By 1912, the sponge bounty in the Keys, once 90% of U. S. supply, was in decline. Its beds had been over harvested. However, with perfect growing conditions still obvious, Mr. Charles Chase, and his brothers of England, via Chicago, invested in the Florida Sponge And Fruit Company. They devised a clever scheme, it seemed, to improve sponge abundance. The Florida Sponge And Fruit Company failed because of hurricanes, theft and miscalculating the time it took sponges to mature. To make matters really unworkable, the Chase funds got

frozen in English banks at the outset of WW I and another Keys venture went under.

Soon after, a Miamian, Richter C. Perky, bought the whole enchilada, established a lodge, gambling business and implemented a grandiose plan to combat the Keys'

Pirates Cove Fishing Camp (Sugarloaf Key), was built in 1930 by New Englander, C. Irving Wright. The camp was a rival in elegance, style, amenities and cuisine to the Long Key Fishing Club built by Flagler. Pirates Cove was designed to meet the needs of the socially elite of the day. The camp accommodated 30, and encouraged women to come. Women could enjoy a saltwater pool, deck tennis and bridge. The road that runs through the camp ended (top) at the Cudjoe Key RR bridge.

In the 1940's, Luther Pinder of Key West, built this fishing camp on Boca Chica Key. Upper left corner of photo shows the Boca Chica Viaduct. NOTE: The Pinder family name is synonymous with Florida Keys history.

worst tourist enemy—mosquitoes. Bat Towers would do the trick. Mr. Perky researched bats, built bat towers, had bat towers built abroad, had bat guano imported and bought a secret bat-attractor formulation from bat expert, Dr. Campbell of Texas. Both were sure the towers would attract bats that, in-turn, would insatiably gobble mosquitoes. This accomplished, Mr. Perky's Keys vacation spot would be a paradise and he and Dr. Campbell heralded, worldwide, as true geniuses. The enterprise, however, turned out to be *Fawlty Towers*. No bats came and Dr. Campbell died with his secret. The mosquitoes, locals say,

ate the bats and Perky's establishment finally went broke. You can see a Perky Bat Tower at MM 17 (Sugar Loaf Lodge), bayside. No bats though.

CUDJOE KEY AND THE SADDLEBUNCH KEYS

The naming of Cudjoe Key has historians still debating. Did the name come from an indigenous wood, joewood, or cudjoewood? Or did the name come from a prominent Key West family's cousin, Joe, who settled there? High ground here was bulldozed by the military for a missile-tracking station during the 60's Cuban Missile Crisis. Not a whole lot a shakin' going on here, but fabulous fly fishing is going on.

BIG COPPITT KEY

Big Coppitt served as a marl quarry for Flagler's railroad. Trestle pilings remain that once carried steam shovels out to the shoals to mine the gunk that engineers discovered could perform, in a dried state, like concrete. Today, only some piling remain and they serve as a roost for birds, as well as a nursery and feeding ground for fish and sea life. The Saddlebunch Keys are a collection of keys, some just mangrove mud flats and others only a few miles in length. The predominant landscape is red mangrove that provides a marvelous nursery for fish. These Lower Keys have very little land, lots of marl, and plenty of scrub pine growth and mangrove anchor it all. They seem to just hover at sea level with their own agenda. Their appearance, however, is not unlike what all the keys look like from a flats boat.

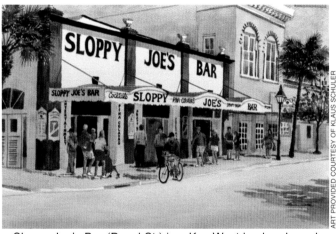

ART PROVIDED COURTESY OF KLAUS SCHULER

Sloppy Joe's Bar (Duval St.) is a Key West landmark, and perhaps the most famous bar in Florida. The original Sloppy Joe's Bar was on Greene St. but is now called Captain Tony's Saloon. In its heyday, Sloppy Joe's Bar was a gambling joint, depression era speak easy and reported to have been whorehouse. It's most famous Hemingway era owner was Joseph S. Russell (1933 to 1937). Sloppy Joe's was, of course, made famous by Ernest Hemingway. Hemingway and Russell became lifelong friends after Russell cashed a publisher's royalty check that Hemingway's bank refused. Russell, literally, became Hemingway's banker thereafter. It is no wild guess that Hemingway had character bait for his novels by spending afternoons in Sloppy Joe's. The Depression era prohibition years meant absolutely nothing in Key West. It remained wide open the entire time. Actually, the local authorities were very much in cahoots. A federal agent, attempting to do his job in the Lower Keys, and especially Key West, was himself in danger of arrest, or worse.

BOCA CHICA KEY AND STOCK ISLAND

These keys are the back-door and, essentially, the industrial back yard of Key West. Stock Island became the place that would handle the Key West overflow. It is a

---

TIDBITS

Mark Twain on Key West in 1837.

"This is really a big town, big enough for 2,000 people, though many houses seem deserted. Business mostly gin mills - that is, for soldiers."

TIDBITS

The Florida Keys, throughout its history, spawned many, many 'fish camps,' some of which matured into fishing clubs, but none lasted. The exception—and with varying charters—The Key Largo Anglers Club, and The Islamorada Fishing Club.

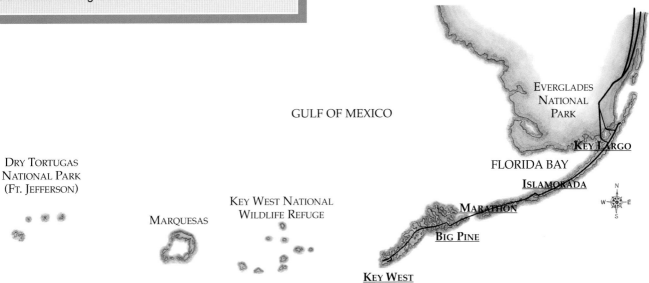

GULF OF MEXICO

EVERGLADES NATIONAL PARK

DRY TORTUGAS NATIONAL PARK (FT. JEFFERSON)

KEY WEST NATIONAL WILDLIFE REFUGE

MARQUESAS

KEY LARGO

FLORIDA BAY

ISLAMORADA

MARATHON

BIG PINE

KEY WEST

ATLANTIC OCEAN

In 1575, Spanish explorer, Hernando d'Escalante Fontaneda comments on turtles (tortugas). *"To the West of these islands (Key West) is a great channel, which no pilot dares go though with a large vessel . . . on the opposite side towards the West, which are without trees and formed of . . . bare and of plain sand. They are seven leagues in circumference, and are called the Islands of the Tortugas (Dry Tortugas); for turtles are there, and many come at night to lay their eggs in the sand. The animal is the size of a shield, and has as much flesh as a cow; it is like all kinds of meat, and yet fish."*

TIDBITS

FEC last published schedule (May 1935).
Miami to Key West - $4.75 round trip. Leave Miami at 7:20AM, arrive 11:50AM same morning. Return, leave Key West at 5:40PM, arrive Miami 10:20PM.
• Sunday Excursion (Miami to Key West) - $2.50 round trip with same timetable as above.
• Miami to Havana - $24 for a 10 day excursion. Leave Miami 7:20AM Sat. or Wed., arrive Havana 6:20PM same day. Included meals and ship berth.
• Many early Keys settlers (1800's) were related by heredity or marriage. Their dialect was similar to 'cockney' of London, misplacing 'h's and using v's for r's.
• There were no doctors in the Upper, Middle or Lower Keys in the 1800's and into the early 1900's. An illness or child birthing required a trip to Key West.

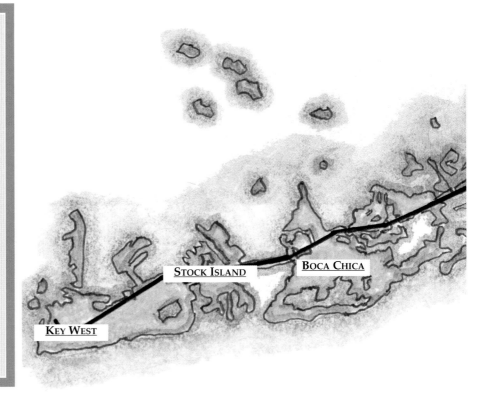

STOCK ISLAND

BOCA CHICA

KEY WEST

microcosm of the mainland: malls, trailer parks, small industries, a golf course, developments galore, and every conceivable billboard to assault, as well as traffic snarls. Boca Chica is pretty much the Navy with a supporting airfield and a popular community park.

KEY WEST - MM 8 TO 0

Frivolous it may be, decadent it is, bigger it wants to be, beauty it claims and marvelous it remains.

The Spanish named Key West the island of bones (Cayo Hueso) because they found the shorelines laden with bones. No factual explanation was recorded as to the origin of these now disappeared bones. There are many theories.

Key West is the window from which you can view the Florida Keys character in its entirety. Its colorful history, filled with accounts of stinging hardships and dramatic rewards for surviving, put a signature on its inhabitants and the Key West Conch persona that is still evidenced throughout the Keys today. Durable people, friendly people, but with an eclectic *carpe diem* outlook on life that most of us would like to own. The participants and events making this all so for Conchs are the fingerprints left by conquistadors, pirates, adventurers, the military strategies of nations, salvagers, speculators, writers, artists, wars, fires, governments, one huge rail-line investment, bull and bear markets, raging fires, a national depression and always, hurricanes. The day-to-day people who came here and continue to come are drawn to it. Always adventurers, always searchers looking for whatever it is they expect to invent new about themselves divines them to this end of the road place. Eccentric pulls Key West along, hour by hour and year by year.

Key West is a town that has learned to live with the influences left by its most singular roller coaster history. It is a city-town that takes on good fortune and bad with equal aplomb. No matter what the Richter Scale says about a setback it faced, or faces, its highly self-absorbed inhabitants, whom it is agreed disagree on everything, always pull together for a common good when the need arises.

If Key West put a current cartographic overlay on a 1500's Spanish conquistador's map of Cayo Hueso's real estate, or one going back to the 1700's, 1800's or even 50 years ago, no overlay would remotely match. The exception, Whitehead's platting of Old Town in the 1840's. Key West has been the product of enormous land manipulation, literally and figuratively. Hurricanes, Mr. Flagler, the military, speculators and developers added to and dredged out a different landscape, made new water boundaries and created a lot of new turf. So much manipulation has taken place that Key West's present land mass is almost double that of its earliest mapped land area.

Key West is worthy of a book and there are many. All delivering differing perspectives, but all in perfect astrological alignment when it comes to describing the sights, smells, sounds and inhabitants of it different. Many leave Key West convinced they visited another country and most come back because they did.

COMMUNITY OF WRITERS

Key West attracts writers. It attracts them in droves because it is an unusual place and an end-of-the-road place. Writers eventually disgorge Key West for the very same reasons they came. It is a place people like Jim, in Joseph Conrad's *Lord Jim*, would come to escape, reinvent, untether and find the stuff of inspiration; newness that only unusual end-of-the-road places promise. And like Jim found, you cannot escape from what you have been accused of, done or become.

Key West did, does and will attract the pen and thoughts of many. Key West is permanently committed

Left: IGFA founder Michael Lerner with his lifelong friend and IGFA VP, Ernest Hemingway. Hemingway fished extensively and wrote prolifically while a Key West resident.

PHOTO COURTESY OF INTERNATIONAL GAME FISH ASSOCIATION PHOTO TAKEN IN BIMINI, CIRCA 1934.

city, Cubans, Africans, Bahamians, English, New England Yankees, whores, gamblers, a cuisine all its own, gays and lesbians, artists, extraordinary sport & commercial fishing, as well as magnificent weather almost 365 days a year. People from around the world have come to this fermenting pot for almost 500 years. They have always left behind ideologies, philosophies, social mores and their signature on its cuisine and architecture.

KEY WEST - HISTORICAL INTERLUDE

Key West got to be important in world affairs simply because of its geography. It was first impressive to nations because its treacherous waters started laying heavy claim to sailing ships utilizing the advantageous currents of the Straits of Florida on returning to Europe with their plunders of the new world. The traffic and cargo got an enthusiastic two thumbs up from the pirating industry as well. Key West had a deep-water port with a nearby reef system and unpredictable weather-perfect combinations to benefit from off-course piloting. Shipping wrecks jump-started its economy, and legal and illegal versions of the salvage business fast forwarded it. Key West would prosper for over a hundred years. Word about its opportunities, even then, traveled fast. Adventurers arrived and Key West had its foundation for being a true frontier. A bounty in natural resources added fuel to the fire of economic expectation. Real and imagined entrepreneurial opportunity put together a population with a most diverse demographic profile, as well as skills. For the most part, Key West relied on enterprise and the common bond of intra-reliance. It combined early on to build an uncommon tolerance for a person's race, religion or any non-traditional belief or practice. Blacks, Cubans, Chinese, Jews and Catholics were, with a few hiccups of intolerance, accepted as integral to the community in every respect.

to writers and the community's events and societies recommend it. Not too many small towns, or for that matter major cities, in America could boast of such a who's who of writers as part of its past, present or part-time community. If you start with writers who wrote about Key West with passion, and made it central to the cohesiveness of their tale, or poetic rhyme, a document would be required. If you just reference those who received the Pulitzer Prize for writing, then this space will do. It is impressive: *Elizabeth Bishop, Philip Caputo, Annie Dillard, Robert Frost (a mere winter visitor), Ernest Hemingway, John Hersey, Joseph Lash, Allison Lurie, James Merrill, Wallace Stevens, Richard Wilbur and Tennessee Williams.* It is no wonder writers come if you just look at the grist this end-of-the-road place can generate with its macro exposures to the world for such a micro place. Pick a subject. Key West is in it with a big colorful footprint: piracy, salvaging, economic boom, sponge and cigar capital of the U.S., one grand entrepreneurial scheme after another, the focus point of a grandiose RR venture gone terribly wrong, a deep-water port

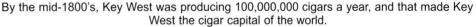

By the mid-1800's, Key West was producing 100,000,000 cigars a year, and that made Key West the cigar capital of the world.

FLORIDA IS CEDED TO THE UNITED STATES

Spain ceded Florida to the newly formed U. S. in 1821.

Twenty years later, Key West was one of the nation's richest per capita income communities with an economy that would see good times roll into the beginning of the 20th century. A prosperity that only a new breed could manage. They would be undeterred by risk, devastating fires and hurricanes. Conchs might just have been the original "Just Do It" folks.

President Truman loved to come to Key West in the spring. He joined a long list of famous people that would make tiny Key West a big stop.

The Lower Keys, especially Key West, by the mid to late 19th century were responsible for 90% of the world's production of sponges.

However, by the start of the Great Depression the bloom was off the rose; all the earmarks of a local economy in decline were well in place. Key West's population had almost been halved to 12,000, the railroad ended in 1935, sponging had essentially moved to Tarpon Springs and Tampa was the new cigar-making capital. The salvage business had been nonexistent since the late 1870's due to lighthouses, steamships and the invention of a chronometer that gave true, up-to-the-minute longitude. Nothing, not even tourism, was a plug-in ledger item.

By 1934, almost every Key West soul was on relief, 80%. In true Key West fashion, however, the town mustered up some unlikely leaders, managed to get more than its fair share of Federal Emergency Relief Act Funds, made an all-out, all-hands-on-deck effort to switch gears and successfully entered the tourist business in earnest. It never looked back on that decision. The new Overseas Highway would open up the entire Keys to tourism and development. The Navy would pitch in a water line, and during WWII the military would improve all roads to better the delivery of supplies. The Keys and Key West were on. By the 1970's, Key West and the entire Keys had a solid economic base. Tourism would become the fuel that drives the Keys' economic engine. Now, over-development is of tremendous concern and, especially, the by-product of sewage disposal. However, that has been addressed and the Keys economy is now solely based on the environment, a first in the U. S.

KEY WEST AND REAL PIRATES

Even before Florida was a territory of the U. S., Key West had a history of salvaging wrecked ships and an economy based on it. By 1821, piracy had matured as an industry, with its Wall Street in Havana. Its sophistication evidenced itself in the special ship models pirates designed for the workload. Shallow-draft schooners with centerboard construction were built to scoot into shallow water and thus avoid the deep draft policing frigates and schooners of the day.

Key West was a deep-water port and therefore a strategic asset worth protecting. Lt. Matthew Perry raised the U. S. flag in Key West on March 25, 1822. Commodore David Sydney Porter was sent by our new government to sort out Key West's free-wheeling salvage business and put an end to piracy. New laws were quickly put on the books, and one such law prohibited all but U. S. citizens from participating in the salvage business.

By 1825, Commodore Porter had summarily dispensed with sea-faring criminality. He had boats built that could overtake pirates in their own specially designed shallow-draft vessels.

PRESIDENT HARRY S. TRUMAN LIBRARY

STATE OF FLORIDA PHOTOGRAPHIC ARCHIVES - TALLAHASSEE

Operating from the mother-ship, *Seagull*, imported from New York City harbor duty, Porter would run up on his quarry and quickly deploy his armada of four shallow-draft vessels. They would chase the pirates out to sea where large naval vessels waited on the single-boat bad guys. By 1825, piracy was not a good business to be in around Key West waters. As a sidebar to all this, the bold and egotistical Commodore was also a loose cannon. He ended up court-marshalled for over-stepping his marching orders by chasing pirates to Puerto Rico and points beyond to destroy, wholesale, any boat under any flag he deemed to be in the wrong business or a potential threat to the U.S. This unauthorized and non-diplomatic activity created a cerebral headache for the bureaucrats of the State Department. After being tossed out of the Navy, Perry hired himself out as a naval mercenary and died in Turkey around 1842. As a deep-water port town, Key West can spin its share of tales with any port town in the world.

SPONGES AND CIGARS

Sponges were big business and Key West waters were a sponge gold mine. By the 1850's, sponging was booming. It was a business for Cubans, Africans and Key West Conchs. For years, Key West dominated the U. S. market with a 90% market share. By 1906, Key West still supported 150 sponge vessels. Sponging would last as a small business until the 1940's when a sponge plague decimated the beds.

A non-Cuban brought the cigar industry to Key West by taking advantage of an in-place and well-established Key West Cuban population. After the Revolution with Spain, Cuban refugees (including Vincente Martinez Ybor) started immigrating to Key West in 1869. The stars were in line and the cigar industry went bull market. Around 1890 Ybor moved to Tampa (Ybor City near Tampa, Florida) having been encouraged there by tax incentives and discouraged with Key West because of a series of labor strikes. Key West's cigar-making influence hung on into the early 1900's. In its finest hour, cigar manufacturing in Key West boasted of producing as many as 100,000,000 cigars per year and had, at one point, one of the highest weekly payrolls in the country at $40,000, a week. A substantial sum in the mid 1800's.

THE FLORIDA EAST COAST RAILROAD EXTENSION

In 1902, Henry Flagler, the many-times-over millionaire partner of John D. Rockefeller set in motion plans to

Depression-era fishermen in Key West.

STATE OF FLORIDA PHOTOGRAPHIC ARCHIVES.

extend his Florida East Coast Railroad from its terminus in Miami to Homestead. From there it would be on to Key West, 128 miles away. The grandiosity of the project was no doubt inspired by the Panama Canal project, the national swell of pride in American ingenuity, and lots and lots of money. Three hurricanes (1906, 1909 & 1910) and 10 years (7 years of actual construction) later, the Rambler, Flagler's lavish personal rail car, pulled into the Key West station on January 22, 1912, with an 82-year-old man who had spent untold millions to ride there. His railroad would outlive him and survive until the infamous and unnamed hurricane of Labor Day, 1935, took the enterprise past its bankruptcy. The railroads' right-of-way was quickly sold to the State of Florida. The rail-bed would become a new roadway providing hundreds of depression-era jobs and change the course of Keys history once again.

Flagler's dream had impacted the lives of many, ended the lives of 100's, and changed the course of history for the Keys, forever. One hundred and thirty four acres of new land had been added to Key West's map, and hotels had been built that would in time introduce a new client, the tourist. Because of the railroad, Florida, the Keys and Key West had a ready made publicity machine. New frontier reading material and photographs would titillate a nation for over 23 years. The rail line would provide the physical foundation for a road that would traverse the land and span the water all the way to Key West. A road that would protect the Keys and Key West from an isolation that would surely have radically altered its 20th century.

KEY WEST, FORTS AND WARS

Construction of Fort Taylor, named after President Zachary Taylor, began in 1845. The building of the original

---

TIDBITS

The first Key West Lighthouse was lit January 13, 1826. It was originally 65 feet tall, but was destroyed by the hurricane of 1846, and replaced at 50 feet tall. A new lantern, in 1873, brought it to 60 feet tall. It was de-commissioned in 1969. Today, there are 88 steps to the tower.

---

fort was 1,200 feet from shore and construction was fraught with labor strikes, material shortages and yellow fever outbreaks. Fort Taylor was never completed and in 1866 it was rendered to mothballs.

Key West at the outbreak of the Civil War was not really a southern sympathizer town. Fifty soldiers secured it for the union, unchallenged. Takeover by the Union soldiers was never challenged by the local population. The forts (Taylor and Jefferson) had more than a small effect on the war. By the end of the war, the U. S. Navy's blockading had laid claim to intercepting 199 Confederate ships, according to federal court records in Key West. Additional blockade-running ships, it is believed, may have been intercepted by the fleet stationed in Key West, but the captured vessels were taken

KEY WEST STATION JANUARY 22, 1912

Henry Flagler's lavish personal rail car, Rambler, pulls in to the Key West station on the rail line's official inaugural trip, a year to the day earlier than scheduled. An 82-year-old, near-deaf Flagler fulfills his dream and silenced critics, but he had spent millions to enjoy the only day he would ride his train. Cost estimates range from $27 million to $49 million. No estimated cost ever deemed accurate. Flagler died in 1913 and, oddly, all those important to his grandest undertaking died relatively young: Parrott, Krome and Meredith.

The dream is realized. A F.E.C.R.R. passenger train pulls into Key West (circa 1927) to unload its Havana-bound passengers on the steamship *Governor Cobb*.

to other ports and the confiscations not applied to Key West dockets. Key West was held by the Union during the entire Civil War struggle. It was the most significant turf ever held south of the Mason-Dixon during the conflict.

Fort Taylor was re-commissioned during the Spanish-American War, WWI, WWII and Cuban Missile Crisis with its battlements technology improved to match the events. Its cannon never fired a wartime shot.

During the fabricated Spanish American War, both forts (Jefferson and Taylor) served as coaling stations. The *Maine* sailed from Key West to its infamous glory in Havana harbor. WWI gave military credence to Key West as a base for the protection of the Panama Canal and also served as a submarine base and aviation training center. Both functions greatly expanded during WWII.

In 1846, construction of Fort Jefferson, 70 water miles away from Key West, began on Garden Key, one of seven coral reefs in the Tortugas. Originally planned by Thomas Jefferson to dominate the Gulf of Mexico, this monument to bricklayers (16,000,000 bricks) was doomed to failure. It was not built on coral rock, but on a base that was of sand consistency. It began sinking while it was being built.

Dr. Samuel Mudd, convicted of conspiracy in the assassination of Lincoln, was a reluctant guest here until 1869 when he was paroled. The fort also served as a prison for union deserters. Fort Jefferson's cannons never fired a hostile shot. Today, Fort Jefferson is part of the Florida Keys National Marine Sanctuary.

Homesteaders delivering fresh foodstuffs to Key West early 1900's.

U. S. Department of Interior.
Fort Jefferson, Dry Tortugas.

Vessels like this delivered the mail, goods, livestock, foodstuffs, and people to locations throughout the Keys, and to the mainland, until Flagler's RR put them all out of business. The ferry system was briefly revived after the RR failed in 1935, but went permanently out of business when the state built the Overseas Highway.

In 1938, the Over-The-Sea Railroad is history, and a new dream begins: The Over-The-Sea Highway. Photo of Long Key Viaduct. A trestle bridge is being readied for the roadway.

NOTE: The RR used the interior girder system, but the state's engineers decide to build the road on top of the girder system. The state took over the RR right-of-way in 1935.

CHAPTER II

THE KEYS ENVIRONMENT: CONNECTING THE DOTS

Marine Science and the Nature of a Fisherman's Paradise.

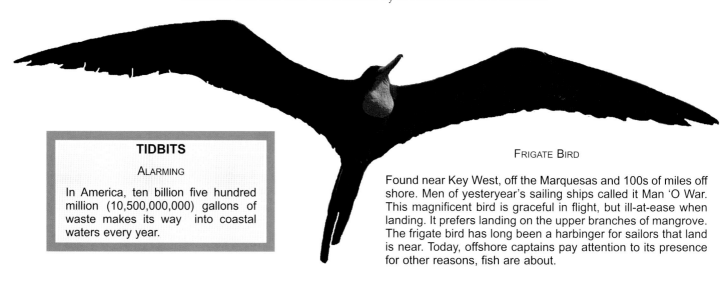

TIDBITS

ALARMING

In America, ten billion five hundred million (10,500,000,000) gallons of waste makes its way into coastal waters every year.

FRIGATE BIRD

Found near Key West, off the Marquesas and 100s of miles off shore. Men of yesteryear's sailing ships called it Man 'O War. This magnificent bird is graceful in flight, but ill-at-ease when landing. It prefers landing on the upper branches of mangrove. The frigate bird has long been a harbinger for sailors that land is near. Today, offshore captains pay attention to its presence for other reasons, fish are about.

". . . We have reached the time in the life of the planet, and humanity's demands on it, when every fisherman will have to be a riverkeeper, a steward of the marine shallows, a watchman on the high seas. We must put back more than we have taken out. We must make holy war on the enemies of aquatic life as we have against gillnetters, polluters, and drainers of the wetlands. Otherwise, as you have already learned, these creatures will continue to disappear at an accelerating rate. We will lose as much as we have already and there will be next to nothing, remnant populations . . ."

—Thomas McQuane, *The Longest Silence*

"Earth has not anything to show more fair. Dull would be the soul who could not pass a sight so touching in its majesty."

—Wordsworth

A TRIP TO BOUNTIFUL
GETTING ON THE EASY SIDE OF GRAVITY

The Florida Keys are a singular environmental masterpiece. The lead architect was nature and construction began about 125,000 years ago with a flow chart of projects that included: rising and falling ocean levels, climactic changes, multiple coral formations, anomalies of nature and ocean currents that would produce a unique mix of water cocktails in a setting of unusual coordinates. The Florida Keys, today, are still one of the most magical places in the world to live, fish, dive, boat and just plain observe the nature of it. Thousands live here and millions come to visit each year. All still willing to testify to the Keys being just like Jimmy Buffet sings that it is, Hemingway and McQuane wrote that is was, Carl Hiaasen's end-of-the-road characters think it is, Dave Barry's Miami people heard it is, and Conchs know it is. Too, for almost a century, fishermen Presidents of the United States have come here to find the best saltwater fishing in the world, and still do.

It is not just the weather, but the water that attracts everyone to the Keys; clean, crystal-clear salt water that is alive with many coveted game fish: sailfish, marlin, tarpon, bonefish, snook, redfish, tunas, wahoo, mackerels, permit and more, lots more. Water that barely hides over 200 miles of magnificent and complex coral reef tracts, surrounds 1,700 mangrove-lined islands in the sun, washes over millions of acres of life-giving seagrass flats, and water that produces multi-hued aqua colors and the psychedelic blues of the Gulf Stream; known to fisherman far and wide as the gamefish highway of the world. Waters that can still produce grand slams on all 365 days a year.

TIDBITS

Tourism is almost the entire Keys economy. Over half the Keys population hold jobs directly, or indirectly, related to outdoor recreational activities. In the 1995-1996 season, over one and a half million visitors snorkel or scuba dive, one million plus go fishing, and just shy of a million and a half visitors view wildlife or study nature.
The economic benefit; $2,100,000,000.

BIRTHING THE KEYS 125,000 YEARS AGO

Acording to Dr. Gene Shinn (SOFIA/USGS), the Miami limestone formations of the Upper Keys are visible today as elongated and relative north-south oriented land masses. Contrarily, Key Largo limestone foundations are noticeably oriented in a relative east-west line, and begin in the Lower Keys just beyond the Seven Mile Bridge on Big Pine Key. Both limestone foundations began about 125,000 years ago when the world's oceans were at least 20 feet higher than present levels. Coral gaps in the Lower Keys, Key West, and as far away as Miami, allowed tidal currents to sweep back and forth over the submerged platform of carbonate spheres, tiny 1mm calcareous oolites (ooids), and form elongated bars of loose sand. These round ooids settled and cemented over time to become the bedrock that is referred to as Miami limestone. Simultaneously, coral formations were developed by the build up of coral islands between the calcium carbonate in the Upper Keys and Middle Keys, and reaching all the way to a portion of Big Pine Key (Key Largo limestone).

FLORIDA KEYS REEF TRACT

From about 125,000 years ago to 80,000 years ago several swings of glaciation (polar ice caps expanding-cooling) and interglacial periods (polar ice caps melting-warming) occurred. The Florida Keys Reef Tract began to form in earnest around 80,000 years ago when the ocean was around 25 feet lower than today. The reef formed, by

Key Largo, FL
The reef then and now.

WATERHOUSE MARINE IMAGES

today's measurements, 6 or so miles offshore and much like its predecessor reef, the Florida Keys themselves, the reef tract followed the same arc. From 80,000 years ago to 25,000 years ago the many swings in glaciation and interglacial periods were not, relatively, extreme. However, about 25,000 years ago the swings became more radical. One so dramatic a glaciation period that it produced new polar ice cap growth that reached an astonishing one mile high and caused the oceans to drop, some calculate, an inconceivable 400 feet. Around 10,000 years ago an extremely rapid meltdown occurred and lasted until about 6,000 years ago. Water began to flood Florida, which was then twice its present width. Florida, before the event of flooding, had a western border that reached into the Gulf of Mexico 100 miles further west than at present. As the ocean level continued to rise, the newly forming Florida Keys reef tract was again under water as a string of corals. Progressively, the water filled the trench behind the reef tract (Hawk Channel), and by 3,000 years ago an Everglades-like swamp took shape west of the Keys and, eventually, Florida Bay immerged and looked much like we know it today. The only remaining land visible on the horizon after this glaciation period was the naked cap rock remnants of the 125,000-year-old reef—the Florida Keys.

The Florida Keys sat naked baking on its cap rock and getting pocked with numerous sinkholes caused by the naturally attacking acidic rain water. In time the Keys collected wind- and sea-borne debris and seeds delivered to it by both, as well as seeds deposited by fowl and game. The old cap rock soon, in geologic time, had several inches of terra firma, seeds selectively anchored in the accumulated debris, and abundant flora changed the horizon again. The growths were hardwood hammocks, pinelands, wetlands, palms and other flora. Much of the growth was similar to that which is found throughout the Caribbean, especially, in the Lower Keys. Many species of birds would soon find a new home or be provided migration layover turf. Animals, as well as reptiles, soon became part of the living Keys, and mangrove anchored where it could and started new islands out into the water on the Atlantic Ocean, Gulf of Mexico and Florida Bay.

FLORIDA BAY: LINCHPIN TO THE FUTURE HEALTH OF THE FLORIDA KEYS

Florida Bay covers about 850 square miles, averages only about 5 feet in water depth, has more than 30 'lakes' or basins and is almost a foot higher in water depth than it was in 1850, which is about a 20% increase. According to Dr. Shinn (SOFIA) and Dr. Bob Halley (USGS) the bay also averages a few inches more in water height than the Atlantic Ocean, which produces a constant, net downhill flow away from the Gulf of Mexico and toward the Atlantic.

Florida Bay is very much an influence on the ecosystem in the Keys, and greatly influences the whole of the fishery. Its adjacent reef tract serves as a nursery for fish, as well as home for wide variety of adult game fish. It also supports acres of sea grass, mangroves and a number of shrimp and crab species, as well as hundreds of organisms. Fresh water entering Florida Bay from the Everglades 'River of Grass' is the umbilical cord on which the bay relies to function. Bay-water salinity, temperature, turbidity, circulation and overall health, as well as that of its bottom life are inexorably tied, in one way or another, to the volume and quality of the water entering it from the Everglades.

MANIPULATING THE ENVIRONMENT

In just over 100 years, man successfully altered the natural water flow through the Everglades by dredging canals and building levies and dikes. All designed to divert water and control coastal flooding, which it accomplished, but it also reduced the amount, and quality, of water entering the system.

Upstream Everglades dredging and canal building began as early as the 1880's. The first confirmable affects of a change in the bay, however, occurred when Henry Flagler built the Over-The-Sea railroad (Florida East Coast Railroad Extension) in the early 1900's. The railroad's bridges and, especially, landfills altered the bay's circulation patterns. Massive manipulation of water flow, however, began almost the day after President Harry S. Truman dedicated the Everglades National Park in 1947. From that date onward, and through the early 1960's, the Corps of Engineers dredged miles of canals, installed over 1,400 levies and added miles of dikes. All done in an effort to save human life, control coastal flooding and preserve the aquifers from saltwater intrusion. Undeniably, it worked to a degree, but the price paid was enormous when considering what would have

to be done to restore historic, or near historic, water flows. Wittingly or unwittingly, the manipulating and reducing water flow through the Everglades dried up acres of historic Everglades turf and created an opportunity for a lot of land reclamation. The timing was perfect as it supported an unprecedented urbanization of South Florida, as well as a burgeoning farming industry. Hundreds of thousands of former Everglades real estate acres would be converted to develop sugar crop production and farming in general. Urban runoff, as well as fertilizer and chemical effluent runoff from increased farm activity, began flushing through the Everglades and into Florida Bay. Nutrient contributions would come from as far away as north of Lake Okeechobee and as close to the bay as Homestead. By the close of the last century, the Everglades had lost thousands of acres of sawgrass, gained acres of nutrient- loving cattails and added a shopping list of non-native flora that started pushing out native plants and trees. Nesting property shrank and a bird population of 170,000 (est. 1870) declined to 40,000 (est. today). Alligators, panthers and a myriad of other species of animals were forced into smaller habitats. Some bird and animal species became so habitat stressed that they closed in on extinction.

The bay itself responded by becoming more saline and marine-like and less its natural estuary-like environment. Reduced water flow and lowered water quality also caused the bay to be subjected to super-heating during dry spells, especially during the summer, which occasionally spawned devastating algal blooms. The bay also lost acres of sea grasses which, ultimately, resulted in increased sediment suspension. The sponge population diminished with a respondent loss of spiny lobster and the bay's vital pink shrimp population.

TODAY

Today, much is under way to restore historic water flow through the Everglades which will, once again, dramatically impact the bay in both terms of water volume, water quality and turbidity. The Everglades Restoration Act is

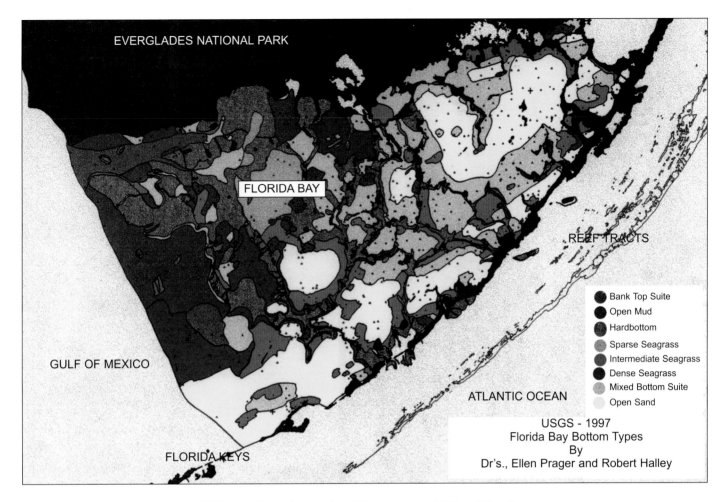

Legend:
- Bank Top Suite
- Open Mud
- Hardbottom
- Sparse Seagrass
- Intermediate Seagrass
- Dense Seagrass
- Mixed Bottom Suite
- Open Sand

USGS - 1997
Florida Bay Bottom Types
By
Dr's., Ellen Prager and Robert Halley

A Rare Look at the Bottom of Florida Bay

MIXED BOTTOM SUITE
Mixed bottom suite areas occur in the west-central area of the bay and can have, within just a few feet, varied bottom types.

OPEN SANDY AREAS
Open sandy areas occur in the transition area from bay to gulf and are primarily made up of a coarse shelly carbonate sand bottom. No significant benthic life forms.

HARDBOTTOM
This is bedrock with little or no sea grass. Gorgonian loggerhead or vase sponges are common to these areas. The bottom is sand carbonate, sand-mud and has relatively little organic matter.

BANK TOP SUITE
These formations are exposed areas, commonly called mud banks and flanked by sea grass. Areas in the north and east of the bay are topped with shelly areas. In the southwestern bay, transition from bay to gulf, these bottom types are topped with both sand and gravel.

OPEN MUD
A bottom is characterized by mud with sparse or no fauna and algal mats. Sedimentation has high organic content of carbonate mud.

SPARSE SEA GRASS
Sparse sea grass areas are where greater than 50% of the bottom is exposed with scattered sponges, muddy carbonate and sand is visible.

INTERMEDIATE SEA GRASS
These seagrass areas are where greater than 50% of the bottom is covered, and sponges, sandy and shell-like gravel-carbonate mud bottoms are visible.

DENSE SEA GRASS
Dense seagrass areas are those where the bottom is completely obscured, and there are sponges, as well as blooms of oyster pearl. Benthic here is high in organic material and it is also shelly.

designed, principally, to restore historic water flows through the Everglades. The planning has recruited scientists of every discipline, and their collective research efforts are being coordinated with the Corps of Engineers, South Florida Water District, Florida Keys National Marine Sanctuary, as well as more local, state and federal agencies, and countless other interests.

Implementing the restoration plan will be slow and issues debated ad nauseum. However, if politicians stay the course and keep funding alive ($7,800,000,000), publication and newspaper editors keep a forgetful public tuned in, science remains a driving force, and special-interest lobbyists can be leashed, then any reasonable implementation of the plan will be a resounding success.

Paradoxically, with all that has happened to Florida Bay in just over a hundred years, it remains a viable linch-pin to the overall bounty of the Keys fishery. In fact, most of the nearly 30 high-caliber guides and offshore captains we interviewed, over a five year period, suggested that the bay is more productive as a fishery now than it has been in the last 20 years. The guides, environmentally clued stewards of the Keys, sighted several reasons: upstream hydro management practices have begun to improve the water flow patterns into the bay; new controls reducing harmful upstream farm run-off; broodstock and shrimp over-harvesting by the commercial fishing industry reigned in; waste-water management in the Keys itself is greatly improved; catch-and-release practices are now widespread throughout the sportfishing community; and the coming of age of the Florida Keys National Marine Sanctuary Program (FKNMSP) is taking effect by placing a lot of sensitive watery turf under "strict-use" guidelines. In addition, research is now being coordinated or sponsored by the FKNMSP. The net affect drowns out special-interest groups' agenda-driven studies with quality research. Nothing kills bad environmental politics better than a good spray of solid scientific research. Additionally, further development in the Keys is coming under much tighter scrutiny, and the public and private sectors of Monroe County's citizenry are favorably responding to needed changes. The endemic beauty and bounty of Florida Bay has not been spoiled.

REEF TRACT HEALTH. IT'S NOT JUST ABOUT SEWAGE

Coral throughout the Caribbean and Florida have, since the 1970's, started suffering in an unprecedented way from various diseases. Staghorn and elkhorn coral, for example, showed evidence of rapid die-off in the late 1970's in Florida and throughout the Caribbean. The worst morbidity occurred in almost a single year, 1983. Some scientists think it's possible that naturally occurring outbreaks of disease throughout history explains why reefs, here in the Keys and elsewhere, never reached their full potential over the past thousands of years.

TIDAL FLUSHING AND THE REEF

Tidal flushing over sections of coral reef tracts in the Middle and some of the Lower Keys retards, or stops altogether, coral growth. Both the bay and gulf are shallow bodies of water and quickly chill during winter cold spells. Florida Bay's runoff is also naturally sediment

Florida Bay and the backcountry. Tricky navigating.

laden. Both the bay and gulf deliver regular doses of cold water and mud sediment, and effectively combine to kill off fast-growing corals. Radiocarbon dating of some of these affected reefs show they have been growth-dormant for over 2,000 years. In the Keys, coral thrives where bay or gulf waters cannot wash over them, which is due to islands (keys) shielding them from tidal flushing. Examples of thriving reefs are those off Key Largo, as well as some in the Lower Keys.

OTHER FACTORS AFFECTING REEF HEALTH

Hurricanes can have a more short-term impact on reefs than any man-made activity. Also, reef species that symbiotically attack deadly coral algae have been over-harvested. In addition, some scientific evidence suggests that water flowing from Florida Bay passes through the porous limestone bedrock of the Keys creating a net flow through the limestone foundation that is significant. This water flush, in and out of the limestone twice daily, pumps a sulfide-rich ground water that reaches the corals and retards coral growth with unnaturally high levels of ammonia. Human activity, of course, has stressed coral recruitment: commercial and residential development, boating, commercial shipping (in the past), fishing, diving and the by-product of human pathogens, and an excess of nutrients.

Some science suggests that increased El Niño events and global warming have a profound effect on reef tracts throughout the world. Other scientists are studying the naturally occurring affects of tons (billions) of African tradewind-borne soil that settles in the Caribbean and southeastern U.S. each year. Within the dust or soil particulate is a fungus (*Aspergillus*) that is believed to be responsible for seafan and staghorn coral disease. Perhaps not so coincidentally, unprecedented seafan and staghorn coral die-off in the Keys and Caribbean happened in 1983 and 1987 when the wind-borne *Aspergillus* fungus was at its highest recorded levels. Another and more subtle reason for reef decline is that the sea level is rising.

A TOUCHY SUBJECT

Near and offshore corals on the Atlantic side of the Keys have, in many places, been replaced by an algae that thrives on nutrients from treated sewage. The algae flourishes in elevated concentrations of phosphate and nitrate, which are by-products of treated human sewage. These nutrients are not, however, considered contaminants. Sewage in the Keys is now treated to near-potable water quality, much of which is discharged at depths ranging from 30 to 90 feet. In the Keys, there are approximately 1,000 shallow wells, several hundred so-called package plants, over 23,000 onsite water-treatment systems, and more than 10,000 septic tanks. Nutrient-rich water, not contaminated water, inevitably, makes its way seaward to the coral reef tract and, eventually, nutrients extort a price.

LITTLE REWARD FOR MILLIONS SPENT ON RESEARCH

Unfortunately, scientists admit they have not yet come up with a solution that promises to solve the problem of coral disease or reef decline. The problem is not just in the Keys or Caribbean, it's actually worldwide. What is possible, many scientists say, is that periodic coral disease and reef deterioration are naturally occurring events of time. However, no scientific study has ever discounted man's negative influence on coral. The litany of abuses is long.

HUG A REEF

If you scuba or snorkel in the Florida Keys, you will at once, and forever, become an addict of the surreal underworld. Each dive is an unforgettable experience, especially for fisherman. It adds a new dimension, understanding what goes on below the waterline and it also changes your perspectives on all manner of things environmental. The Florida Keys Reef Tract is the third largest in the world, the Belizian Reef is second, and Australia's Great Barrier Reef is the largest. Florida's Reef Tract is 10 times smaller than Australia's, but it hosts 10 times as many visitors per year. The Keys Reef Tract is also the only living barrier reef in the continental shelf of North America. It extends from just south of Miami (Fowery Rocks) to the Dry Tortugas. The Keys Reef Tract is host to 80% of the known coral types in the tropical Atlantic, with over 100 coral species and over 500 species of tropical fish. The interaction and interdependence of reef-dwelling inhabitants is so tied together that several species of fish could not survive without the coral reef. Principle in the coral reef tracts' health is the warm Gulf Stream waters that wash over them with nutrient-free, clean, clear water that is packed with life-sustaining plankton.

NOTE: The reefs have long been a blessing as a storm barrier. They also play an essential role in sand production with an annual production of about two and a half tons of sand per acre per year, which is essential for beach and sea grass build-up.

NOTE: The coral reef tract in the Keys, usually, has well over 1,000,000 visitors a year: fishermen, divers, boaters and sightseers. The monetary value of the reef tract to Monroe County is immeasurable.

TIDBITS

The Keys are similar to the southern peninsula of the Florida, but only the Keys support several terrestrial, marine plant and animal species indigenous to the Caribbean. The Gulf Stream and trade winds, rather than longitude and latitude, allowed for colonization of indigenous Caribbean plants and animals. Singularly, the Keys have produced a number of subspecies, adapted only for life on the Keys.

SEA GRASSES

Every flats guide in the Florida Keys is a jealous guardian of sea grasses. Those who dare to abuse sea grasses, or disregard them when boating, are likely to hear about it. To the Keys flats guides, robust watery fields of sea grasses are a grant of continuance. Without sea grasses there are far fewer and, possibly, no bonefish, shrimp, redfish, crabs, permit, spiny lobster or a long list of seasonal show-up species. For fish, sea grasses are a nursery and repository of a most useful by-product of mangrove: detritus nutrients. For juvenile fish, sea grasses are a place to find daily sustenance and cover. For other species, sea grasses are an ambush cover in one big grocery store.

Sea grasses serve the Keys environment in many ways. They host over 100 species of algae, more than 130 species of animals; not counting fish, which there are an additional hundred or so known species. They are also primary to pink shrimp, mollusks (conch) and other crustaceans (other shrimps, several varieties of crab, and lobster). Sea grasses are also a principle component in aiding water clarity and stabilizing the sea floor. They perform the latter functions by baffling wave action, trapping naturally suspended sediment with their long leaves, and anchoring their roots deep into the bottom, which aids the advance of more grass. The reduction in suspended sediment also improves the process of photosynthesis, which has a ripple effect that reaches all the way to the reef tracts. The clearer the water that makes its way to the reefs during tidal exchange, the more beneficial it is in the promotion of growth and overall health of the corals, as well as sea grass itself.

Of 52 known species of marine grasses in the world, only four are part of Florida's waters. Three, however, are primary to the Keys: manatee-grass (*Syringodium filiforme*), shoal-grass (*Halodule wrightii*), turtle-grass (*Thalassia testundinum*). Widgeon-grass (*Ruppia maritima*) is the fourth Florida sea grass. Manatee grass is the easiest to identify as its leaf blades are rounded. Shoal grass leaf blades are not as big (wide or long) as those of turtle grass. Turtle grass leaf blades can be as long as one foot and have a blade width approaching an inch. Shoal and manatee grasses are pioneer grasses that can establish growth in soft sandy bottom terrain that turtle grass cannot. However, once growth is established by the forerunners, then turtle grass will introduce itself and, usually, takes over.

7 TO 10 YEARS OF HARD LABOR

A prop dredge-damaged sea-grass bed will take 7 to 10 years to regenerate. Sediment plume is as harmful to sea grasses as prop dredging itself because it can also cut roots (*rhizomes*) that anchor as deep as 5 feet. Dredged sea-grass paths are a sure sign of abysmally ignorant boaters, who have raped everyone's fishing future. Sea grasses are disappearing from the Florida Keys at an unacceptable rate. Guides in the Keys state that acres and acres of propeller and plume damage to sea grasses are almost always caused by, with no malice intended, casual boaters, jet-ski operators (almost all personal watercraft operators are clueless according to guides) and novice sport fishermen boaters who are both impatient and unfamiliar with where they are, what they are getting into, or doing.

MANGROVE

Man's most noticeable impact on mangrove has been dredge and fill operations. The Keys, at one time, were entirely bordered by mangrove, as were all its islands. Mangroves service the Keys environment and its fishery in many, many ways; some of which are just like sea grass: filtering the system and trapping suspended sediment. They also have the ability to create land and stabilize shorelines by establishing a foothold on the tiniest spit of turf. Once anchored, mangroves begin trapping debris, which continues to consolidate more turf and expand more mangrove growth. Only water depth retards their advance, or the clown who illegally has them torn out to improve his view. Mangroves are now protected by law. One very big benefit mangroves provide man is protection from violent tropical storms and hurricanes, as they capably baffle wind and reduce the affects of storm surge. Mangroves, below the water line and within the root system, host many species of fish, crustaceans and shellfish. Their leaf litter alone has been determined to be the first link in the food chain. The fallen leaves, broken down by microorganisms, produce sustenance for as much as 75% of the Keys tropical aquatic community, which includes the early-in-life needs of snook, tarpon, redfish, snappers, shrimp and more. Mangroves, at the water line, host animals (key deer and raccoons), and skyward in their branches, nest rookery areas for birds (pelicans, roseate spoonbills and frigate birds). Three species of mangroves are indigenous to the Florida Keys (button-

Sea grasses teeming with life.

Queen conch surrounded by healthy sea grasses. The conch is the source of the Keys, calling itself the 'Conch' Republic.

wood is also considered mangrove and indigenous to the Keys). They are also all common to the Bahamas, West Indies and Africa. All can thrive in saltwater environments with varying degrees of tolerance and have species-specific reproductive systems, as well as abilities to deal with salty environs. Red, black and white mangroves all have unique desalinization plants enabling them to exclude or extrude salt.

The red mangrove (*Rhizophora mangle*) is easily identified because it is the most shoreward of the mangrove types, but can survive deeper into the mangrove forest where other mangrove reside. Its reddish-brown roots

Prop scars, unfortunately, are a common sight on the Keys flats and backcountry. The damage shown will take a minimum of seven years for a full regrowth, but more likely 10 years. In the past 15 years, water toys and small boats captained by novices with little knowledge of their conveyance and ignorant of the environment, have dramatically increased. Plowed-through "No Combustion Zones" (well marked) and indiscretions on the open flats are of great concern to environmental authorities, professional guides, professional dive-shop owners, qualified boaters and responsible sportsmen.

are tall and arch from branches, so as to appear to be walking. Red mangroves can reach a height of 60 feet or more, or be as stubby as a bush. Its leaves are thick, rubbery and elliptically shaped. Their shiny leaf is a dark green on top and pale green on the underside accompanied by dark spots. Its flowers are yellow and found in clusters of two or three separate blooms. Its propagation, like the other two mangrove types, is via a propagule. With the red mangrove, the propagule is a long pencil-shaped, fully germinated seed before it falls to the ground. It can establish itself by puncturing the ground it falls on or lodge later at a great distance from its maturation drop point. Propagules can be seen germinating from any of the mangrove type during the early summer, and found floating late in the summer when they fall. They can be seen floating well into the fall of the year. Red mangroves exclude salt, using a reverse osmosis process powered by high negative pressure, which all happens in the xylem, and results from a transpiration at the leaf surface.

Black mangroves (*Avicenia germinans*) are found on slightly higher ground than red mangrove. They grow to 60 feet or more and are easily identified by their root system as well, which protrudes around the tree's trunk as pointy fingers called, *pneumatophores*. The pneumatophores are short spikes that carpet and surround the mother tree. The black mangrove's flowers are yellow, but are short, spike-like and in clusters. Black mangroves have large, spread-out branches that are dark brown. Its leaves are opposing, leathery, dark green on top and elliptically narrower than the lance-like red mangrove. The underside of the leaves are a noticeably paler green, have deposits of salt, and a hairy feel to them. Black mangroves are the hardiest of the mangroves as they can endure extreme cold (for the Keys) without damage.

White mangroves (*Laguncularia racemosa*) grow in muddy tidal water of bays and lagoons, more upland than its rivals, and have no visible root system. Its wood

I

Tropical hardwood hammock: Found on higher elevations of the Keys. Varied tropical plants, hardwoods and protective coverage for key deer and many other animals.

II

Mangrove and nearshore hardbottom: Mangrove fringe the entire Keys, Florida Bay the southern tier of the Everglades and all intertidal shorelines. Mangrove root systems and nearby sea grasses provide shelter, food and act as nurseries for many fish larvae, juveniles and eventual reef-dwelling creatures. It is also a predator's mecca for several gamefish species.

III

Inshore Patch Reef: Small, scattered cluster reefs appearing often on the flats. Generally, a halo of sand surrounds these outcroppings, which are created by grazing juvenile fish and invertebrates.

IV

Mid-Channel Reef: Found in the deep part of Hawk Channel, between the Keys and main outer reef. Coral can rise to 15 feet. A holding station for maturing fish and invertebrates.

V

Offshore Patch Reef: Located on the seaward edge of Hawk Channel, paralleling the outer reef tract. A diverse habitat of tall, soft and stony corals.

VI

Reef Flat (back reef): A scattered and sheltered environment. These ridge outcroppings include sea grasses and provide refuge from wind and waves for many organisms.

VII

Fore Reef: Shallow and sometimes an exposed crest of coral fingers, forming high-profile slopes and ledges, separated by deep sand channels known as 'spur & groove.'

VIII

Intermediate to Deep Reef: Intermediate: a gradually sloping, low-profile 'spur & groove' coral reef. Deep reef: locations where the intermediate reef drops off abruptly to a sandy bottom.

is hard, strong, dark yellow-brown in color, and its bark is loaded with tannin. It, too, can grow upwards of 60-feet. The largest stands in Florida are found in the Keys. Its flowers are quite fragrant, bloom almost all year long, are round greenish-white, and set around a central spiky stem. Its leaves are more oval than red or black mangroves, and have a notch at the tip, and two small bumps on either side of its stem just below the leaf blade. Its leaves are uniformly pale green on both sides. White mangroves lack pneumatophores and its propagule are small in comparison to the red and black mangroves, wrinkled and 10 ribbed. Both black and white mangroves extrude salt through the petiole at the base of each leaf. NOTE: The sap of a red mangrove is one seventh the salt concentration of sea water, but 10X that of freshwater plants. The sap of a white mangrove is 10X saltier than red mangroves.

TROUBLE BREWS IN THE 1970'S
Environmental failing in the Keys was noticeable to many scientists of several different marine and wildlife disciplines by the 1970's, but very, very little was ever done to curb the slide. There were hardly any coordinated research efforts and no one to deliver a decipherable message. In the 20 years that followed, dozens of agencies were spawned with an alphabet of acronyms that were full of sound and fury, but signified nothing in the way of change. Abuses to the environment escalated as the calendar rolled forward. Ship groundings and boat anchorings on the reefs were all too common. Overharvesting by the commercial interests and party boat hauls began to reduce broodstocks. Table fare fads decimated some species, and seasonal runs on several species were more than occasionally over-fished by commercial interests. Personal watercraft and small boats proliferated and their collective intrusions on the shallow water flats environments started taking a heavy toll on sea grasses. A new term made its way into the guides vocabulary: "flats rage." Coral reefs and sea grasses were producing clear evidence of physical abuse, and unprecedented over-development taxed the Keys infrastructure. By 1990, it was no longer heresy to say the Keys were environmentally stressed.

Dive-shop owners, guides and offshore captains noticed a decline in water clarity, but still this disturbing fact generated little press. Water quality was the most troubling by-product of exhibited environmental stress and suggested to many an apocalypse if not corrected. The Keys only capital stock, clean, clear water, was taking a hit. Clean, gin-clear water is, quintessentially, the Keys. It is the most critical resource, and the benchmark by which the Keys are measured. If the Keys waters run foul then everything they embraced will be affected. Property values will decline, businesses will be severely hurt and jobs will be lost. Without clean, clear water there is no scuba diving because polluted, cloudy water and dead coral are not sought-after sights. Without clean, clear water there are no tourists and without tourists the Keys economy is impounded.

Polluted water is cloudy water that kills coral and sea grasses by retarding light transmission and produces unmanageable sediment deposits. It also spawns voracious forms of un-natural algae, which denude sea bottom life, quickly. Without healthy coral, sea grasses and mangroves there are no broodstocks, no baitfish, no reef fish, and no inshore game fish. Finally, no pelagic gamefish species would have reason to seasonally visit because the food chain's essential links would be missing.

CALAMITY MEETS OPPORTUNITY
In 1989, a plethora of newspaper and magazines articles serendipitously drew national attention to the Keys quiet environmental suffering. Three horrendous ship collisions with Keys Reefs Tracts (1989 and 1990) were, sadly, the catalysts. Senator Bob Graham (FL), a long-time proponent of saving the Everglades, protecting the Keys and environmentally clued well beyond most of his colleagues, quickly mustered bi-partisan congressional support for a plan that would expand the presence and power of NOAA's (National Oceanic and Atmospheric Administration - Department of Commerce) already in-place Florida Keys National Marine Sanctuary (FKNMS) with an all-encompassing Florida Keys National Marine Sanctuary Program (FKNMSP). NOAA was charged with the responsibility of curbing past and potential environmental abuses on the bountiful waters of the Keys. In essence, to protect the Keys waters from being further damaged, degraded, resource plundered, and to restore a fishery. The Florida Keys would never be the same, just better. Enter NOAA's FKNMS man, Billy Causey. With alacrity uncommon to a bureaucracy, and with the skill of a true CEO, Billy Causey, a highly motivated and educated team of the FKNMS staff put together a program, then regarded as radical, called the Florida Keys National Marine Sanctuary Program (FKNMSP). The program was much debated, hated and loved. The FKNMSP, in effect, replotted the sailing course for the Keys by redefining environmental awareness, responsibilities and direction that research would take. The FKNMSP would impact every diver, sport and commercial fisherman, boater, recreator of any kind, employer, visitor, citizen and institution in the Keys, forever.

For the decades before the FKNMSP came into being, double-digit federal, state and local agencies spent millions of tax dollars on hundreds of niche research

---

TIDBITS

Key Largo National Marine Sanctuary
Administrative Office
POB 500368
Marathon, FL 33050
305 - 743 - 2437

Upper Keys Regional Office
POB 1083
Key Largo, FL 33037
305-451-1644

Lower Keys Regional Office
216 Ann St.
Key West, FL 33040
305-292-0311

Red mangroves, commonly called walking trees for obvious reasons. A typical tidal flush piece of real estate where water rises and falls, in and out of a root system, and provides both safe harbor for fish and a place from which many an ambush takes place. This is prime snook, redfish and small tarpon turf. The Keys, unfortunately, have been subjected to much development, which has reduced the populations of mangroves. Law now, however, prohibits removal or trimming. It's a good law.

White egret.

projects that produced some legislation, but many times they were impotent restrictions or do-nothing pain-in-the arse laws. Clearly, there were too many cooks in the environmental kitchen, and many powerful groups had agendas that slowed down, or abrogated, the process of rejuvenating the environments of the Everglades, Florida Bay and the Keys.

By July 1, 1997, after much tumult, the FKNMSP was fully operative and, literally, encircled the land masses of the entire Florida Keys. Some 3,600 square miles of watery turf were now theirs to captain. The FKNMSP had already moved historic shipping lanes way away from the reefs, forbade future mining, oil & gas exploration, artifact hunting and were heralded by most for those successes.

Thus far, and into the new millennium, the FKNMSP has proven itself a reliable research information clearing-house, a capable referee and a good traffic cop when it comes to quantifying and qualifying research project information. They have also taken on the much needed role of educator by involving the Keys community. An

TIDBITS

The most western boundary of the Florida Keys National Marine Sanctuary are the waters surrounding the Dry Tortugas. Its most extreme northeast boundary is where 125th St. (Miami) intersects with Biscayne Bay.

Advisory Board, made up of 22 Keys citizens, representing every professional, as well as private, interest focus in the Keys, deals with the impact issues proposed by the FKNMS. The FKNMSP has proven to be a capable arbiter and responsive listener on environmental water, and fishery, issues affecting the Florida Keys. In the new millennium, the FKNMSP's, Monroe County and the state's biggest challenges will be the improvement of the collection, and treatment, of storm runoff water, and influencing the continuation of improvement in water quality that flows through the Everglades and into Florida Bay.

"THE EYES OF THE WORLD . . ."

So far, the FKNMSP has put forward several coherent and widely understood plans. Many have been put into effect, and they have all come about, for the first time, through high-level, coordinated research.

In the next 20 years, the loomimg task for Monroe County, and the FKNMSP, will be to keep the pressure on the state and federal authorities, south Florida water management engineers and scientists, and private interest groups to stay the course of continuing to move forward with the Everglades Restoration Plan. A plan that can undo a lot of man-made water-flow constrictions on three quarters of the natural flow through the Everglades' "River Of Grass." The restoration of as much of the natural order as possible is vital, and will profoundly affect the environmental future of several of this country's most unique resources: the Everglades, Florida Bay, Florida Keys and an entire fishery.

A majority of the Keys guides and offshore captains we spoke to are solidly behind the FKNMSP's closures (Tortugas 2000) that offer species a chance to recover, and other proposals that limit species takes. The guides and offshore captains support the FKNMSP's actions and that, oddly, runs contrary to many in the sportfishing editorial business.

Eagleray. Several species of rays are common to the Keys flats. Guides will pay attention to the presence of rays as they invite followers, cobia, mutton snapper and permit, for example. All can find a crustacean or two loosened from its bottom dwelling by the ray's powerful wing action.

Unfortunately, restoring the environment of the Florida Keys, Everglades and Florida Bay have components of natural conflict. First, an economy based solely on the ability of an environment to perform while thousands make a living off it, and for the millions who recreate in it. A very complicated accommodations equation. One that now rests with the Florida Keys National Marine Sanctuary.

"The eyes of the world are watching what's happening here (Florida Keys)."
Bill Causey, Florida Keys National Marine Sanctuary

". . . Keys will become the world's center of marine environmental intelligence in the 21st century."
Naturalist, Edna Gould Clement, 1990

WHAT LIES AHEAD

The FKNMSP is not really a park program and not really a policing agency. It is, after all, a branch of the Commerce Department, required by charter to encourage both commercial and recreational use. All kinds of recreating are welcomed activities in most of the NOAA sanctuaries. Additionally, marine science, unfortunately, is relatively new, as are marine sanctuaries themselves. Not much is known about what really makes marine environments tick, especially down there in leagues under the sea, so expect some hiccups and flawed proposals to emerge.

The FKNMSP may be relatively new to the Keys, but NOAA's history with other sanctuaries is not. Reports about them are excellent, and no matter how you slice it, the FKNMS holsters the only gun in town that is loaded. Who, if not the FKNMSP, would be the best Keys 'river-keeper, steward of the marine shallows, watchman on the high seas . . .'? They are probably the last real big-league quarterback we'll see in the Keys and, so far, they are doing pretty well.

The event of installing the FKNMS as the new steward for the Keys waters started a chain reaction and created a catharsis. Their presence produced a defining self-examination process within the institutions of Monroe County and the State of Florida resulting, today, in a new all-hands-on-deck priority: the environment. The Keys entire capital stock is now the environment, and a new market economy is based on it. In the short run, the new economy of the Keys will cause hardships, but Conch's were weaned on hardship.

FOREVER TIED TO THE ENVIRONMENT

With the economic future of the Florida Keys now tied entirely to the environment, every effort to maintain and improve that capital stock is now an all-institutions focus, with Monroe County and Tourist Development Counsel taking the lead. All available technology, research and education to improve individual behavior is presently under way. The Monroe County Comprehensive Plan and Land Development Regulations have implemented plans for a new water-treatment system which will favorably impact the Keys water quality for the next 20 to 30 years. The costs of implementing that plan, authorities have said, are just peanuts when weighed against the billions in compensating yearly GNP for the Keys.

"Any cost analysis one does to favor whatever position he holds still ends up a pittance of an investment to improve the waste water facilities and favorably influences the most critical element of the Keys; protection of its environmental magnificence: coral reefs, sea grasses, mangrove and bountiful fishery."

Sage Author Unknown

THE BARELY CHARTERED WATERS OF MARINE SCIENCE

WHAT FISH CAN HEAR

While quiet has always been a priority when approaching game fish, especially on the flats and backcountry, it has never been well understood just how fish hear and what they hear. Marine science has, however, reached some interesting conclusions. All fish do hear, and like humans, some are better equipped than others. A fish's sense of hearing, to the degree that it's developed in each species, is relational to how it adapted itself to hearing and discerning sounds at the distances it needed to escape, find food and mate.

Sound travels five times faster (1 mile a second) in water than in the air and can be heard at much, much greater distances, carrying a thousand miles or more (water is at least a thousand times more dense than air). The ocean, therefore, is a very noisy place: waves, boats, fish themselves engaged in all manner of activities, storms, earthquakes, volcanos, ocean currents, the movement of your fly and that clumsy guy who bangs around on the boat deck. Fish rely on sound, as well as other senses, for their survival.

A fish hears near-field and far-field sounds. Near field is at about 30 feet away and heard through the inner ear and by its lateral line. The lateral line performing so well at about 6 feet that it is often as accurate as our sense of touch. The lateral line is also used to detect objects by rebounding sound, which would include a fly. Far-field sound is heard as sound pressure (sign waves) and detected/analyzed through the inner ear as well as the resonating of the swim bladder, if they have one. Fish have only one ear. It is internal to their body and located in the head. Fish do not have an outer ear as its body tissue is, approximately, the same density as water. Sound, therefore, passes un-impeded and not mutated. The inner ear also enables a fish to keep its balance. There are several chambers and canals in a fish's ear, some hold fluids and some have stones called, *otoliths*. Each otolith and chamber/canal detecting a myriad of distinctive sounds, which the brain then computes - who, what and where. As a side bar, otoliths are distinctive rings (similiar to trees) the age of a fish and species can be determined from them.

Tarpon have superior hearing and they have swim bladders. The latter acting as a resonator that aids the inner ear. For example, from about 6 feet away a tarpon can pinpoint your fly from the sound made when you twitch it. Even in pitch-black conditions, tarpon can instantaneously determine whether it's a threat, opportunity or an unnatural sound. A tarpon can also orient itself to the origin of that same fly from about 30 feet away.

Fish use the information of detected sound in many ways: to avoid objects in murky water, to determine prey or predator, to determine the distance from an emitted sound, to maintain position when in a schooling profile, and in some species, to detect sounds made from the opposite sex, and to communicate. Some fish, sharks for example, also have highly developed abilities to detect electrical fields (muscle twitches of prey) in their lateral line. Sharks are true predators, first on the scene of an accident and ready to take advantage of a bad situation.

Most fish become stressed by unnatural sounds and scoot immediately when they feel threatened. Flats and backcountry game fish of the Keys are particularly sensitive to sound and they compute unnatural noises such as a poor presentation with the fly slapping the water, noisy hull design, loud conversation, or banging around on the boat deck as threatening. Paradoxically, some species seem to be attracted to the noise of the engine/propellers (sailfish and tuna), and some seem attracted to the sound of a popper (seatrout). Constantly changing the RPMs of your boat will frighten most fish.

WHAT FISH CAN SEE

What marine scientists know about how a fish's brain translates what it sees is useful to anglers. Most fish are nearsighted, but sharks are believed to be farsighted. Large, open-ocean, big-eyed predators can, generally, see great distances while tidal, inshore and smaller-eyed fish see only short distances. Most game fish found in the Keys see well left and right, but not directly in front or behind. Their eyes protrude from their head and move independently, giving each eye a 180-degree view. Each fish species' eyes have an orientation, or characteristic, which allows them to see predominantly up or down, and that determines how and what they feed on. Most game fish in the Keys have their eyes dedicated to the water column in which they swim and are considered up-looking fish. A bonefish, some snappers, redfish and permit are modified exceptions, but their eyes are not downwardly developed, thus the tailing/mudding profile. A fly presented below the water column in which game fish swim is almost always a true waste of time.

The sense of sight always allows predatory fish to isolate prey for the final assault. Seeing a prey's final movements, or movement in general, is essential to instigating the strike itself. The final focus of an attacking predatory fish will be on the eyes of its prey.

A fish's eyes have cone cells and receptor cells (rods). Cone cells respond to color, providing higher definition, and rod cells respond to black and white, or contrast. Fish that feed on the surface during the day have more cone cells than fish that feed in the low-light conditions of early morning, or dusk. When fishing in the first transition hour of night or day, you fish when all fish are making at least an hour-long vision adjustment to their rod/cone cells, and fishing will tend to be poor. However, just before the light change occurs (dawn or dusk) fishing tends to be very good if all other conditions are right.

Fly color is an argument not quite 100% put to rest, but shape, use of eyes, matching what the fish feed on and contrast are all critical considerations, but not necessarily color. Red, for example, is completely invisible in 10 feet or so of water. White is good in deeper water. Dark colors are good in low-light conditions because they produce contrast, or silhouette, and bright colors work best on bright sunny days. Paradoxically, permit, bonefish, snappers and redfish (tidal flats species) are not fish that respond well to contrast. All their normal prey mimic the color of their (bottom) surroundings. Larger flies work better when there is rough, choppy water. Fluorescence in flies does attract fish and it does frighten fish. The theory, and some laboratory experiments suggest, that on cloudy days when ultraviolet rays increase, which some species can see (humans cannot), it energizes the flashy material and creates interest. Too much flash, however, will definitely scare any game fish away.

WHAT FISH SMELL

Chumming, of course, is a smell inducement for game fish, and smell is probably the most relied on sense of a game fish in the Keys. The smell sense is not, however, 100% understood by marine scientists. What they do know is that smell is important in finding food, some migrations, communication and the reproductive process. Fish have two nostril openings on each side of their head. Each nostril takes in water in one opening and passes it through the opening right next to it. Olfactory nerve endings at the base of the nostril are titillated by the water rushing over tiny hairs (*cilia*). Cilia send the odor message. For example, when the skin of a fish is injured a scent is released. It alerts all nearby fish of danger or opportunity. A bleeding fish, of course, notifies all predators that the feed is on.

Fish attractors, although very popular with bass fisherman and sold widely in tackle shops, are not the answer in salt water, even though fish have a keen sense of smell. Each species, actually, reacts differently to the same chemical compound. Also, that reaction can change from location to location, tide to tide, month to month, or season to season. For one species a particular odor is an attractor and for another it's a repellent, or, today one odor is good and later in the month it's not. This fact is not well understood by marine scientists.

Conversely, some chemicals are always repulsive to fish. Namely, those that are exuded from the skin of most caucasians called *L-serine*. Other known chemicals that offend all fish are: gasoline, oil products in general, sunscreen, mosquito repellent and tobacco residue. More importantly, all the aforementioned odors are quickly absorbed by monofilament, leaders and flies. Worse yet is that the chemical residue on mono line is an irreversible

A barjack takes a look at today's menu (silversides).

odor impression. Oddly, your own saliva will lessen the chemical print, and liquids from baits do the same, along with fruit juice, sugar and dairy products.

HEARING, SEEING, SMELLING AND FISH CATCHING

Taking advantage of marine science is not particularly new to experienced guides and offshore captains of the Keys. They have been inputting data by guiding and captaining marine scientists around Florida Bay, Gulf of Mexico, flats and Atlantic Ocean for years. Their collective input is more valuable to clients than any X-marks-the-spot map that, falsely, promises delivery to the promised land of great fish catching. The conclusions, or realities, about what a fish hears, sees and smells are just a part of useful information that has come from this budding science.

A summary of the above as it relates to marine science and fishing might be helpful on your next trip to the Keys.

• Bright-colored fly lines are detected by fish. Try light green to avoid alarming a fish.

• Heavily applied fluorescent (flash) material on your flies will not attract, but alarm, fish.

• Sending your fly below the water column in which game fish swim will produce nothing. A fish may rise to a fly, but it will not descend to one.

• In the open ocean where fish are schooling on the surface you can almost be assured that larger fish are below them and probably not of the same species.

• Fresh chum works a lot better than frozen chum.

• That cigarette habit you have is not only harmful to your health, but is repulsive to fish and will permanently imprint on your line (mono) and flies.

• Varying the RPMs of your boat will chase fish away.

• Your voice and banging around on the boat deck will chase fish away.

• Limit your false casting as it can invite detection. Your fly slapping the water is an unnatural sound that will frighten fish. Your shadow cast over, or even near, a fish will spook it.

• The twitching of your fly, it's speed and length of pull, have a lot to do with getting and keeping a fish's interest, especially the all important strike. Each game fish's natural instincts for reacting to the latter must be known. A lazy pull will not interest a barracuda, for example, and a fast retrieve will spook a bonefish. Your guide or

---

TIDBITS

SLEEPING

Fish do sleep, but not in the sense of the word relevant to our understanding of it. With no eyelids, or poorly developed ones, we've long assumed that fish were not capable of sleeping. Fish, however, spend a lot of time doing just that. They go into a floating or rest state in which they conserve energy, and will do so for hours at a time.

---

offshore captain will have that all important understanding down pat.

• When a fish strikes, each species is a little different. Knowing when to set the hook is critical. Again, your guide will have this down pat.

• Fishing when the light is changing is not a good time period because all species' eyes are in mid-adaptation from predominantly using rod cells or cone cells. Some species adapt faster than others, but the process can take an hour or more.

• Generally, the color of your fly should correspond to: natural baits presently available (size and color), darker colors on cloudy days or in murky water, brighter on sunny days, larger when the water is choppy, and for bottom-feeding tidal-flats fish, matching the color of natural foods. Many guides and offshore captains have a definite color and size preference when it comes to flies. They may well be contrary to current thinking and wide of scientific conclusions. Always, however, go with your guide or offshore captain's choice as they have come to their color/size selection from repetitive successes, not failures.

TIDES

Tidal currents are perhaps the most important by-product of tidal changes in the Keys. Tide changes absolutely affect flats fishing. The current created by tidal changes may make for a favorable feeding station at one part of a tide, at a given place, and not favorable at that same location, in another phase of the tidal change. Tiny organisms to small baitfish are swept into currents during a tide change or are activated by them when water covers a tidal plane. All gamefish predators of the tidal flats—permit, tarpon, bonefish, redfish, snook, spotted seatrout, barracuda, sharks, snappers and others—know when and where it's most favorable for them and can be counted on to be present or nearby. Knowing when and where these changes take place is, of course, the advantage, and local knowledge of them is paramount to catching fish. Without local knowledge you can only guess.

The effects of tides are primarily determined by gravity and inertia, and they are relative to the moon's phases (apogee: furthest from the moon; to perigee: closest to moon). Also, when the sun lines up with the moon, the excessive pull of gravity causes spring tides (spring tides have nothing to do with the spring of the year). These tides occur about every two weeks. A neap tide is a lower than normal tide and also occurs every two weeks, but only when the sun and moon are at right angles to the earth. A spring tide range averages about 20% greater than a normal tide and a neap tidal flow averages about 20% lower in range than is normal. The sequence, spring tide to neap tide, takes twenty nine and a half days.

Tidal flow in the Keys can vary greatly in just short distances, and the effects on fishing can be dramatic. Some of the elements that effect great flow differences are: the influence by both the Atlantic Ocean's two high and two low tides and the Gulf of Mexico's one high and one low tide, Everglades freshwater discharges into Florida Bay, thousands of mangrove islands redirecting water, land masses creating bottlenecks, channels collecting and moving water at greater speeds, bottom topography, interference of structures (bridges), and wind. It would be impossible for a visitor to know where these vastly different flows take place or what effects they have on fish. No book or chart, thus far printed, reveals them accurately. Guides have told us that to be schooled in a relatively wide area it would take about two to three years of vigilant surveying to understand the nuances of currents and tides, and know when, where and how better fishing plays into those subtleties.

Flats species are highly tuned to the tidal swings that occur on their turf. All flats species are very easily spooked because of potentially being trapped by a receding tide and are therefore never far from an escape route. Also, these same species are far more vulnerable to predation in the corral-like real estate of the flats. Their senses of sight, smell, acuity of hearing and bearings have been highly developed over an eon of time, and keep them ever alert to the relatively quick changes of opportunities and dangers that occur during tides.

ABOUT FLATS REAL ESTATE

Flats in the Florida Keys, as elsewhere throughout the world, are large areas of salt water with decidedly skinny water of just inches or feet. In the unique coordinates of the Keys there are miles and miles of flats on both the bayside (Florida Bay and Gulf of Mexico) and oceanside (Atlantic Ocean). The flats run from Biscayne Bay to the Marquesas Keys. They are interrupted after Key West with open water, but restart in the Key West National Wildlife Refuge, after which there's more open water and then flats again on the only atoll in the Atlantic Ocean: the Marquesas Keys. The entire shorelines of all 1,700 islands that make up the Florida Keys are surrounded by flats. Many have internal lagoons, and some are large enough to have named bays. All these islands interrupt tidal flows. They have channels and other bottom irregularities

---

TIDBITS

Air currents move smells about 10 times faster than in water. A fish's ability to smell, however, is so keen that it can be measured in parts-per-billion. A dog can smell in parts-per-million and its ability to smell is greater than that of a human by a thousand times. A fish can differentiate smell so well that it can distinguish parts within a chemical compound.

Note: For a reference point, smelling in parts per billion is the ability to distinguish the chemical compounds, within one eye dropper of foreign liquid, in a rail train car that is 17 miles long!

---

that can produce varying current speeds through and around them. The flats real estate in the Keys sustains life for hundreds of organisms per square yard, and some grow up to be 100-pound tarpon or 15-pound bonefish. The health of the flats fishery is one of the dip sticks by which the entire Keys eco-system is measured.

BAROMETER AND TEMPERATURE

Many excellent fishing books by very accomplished fishermen attest to barometric pressure as the reason for change in fishing, but in truth it's the accompanying weather that influences fishing, not the rise or fall of barometric pressure itself. Only a few species are actually known to have the ability to sense a change in barometric pressure, and none of those are game fish found in the Florida Keys. Ocean fish, in fact, are relatively undeterred by barometric pressure changes and the resulting conditions of weather that accompany fronts. However, water temperature, a post condition of a barometric pressure change, is the real influence. All bets are off when a hurricane is approaching as all fish hear it coming.

For bonefish, permit, snook, redfish and other flats inhabitants the same effect of water temperature change associated with fronts is influential in every aspect of their life on the flats. Tidal-flats fish also face another huge interruption in lifestyle when a front comes through the Keys, as the tides may be greatly effected. For example, where there were a few inches of water yesterday at high tide there may be no water at all today, or there could be several more inches. A front, however, can also bring a favorable change to fishing opportunities as it may induce one or more species to frequent an area they had been avoiding because of high water temperature.

Water has high heat capacity and therefore will not quickly lose or gain heat. Fish and organisms of the Keys, generally, never have to endure major swings in temperature, but there are many decided temperature zones found in the Keys both in the vertical and horizontal. The Gulf Stream's outer-edge waters, for example, differ in temperature from water internal to it. The phenomena of the Gulf Stream's edge also creates a current which hosts baitfish densities as well as flotsam, where predators find an opportunity to enjoy a free meal.

Each species has its own optimum range of temperature. The influence of water temperature induces feeding, spawning and migration. The range of water temperatures surrounding the Keys is about as unique as there is in the world with factors of influence (besides longitudinal and latitudinal) such as: the Gulf Stream, Atlantic Ocean, the third-largest reef system in the world, the Gulf of Mexico, Florida Bay, Everglades freshwater outflow and acres of quickly heated or cooled skinny-water flats.

BACKCOUNTRY AND EVERGLADES REAL ESTATE

The backcountry goes from Key Largo to Key West, and it is all bayside or gulf side. For North Key Largo, backcountry is southern Biscayne Bay, Card Sound, Barnes Sound, Blackwater Sound, Little Blackwater Sound, Long Sound and Manatee Bay. All of the latter are accessible from Florida Bay. Local guides divide backcountry real estate up into "near" backcountry and "far", and the line of demarcation is always a point of interpretation. Near backcountry being pretty much most of the mangrove islands, but not all, that stretch into Florida Bay and the Gulf of Mexico. Far backcountry, most agree, is near the Everglades shoreline from east and west of Flamingo, as well as the more open water of Florida Bay and the Gulf of Mexico. The freshwater outflow into Florida Bay and the influence of the Gulf and Atlantic tides make these backcountry waters a cauldron of sea life, and as complex a tide puzzle as exists in the world. Master it and you are a guide. A word of caution, however, for do-it-yourself folks. The backcountry is more than complicated and can be treacherous.

OFFSHORE

Keys big-game, offshore fishing begins in the deeper water off Biscayne Bay National Park and, generally, ends around the Dry Tortugas. Big-game fishing is also a part of the Gulf of Mexico. The Keys offshore fishery is enormous in both terms of square miles and species.

TIDBITS

Tidal current is the horizontal movement of water and tide itself is a vertical movement of water. The tidal pattern is repeated every 24 hours and 50 minutes. Most of the Keys fishing turf is governed by semidaily tides or semidiurnal tide (2 highs and 2 lows). The Gulf of Mexico has only one high and one low tide (diurnal tides).

RED TIDE AND HABS

HABs are harmful algal blooms. Harmful algal blooms, or "red tides," are algal blooms that can occur in fresh water, salt water, and brackish estuarine waters of coastal areas. Algal blooms are naturally-occurring events that have been making an appearance throughout the world for centuries. The event is caused by an excess growth of algae due to a changed environment. In recent years, algal blooms, and HABs especially, have gotten the attention of researchers and epidemiologists here in Florida, as well as several other coastal states, and around the industrialized world. The reasons: frequency of occurrence, influence on coastal resort/tourist businesses, genetic morphing of the microorganisms, the possible harmful effects on humans from eating fish or shellfish exposed to red-tide toxins, inhalation of aerosolized contaminated water and the long-term effects on fish, fisheries, sea birds, sea mammals, shellfish and plant life.

Oddly, the organisms that are responsible for red tides are the most basic life forms on earth, unicellular and microscopic (*cyanobacteria, diatoms* and *dinoflagellates*). New marine organisms (genetic morphing) have been identified with HABs, but it is not yet known if they are truly genetically morphed versions of known algae. Human impact is the likely suspect in the increased red-tide occurrences, and outbreaks of *pfiesteria* are clearly linked to sewage, human waste and farm runoff.

The events of algal blooms have been infrequent and short-lived in Florida Bay. Portions of the Lower Keys, Key West and beyond have been, occasionally, effected from diluted versions of red tides. The latter, born on the west coast of Florida, with phospahate mining runoff suspected as the primary initiator, drifts southward in the Gulf of Mexico before contacting the Lower Keys/Key West.

CHAPTER III

ABOUT GUIDING AND OFFSHORE CAPTAINING IN THE KEYS

They Wrote the Book On Light-Tackle Fishing and Saltwater Fly-Fishing.

" . . . and without local knowledge we fished only as hopefuls."
Zane Grey, 1922

"He who is a traveller learns things at second-hand and
by halves, and is poor authority."
Henry David Thoreau, 1846

PHOTO PROVIDED COURTESY OF SANDY MORET

Captain Norman Duncan, above, invented the Duncan loop (UNI-knot). Flip Pallot (ESPN's Walker Cay Chronicles), Chico Fernandez (TV, books, articles and many endorsements) and John Emory (thought to be, along with Steve Huff, the best fly-fisherman ever to have cast a line in the Keys) were all guides in the Keys. What is little known is that they were high school classmates in Miami. Combined, they have played more than a small part in defining light-tackle saltwater fishing as the world knows it today. They developed knots, fly patterns, fish-catching strategies, wrote books, articles and produced videos that are still considered bibles of saltwater tactics. Fernandez and Pallot continue consulting assignments for producers of rods, reels, boats, fly line, leader material and more.
Fernandez and Pallot also teach at Sandy Moret's Fly Fishing School (Cheeca Lodge). Norman Duncan and John Emory have passed away.

THE EVOLUTION OF LIGHT-TACKLE FISHING

The Keys evolved into a place where guiding is a singularly exceptional vocation. High-caliber guiding is more readily available in the Keys than in any other place in the world. Fly-fishing guiding and offshore fly-fishing captaining were not initiated in the Keys by mandates from the state, derived from a written code devised by the Keys guides themselves, nor has it been an evolution from a managed apprenticeship program. Instead, it has been a serendipitous evolution of coincidence, as well as pure Darwinian survival.

A spectacular fishery seduced, early on, a handful of men, and a few women, who would devote themselves to the Keys life: fishing, an intellectual curiosity about it all, an honor code of ethics, an environmental awareness beyond the times, and a willingness to share the Keys experience with all comers. The men and women who made the high mark on the wall for guiding standards in the Keys also helped write the book on saltwater light-tackle fishing as the world knows it today. Their early discoveries have been delivered to us by many articulate messengers, some even claiming to have discovered much of it by their telling of it, but most of it has the ring of Keys guides and offshore captains authorship.

Manufacturers of rods, reels, lines, boats, motors and all manner of fly-fishing accouterments sought, and still seek, the Florida Keys guides and offshore captains counsel on design, commentary on product performance, as well as outright endorsement.

There is an unwritten sportfishing industry strategy that mandates: if it is made to sell for saltwater fishing it better be test-driven by the Keys guides and offshore captains first.

Above: Legendary Captain Jimmy Albright with another Jimmy. Not a bad catch for a novice from Hollywood. Photo taken in the 1960's. Photographer unknown.

Fly patterns continue to evolve from the Keys guides and offshore captains' tying tables. Many fly patterns that take saltwater fish worldwide, were and continue to be, Keys-born. Several of the world's most utilitarian fishing knots are the invention of Keys guides: the Duncan loop (UNI-knot) and Albright knot. A major portion of salt water fish-catching techniques are original to Keys guides and offshore captains and they play a big part in having introduced a new venue to the fly-fishing community: saltwater.

Today's Florida Keys professionals, as well as yesterday's legends, have always served as an invaluable source of information for fishery ichthyologists, fish biologists, environmentalists, marine scientists and researchers of every discipline. Over the years, these marine studies contributed to the growing wealth of knowledge about the Keys' complex environment and, especially, its fishery.

JIMMY ALBRIGHT

Many guides and offshore captains have contributed and still contribute to the specialness that has become the Keys professional guide and offshore captain's signature. One man has been singled out and eulogized by his peers and sportfishing outdoor editors as typifying those attributes best. His name, Jimmy Albright. Almost everyone acquainted with fishing in South Florida, or saltwater fishing for that matter, knew who Jimmy Albright was. Anyone who knew him personally spoke volumes about how special he was to them, just ask any Keys guide or offshore captain with a few miles on his face. They will tell you he is the stuff of real legend and, oddly, not because he was such a talent as a guide or even inventor

of the Albright knot, but because he was, inexplicably, a man of special rank among them.

Albright was a favorite guide of the rich and famous because he possessed an aura that few own. He respected what he did for a living, defended the Keys environment (past president of the Islamorada Fishing Club) and this all helped to elevate his fellow guide and offshore captain colleagues vocation. Today, perhaps because of Albright, Keys guides and offshore captains seem to work harder and smarter than guides anywhere else to ensure each clients' success, and to jealously protect the environment in which they ply their trade.

Albright would be proud to know that the high standards he set for guiding lives on. It's a standard that separates the Florida Keys fly-fishing guides and offshore fly-fishing captains from all others of such a claimed degree of accomplishment.

SORRY CHARLIE, NO SHORT CUTS

If you have expectations of connecting with lots of game fish in the Keys because you paid for an "X marks the spot" chart, or decided to rely on a do-it-yourself and "stand here" fishing publication, plan on being a calamitous witness to your own fish-catching failure,

left: Bart Froth is still the holder of the world's record on a fly for a jewfish (1967/356-pounds.). The jewfish pictured is not the world record. **Right:** Captain Ralph Knowles. Photo believed taken in the 1950's.
NOTE: The jewfish is now correctly called goliath grouper.

and be prepared to accept that you have been profligate with both your time and money. The gateway to bountiful Keys fishing cannot be divined to you by a map of coordinates or a book claiming it can guide you to the promised land. Where-to books and "X marks the spot" charts, at very best, deal in "possible" and "possible" simply does not cut it in the Keys for fish-catching hopefuls.

Above: Believed to have been taken in the 1940's. In this photo, upper left: guide unknown, bottom, 2nd from the right is Captain Jimmy Albright. Woman (seated) is Captain Jimmy Albright's wife, Franki. Franki guided extensively, especially when her husband was called to serve in WWII. Franki was well respected in the community of guides in the Keys and was influential in environmental matters.

Below: Photo believed taken in the late 1940's. Captain Jimmy Albright (left) with George Coughlin. Significance of photo is that this is the first-ever 100-pound tarpon taken on a fly (Islamorada).

PHOTOS PROVIDED COURTESY OF SANDY MORET

The saltwater hydrology of the Keys is as complicated as it gets, and known only to the inhabitants of the brine and a select company of professional guides and offshore captains that have been revealed its secrets through thousands of hours on the water. If you chance coming here to be self-guided or even guided by a lesser-than-expert fishing guide or offshore captain, you chum with little more than that which will tease up disappointment all day, all month and all year. You might, however, get the hang of it after a couple of years if you can afford to quit your job and devote 365 days a year to on-the-water schooling.

Fish in the Keys are a moving target; always. Yesterday's tide and yesterday's bait migration belongs to yesterday, not today. The variables of change that will effect where the fish will be each hour of each day is almost infinite. Several thousand square miles of watery turf requires arriving prepared for eventualities, being informed about the realities, being as knowledgeable as possible and hiring an expert guide or offshore captain. These are the only roads to salvation. So if you are willing to learn as much as is possible before you arrive, then keep on reading. If you are sure you know it all or you're committed to the final, inglorious destiny of doing it all on your own, then put this book down now.

COME TO THE KEYS ABLE TO CAST

To be successful as a saltwater fly-fisherman in the Keys you need a reality check. The Keys are just what the doctor ordered. One miracle prescription is arriving here able to cast. If you are unable to double haul and cast to at least 50 feet, or better, then either stay home and wait for trout-stocking notices or spend your first days with your guide learning how to double haul and cast the required minimum. If you spend a little time practicing with your guide, your fish-catching potential will improve, a lot. The real bonus, however, will be that you and your guide are on the same page from the get-go, a marvelous serum for success. Your captain will be delighted to give you a lesson if you are a little rusty. The time taken to get it right will pay big dividends. For example, (and it happens too often to be an anomaly) the very first fish that your guide puts you on might just be the very fish you dreamed about, and it could end up the best opportunity you will ever have. If you were too embarrassed to tell your guide you were rusty at casting before you left the dock, just take a guess at how you would feel when the best tarpon, cobia, redfish or bonefish gets away. Your captain may say little, but he'll be seething, and you, well, you get the idea. Your captain wants you to catch fish because that's what he does for a living. Stay on the same page, always.

If you are honest with your captain about your casting competency, at the outset then he'll know how well you can cast. He can then spend all of his efforts and all of your collective time putting you in the very best position to catch a fish, given your abilities. It works; take it to the bank.

AFTER THE BALL IS OVER

Every qualified fly-fishing guide or offshore captain we ever met in the Keys has another life. A wife or girlfriend, family, other clients and a business to run. When you close out your engagement with them you probably have made a relationship that will last. Do not, however, think that your gracious offer of enjoying a few libation's or

Photo taken in the 1930's Depression era.
Manual Lopez, one of the first fishing guides in Key West.

hors d'oeuvres has tip-replacing clout. Your captain will almost always decline you. Two beers or duck paté on toast points buys no fuel. Remember, the day is not at all over for them when you drive off.

The best guides and offshore captains are always busy. They earned that right. They began their day before you even thought of turning over and will end it cleaning the boat, checking everything that has a moving part, spending time with his family, checking messages, returning calls, tying new flies and repairing equipment. Their days are long and they are just as conscientious about their job as you are about yours. They may love their job, but they are not on vacation.

PROTOCOL IN THE KEYS

It is customary in the Keys for the client to provide both lunch and drinks for the boat. Fear not, it's usually bottled water, ham & cheese sandwiches, chips and a piece of fruit. The same low-budget items you would buy for yourself. Your hotel or motel, as well as local stores in the Keys, are familiar with the drill. Most clients realize they are far better served if the captain tended to preparing the boat for the day rather than preparing a gourmet, Martha Stewart meal for them.

FROM MAKING ARRANGEMENTS TO TIPPING

See last chapter, Practical Information, for best guiding and offshore captaining arrangements.

Always try to book as far in advance as possible. You can expect to pay a 50% deposit. For flats guides, the fee for a full day is around $425. Offshore can be more than double that. It is a lot of money, but remember a well-equipped flats boat costs more than $30,000, and an offshore fishing boat well over six figures. There's fuel costs, thousands of dollars in fishing equipment, meeting strict Coast Guard standards for safety, insurance, licenses, bait, maintenance and more, lots more. The best part is that your guide or offshore captains knows where to fish. You, on the other hand, get to fish in one of the world's greatest saltwater venues with one of its expert fly-fishing guides or offshore captains. Nice, real nice!

Tips are usually 10% to 15% of each day's trip fee. More, of course, if you have had an outrageously successful experience. If you like your captain, book another trip with him.

PROFILES, GETTING TO KNOW THE PLAYERS

Today, there are many Keys guides and offshore captains skilled at fly-fishing. We only profile a few among the many that are special. Our profiles are a cross section of the Keys real estate in which these exceptional professionals guide and captain their clients. We have included a mix of true legends, proven newcomers, and a few who contribute to the fly-fishing community in the Keys just by their avocation.

CAPTAIN JEFFREY CARDENAS. KEY WEST

Jeffrey Cardenas is different from the rest of us. His fascination with the water, fishing and exploring has produced an uncommon approach to life, and an uncommon man with singular accomplishments. It's difficult, impossible actually, for Jeffrey to be anything less than someone admired because he is a true renaissance man and modern-day Marco Polo. True adventurers are always apart from all others.

For most of us, our avocations are not accomplishments, but for Jeffrey they are, and Herculean to boot. No one we know makes transatlantic voyages alone on a 27-foot sloop, dives alone in the Marquesas deep into the mangrove to see where a mighty tarpon might go, floats alone for days on the Gulf Stream's current just to observe the nature of it all, escapes the distractions of life's agendas to fly a plane, low level, over the Keys all the way to the outer islands of the Bahamas just to observe the fishery, or makes it a quest to catch a huge bluefin tuna on a fly in freezing winter weather off the coast of North Carolina.

Jeffrey Cardenas also taps into a clock that provides him with more than 24 hours a day, or he has an undiscovered double. His list of adventures and accomplishments already suggest the advantage of having been around for two or three lifetimes.

For more than two decades he has made a living from the water: fishing, diving, photographing, traveling and writing about it all. His penned words and photography delivering us all to as far away as Russia and as near to home as the Spanish galleon *La Senora de Atocha*. Many of you may recognize Jeffrey Cardenas' name as the author of the McQuane caliber read, *Marquesa: A Time & Place With Fish*, or for his articles that have appeared in the *New York Times*, *Time*, *Outside*, *Sports Illustrated* and *Playboy*. Most know him for the saltwater column he writes for every issue of *Fly Rod & Reel*. His new book, *Sea Level*, is a collection of essays and equally as fascinating as *Marquesa: A Time & Place With Fish*.

Jeffrey's fascination with the Keys began with family vacations there and nurtured an intuitive love of the sea. He has mastered every aspect of the Keys' unique environment, including fishing, diving, sailing and photography. After getting a degree from the University of Florida in Photo-Journalism, he met and married Jenny Stone, a

Jeffrey Cardenas.

University of Miami law school graduate, whom he says made his lifestyle possible. *"While I freelanced at writing and photography, Jenny provided a solid economic base for us as a prosecutor for the state's attorneys office. Jenny always encouraged me and never tried to dissuade me from my predilection to pursue fishing, adventurous outings or criticized me for not having a steady income in those early years. It is she who made it all possible."*

Some 20-plus years ago he decided to be a guide and, as only Jeffrey would, he plied the Key West waters alone for a year in order to discover for himself the fisheries' subtle rhythms and its solitary places. As a guide he soon became recognized as the very best, even amongst his peers—an unheard of confession. John Cole's book, *Tarpon Quest*, refers to Jeffrey throughout for his skills, knowledge, patience, encouragement and competency as a guide, but more importantly as a true friend. Interestingly, it was John Cole that provided Jeffrey his first opportunity to pursue the fly-shop business in Key West. *"John got me a small space (5-foot by 10-foot) at the Key West Anglers Club. There, I was able to build rods and tie flies for my customers and clients."*

Jeffrey has won several tournaments, but one of the Mercury/Redbone SuperFly events stand out. The regulations for it stipulate that only one fly pattern can be used. He won the championship in 2000 and 2001. In one event he made it a Grand Slam by catching a bonefish, tarpon and permit all in the same day. Jeffrey used a single pattern, a Merkin crab with the legs removed. In 1989, he won *Fly Rod & Reel's* coveted Guide Of The Year Award.

Jeffrey's remarkably distinct photography appears in books, national and international magazines, and can be seen at many of the best galleries in Florida. His photographic credentials have earned him a grant by the State of Florida to shoot underwater landscapes in the Florida Keys.

Today, Jeffrey serves on the Board of Directors of the UFA Conservation Foundation and, somehow, finds the time to run a 4,000-square-foot outdoor specialty retail store and fly shop, The Saltwater Angler. He also shows up around the globe to either help a cause or put his foot on the threshold of something new.

Jeffrey's Key West shop is, of course, your Key West fly-fishing headquarters. The shop has everything you need to outfit a convention of fly-fishermen or a conventionally-inclined fisherman. Jeffrey does not guide anymore, but as a full-time outfitter he has hand-picked the guides that you'll be chartering, and they all meet his high standards, and yours. NOTE: See last chapter, Practical Information.

CAPTAIN DOUG BERRY - ISLAMORADA

Doug is one of those quiet, polite guys who always knows what he's talking about. The kind of guy you know you can trust and one you can count on; the perfect captain.

Doug Berry grew up in Ithaca, NY, in a household where the out-of-doors was a tableside language. His connection to the Keys goes back to the late '60's. As a young man his lifestyle was fishing the Keys, and in the summers, Steamboat Springs or Alaska. By 1980, he decided to take advantage of an opportunity to captain an offshore charter boat, and by 1983, he moved full time to Islamorada.

Doug would become one of the best offshore fish catchers in the Keys, and his skills would earn him a reputation that was reflected in his bookings. Seeing a rise in fly-fishing popularity, improvements in fly-rod technology and realizing there were new potentials for offshore species on the fly, he decided to be the first to stock his boat with rigged fly rods. Captain Doug Berry soon became the man to see if you wanted a shot at an offshore game fish in the Keys on a fly rod.

A younger Captain Doug Berry "Outstanding Captain Trophy" 1989 Junior Sailfish Tournament.

His tournament titles are many (25), but one stands out, *The Lou Steiner Award* (biggest Marlin of the year). Doug was both a fisherman by vocation and avocation. While in Cabo San Lucas, Mexico, he caught the Grand, Grand Slam of offshore fishing: blue marlin, black marlin, striped marlin and sailfish all in one day. A worldwide feat with less than a handful of claimants.

Doug, like every Keys captain we spoke to, reflects remorsefully on the past practice of killing non-eatable game fish just for a client's dockside boasting. Doug became so uncomfortable with that by 1989 he began working with The Billfish Foundation, participating in the OTC tagging program. He was the first participant in the continental U. S. to successfully OTC tag billfish (5).

By the late 1980's, on a charter with Captain Berry, you were advised that he was not going to let you kill a billfish if it was not a possible IGFA record.

Captain Berry opted out of the charter business in 1995 to take a job with the new World Wide Sportsman and to spend some time doing radio talk shows. Doug is now comfortable in a time-demanding executive position as a store manager with the Worldwide Sportsman in Islamorada. He is content these days with family fishing outings and, especially, teaching his son the nuances of fly-fishing.

"Bill fishing in the Keys is as good as it ever was. It's still a place to come for the fly-rod enthusiast wanting a shot at sail or marlin on a fly."

CAPTAIN TIM CARLILE, SUGARLOAF KEY

Tim was commissioned into the world of fishing; his father was a career Navy man, Sugar Loaf Lodge's marina manager and a top guide. Tim grew up on Sugar Loaf Lodge's property right next to integral parts of Lower Keys history (Perky's Tower and the remains of the Chase Sponge Farm).

Captain Tim Carlile is a fish-catcher first, last and always. If you arrive unable to fly-cast well enough to suit him, he'll insist you go to spinning gear or a bait-casting rig, which he'll provide. Tim gave up carrying fly rods on his immaculate flats boat and he's not about to give you a casting lesson. Captain Carlile's orientation is catching fish, so be prepared for that, and he's as expert as any guide in the Lower Keys. He can see what no one else seems to be able to see and if you heed his coaching you'll be rewarded. Tim is all business and as matter of fact in every aspect of his guiding as is possible in the Keys. What distinguishes Tim among his guide peers is not that he is a skilled fly-fisher, but that he knows the tricky waters of the back-country, literally, like the back of his hand. He's been wandering the mangrove snarls of the Lower Keys since boyhood. The Lower Keys, bayside and oceanside, are mind-boggling mazes of mangrove islands that can lose you in its tangle 200 yards from the dock. The effects these islands have on incoming and outgoing tides

Tim Carlile.

and species show-up probabilities defies all charts. A tides chart on Tim's turf is invalid due to the influences of hundreds of islands that interrupt tidal flows. The Lower Keys are pristine, a healthy fishery and a piece of real estate that beckons more adventurous souls to take a shot at some seldom over-fished tarpon, permit, barracuda and snappers. There are a host of shark species and, possibly, the best opportunity for cobia in skinny water in the entire Keys. Bonefishing here can be very good, but it will take a commitment to be with Captain Tim Carlile to find them. Tim is an expert at finding and approaching tarpon and permit. You'll find the thrill of hooking up with either in the labyrinth of the Lower Keys mangrove to be one of the best experiences you can have on a Florida Keys fly-fishing outing.

Tim's tournament credentials are many, but one stands out. He guided Pepe Lopez of Miami to double slam in a Key West celebrity tournament. You might recognize Captain Tim Carlile as he has appeared in *Florida Sportsman*, produced a good fly-fishing video, been the featured guide on ESPN and is often heard on local radio in the Keys. If it's a Lower Keys adventure you're after, then stay at Sugar Loaf Lodge and book Tim. You'll stay busy catching fish and immersed in the Keys of yesteryear. NOTE: See last chapter, Practical Information.

BILL CURTIS, BISCAYNE BAY, EVERGLADES AND THE FLORIDA KEYS

Bill Curtis began fly-fishing in 1934 when a good fly rod cost $3 in Oklahoma. He's been fly-fishing the Keys from Biscayne Bay to the Everglades to the Dry Tortugas since the late 1940's. He's watched the fishery go from fabulous to poor and back to spectacular again, and says without hesitation, commercial fishing and netting regulations are the sole reasons for the fishery's ups and downs.

"I was a reconnaissance photographer during WWII. After discharge I had a little portrait business in California, but ended up in Miami in 1947/48 working for an ad agency, J. Walter Thompson, as their account photographer for Pan Am and others. During that time I always fished the Everglades, Biscayne Bay and the Keys every chance I got. By 1948, I had started guiding as a side business.

Joe Brooks would stay with me when he was in town and we often fished Biscayne Bay and the Keys. I can remember taking Joe and the legendary Islamorada guide, Jimmy Albright, out to show them how to catch bonefish on a fly. One day Joe caught three, and from then on bone fishing with a fly rod became part of the Keys sportfishing culture.

In 1952, I met an ex-Navy pilot who was flying for Pan Am, named Stu Apte. For the next several years, I took Stu fishing up and down the Keys, Biscayne Bay and the Everglades. When Stu was laid off in the late 50's, I loaned him a boat and he started guiding out of Little Torch Key. He went on to become one of the best tarpon guides in the Keys.

By 1958, I quit photography for good and spent 100% of my time at the business of guiding. By the 70's and 80's, I was booked and on the water over 300 full days a year. The most

Bill Curtis.

I've ever fished in one year was 330 straight days. Funny, in those years I was never skunked on a full-day charter, but I would never guarantee anyone that it couldn't happen. In 1960, the only guides in the Keys were based in Marathon or Islamorada. I would spend, usually, April and May in Key West guiding during the 'Spring Tarpon Run' or taking clients to the Marquesas or Lower Keys for permit, if that's what they wanted.

When Curt Gowdy and I made the segment on fly-fishing for permit in Key West for his hit TV show, "The American Sportsman," there were no guides in Key West, but that TV show changed all that. We were catching six or seven permit a day every day we filmed. It was so good then that one of the film crew quit to become a Key West guide. Curt and I did two other "American Sportsman" shows on fly-fishing the Keys, barracuda in the Tortugas and bonefish in Biscayne Bay. I think those shows told millions of viewers that the Keys were an incredible fishery. From then on several Marathon, and even a few Islamorada guides, headed down to Key West to set up shop.

My proudest memory is playing a measurable role in saving Biscayne Bay, at least the lower part, by getting it turned into a national park. In 1960, there was a move under foot and a lot of money behind getting a refinery built at Turkey Point, next to the power plant (near Miami). The plans called for a trench to be dug 50 feet deep that went from Turkey Point to the Ragged Keys to support mega-tankers moving through the bay. It would have, in one stroke, decimated Biscayne Bay. My friend, Bud Hoover, the Hoover vacuum heir, enlisted my support to make his stand against the project. It turned into a real dog-fight. Bud, however, was no fool and had friends and influence in high places. He got the Interior Secretary, Stuart Udall, to come down and see first-hand what was at stake. The plan was that I take him (Udall) out fishing, show him around, give him the lay of the land and tell him what would no longer be if the project was allowed to move forward. I saw to it that he was put on a lot of fish. Further, Bud got the Secretary of Commerce, Luther Hodges, to visit and spend time with me. I gave him the tour and put him on a lot of fish. Both Udall and Hodges were, as the records show, instrumental in getting the bill passed that salvaged Biscayne Bay by turning it into a national park. Oddly, 60 years later, it was Bud Hoover's daughter, Lacey, that put an end to yet another sinister plan. A plan that would have destroyed both the Everglades National Park and Biscayne National Park for good with a monstrosity of an airport plan for Homestead (FL) that encroached on and straddled them both.

It's not hard to draw Bill out when it comes to speaking of his accomplishments. Bill has developed several fly patterns, but one, the Super Bug, is a winner. It works on both bones and reds. He also has a leader-connection system that is real easy, and fail-safe, called the Curtis Connection. Bill once held the world record for snook (27 pounds). He introduced the Bimini twist (name has nothing to do with the Bahamian Island) to the Keys after learning it from a Venezuelan marlin fisherman, and has several Lifetime Achievement Awards. Two of the latter were for helping shallow-water boat builders, Bob Hewes and Bob Stearns, develop the "flats" boat as we know it today, and the other was for playing a part in inventing the poling platform.

Bill is a robust, powerfully built man close to 80 years old. When he's not guiding in the Everglades, Florida Bay, Biscayne Bay or the Keys he works at the incredible Johnny Morris' Outdoor World in Dania Beach, FL. There he teaches casting, puts customers straight of any predilection (spin, baitcast or fly) and delivers a meaningful environmental story.

And last, but not at all least, Bill is one of the founders of *Bonefish & Tarpon Unlimited*, an organization that supports projects and research to help understand, nurture, and enhance a healthy bonefish and tarpon population. The membership roster reads like a Who's Who of sport fishing. Memberships are available by sending $50 or more to: Bonefish & Tarpon Unlimited, 24 Dockside Lane, PMB 83, Key Largo, FL 33037. Telephone: 305-367-3416 and FX: 305-367-3546. NOTE: See last chapter, Practical Information,

CAPTAIN PAUL DIXON, NORTH KEY LARGO AND KEY LARGO

Paul Dixon grew up in Newport Beach, California listening to the music of the Doors, the Grateful Dead and

Paul Dixon.

learning how to fish. At age 16, on a trip to Idaho with the San Francisco Casting Club with none other than Gill Day and Ed Landry as tutors, Paul was pitched into a fascination with the fly rod. He was seduced on the fabled Henry's Fork and its sirens' song is still playing in his soul. Upon returning to California, his head buzzing with new ideas, he headed to more familiar waters and applied what he'd learned to the striped bass fishery. By the time Paul had graduated from college, he'd fly-fished from the northern extreme of California's coast to the tip of Cabo San Lucas in Mexico. In the late 1980's, he headed east to work for Orvis in New York.

BONEFISHING IN MANHATTAN?

Already an expert fly-fisherman and living on Long Island, Paul began the pursuit of fly-fishing for eastern striped bass and was soon on to something altogether new, stripers in very shallow water. He had noticed stripers moving onto the flats as the tide came in and realized the net bans were bringing stripers back in good numbers. Paul, and a few others, bought Keys-style flats skiffs (very shallow draft boats) and began studying striper habits in relation to the tidal flow. He could soon correctly predict where and when they would show up to feed on the flats. He was, essentially, bonefishing for stripers with Manhattan's steel-and-glass canyons as backdrops.

TIMING IS EVERYTHING

The sudden boom in the fly-fishing industry, coupled with extremely successful net bans, sent Paul's budding guiding business, To The Point Charters, into overdrive. New Yorkers and Jerseyites couldn't believe that sight fishing was now available to them in crystal-clear shallow water just an easy day trip from Manhattan. Because of his timing, innovations and some interesting new fly patterns he developed (Dixon's Devil Worm), Paul became nationally recognized. He was the pioneer of flats fishing for striped bass. That recognition has gotten him featured on Flip Pallot's, *Walker's Cay Chronicles* (ESPN), *The Spanish Fly Show* with Key West native, Jose Wejebe, and several other outdoor fly-fishing programs, as well as a recent documentary made by Barbara Koppel on the fall blitzes off Montauk, Long Island.

Paul has written numerous articles for fly-fishing publications and was recently featured by outdoor writer, Peter Kaminsky, in his book, *The Moon Pulled Up An Acre Of Bass*, a great read and well reviewed by the *New York Times*. The book takes the reader out to Montauk with Paul, Peter, and fellow guide, Amanda, for the celestial phenomenon that brings huge schools of south-migrating herring to Montauk. Where the herring go, so go the stripers; fat stripers. Kaminsky's book logs the account, which Paul refers to as, " . . . *best striper fishing I have ever experienced, straight through to December 15th*."

Paul has a core clientele of expert casters: musician Jimmy Buffett, screen celebrities Ed Burns, Minnie Driver, Rip Torn and a long list of heavy hitters from the world of high finance, Henry Kravis, Julian Robertson and Bob Rubin to name a few.

In the 1980's, from late December to spring, Paul began vacationing in the Keys, but true to form his friends and clients found out where he was and wanted to visit. Serendipitously, and at about the same time, Upper Key's Guide, Bruce Miller had just opened a fly shop at the Ocean Reef Club in North Key Largo. Bruce knew Paul, about his elect clientele, their eagerness to participate in the Keys experience and they struck a deal. Soon after, Paul's followers (Kaminsky, Outdoor Editor for the *NYT*, chronicled some of his trips with Paul), began making frequent pilgrimages to the Keys; the graduate school of saltwater fly-fishing. Hundred-pound tarpon, double-digit bones, and big permit were attractive bait, and Paul's time alone on winter vacations to the Florida Keys ended. You can find Paul in the Keys every winter through spring, guiding seven days a week.

What separates Paul from most guides is his insatiable curiosity. He's always tinkering, experimenting, pulling flies made of some new material through his swimming pool, trying new approaches and adapting. Paul takes little credit for anything. However, his fingerprints appear on many fly patterns. "*That's a touchy subject with me. I don't really believe many people invent flies even though they put their names on them. Other than Lefty Kreh, Bob Clouser, Bob Popovics, Lenny Moffo and a few others, most flies are really just adaptations.*"

Paul is an excellent teacher, but also one who expects a lot of his students. He is a willing instructor for a willing learner who practices. He stresses the importance of listening to the guide through the entire presentation to the fish. His first advice to beginners is to "*practice your casting*" before you come to the Florida Keys. While he does place great importance on fly selection, Paul feels, "*. . . how you wiggle the worm is more important than what the worm looks like.*"

Paul feels Lefty Kreh has been the biggest influence in his fishing career. Oddly, what he admires most about Lefty is what everyone admires about Paul. Paul on Lefty: "*Not only is he one of the all-time greats, but he is such a willing teacher. He really is into helping people more than anything. That's what I love about Lefty. He is always giving you little things, not only in casting, but meaningful anecdotes, a good belly laugh, a great new way to clean your sunglasses, little tidbits of information, and he is such a generous and sharing soul.*" Paul also credits other friendships as big influences, such as world-renowned fly tier Bob Popovics and Nick Curcione, an all-around fly-fishing guru. "*Those guys, because of the true friendship we have, enjoy a fascination with pulling feathers or fur through water. I learned a lot of stuff from those guys.*"

On the boat with Paul Dixon, it's rare to go five minutes without a good laugh, shared anecdotes of life's winding course, a fish tale or two, a yarn about experiences with the Grateful Dead on ranches in California, loves lost and lunkers lost. He will share with you just about anything. NOTE: See last chapter, Practical Information.

CAPTAIN GARY ELLIS, ISLAMORADA

Gary Ellis is that rare kind of person who possesses a commanding presence. He always energizes a room in a friendly and engaging way, becomes the center of attention without any noticeable effort. There isn't a guide in the entire Keys who doesn't know and like Gary and, amazingly, Gary knows them all by name and always boasts of their accomplishments when queried. There is one thing that is uniquely Captain Gary Ellis. He never speaks in the negative.

This Iowa corn-bred, jazz-loving, hunter/fisherman backed into becoming a Conch in 1967 when he decided on a Keys vacation, a break from his hectic in-front-of-the-camera job in Chicago, and a break from harsh winter blizzards. Gary's other life was TV, commercials, industrial films, bit parts in movies and interviewer of prospective 'bunnies' for Hugh Hefner's magazine, *Playboy*. We're not at all convinced the latter assignment necessitated a vacation.

"*On my first day in the Keys I went out fishing, offshore, and caught a sailfish, which I managed to lose right at the boat. I think it was that one event, that single sailfish, that triggered in me a need to be here (Florida Keys). I decided I'd stay here (Islamorada) and learn the water. I hired on as a mate for Captain Skip Bradeen out of Whale Harbor, but I kept one foot in my other occupation. I hired an agent in Miami and I got work doing travelogues, bit parts in movies and doing commercials."*

Gary got his captain's license in 1968 (he's on his seventh renewal) and took his 25-foot boat into the backcountry. It would take a long time to master the backcountry, years in fact, but Gary had mentors, Captain Kirby Carter and a neighbor who was already a Keys legend, Captain Jim Brewer. Carter and Brewer would show Gary the backcountry of the Keys.

In 1969 and 1970, there were only a few fishing tournaments held in the Keys and none in Islamorada or the Upper Keys. The Islamorada Fishing Tournament was put in motion, and Gary was named co-director. The event had to have a celebrity speaker. Lefty Kreh committed at the last minute and saved the day, but for services rendered he wanted to be guided in the backcountry. A place Lefty actually knew very, very well. Gary was appointed guide for their speaker. *"Lefty provided me with the most indelible fly-casting and fly-fishing lesson I've ever gotten. He showed me more of the backcountry than I knew existed."*

In the early '70's, Captain Jim Brewer, lead rep for Shakespeare, got Gary on the Shakespeare staff. Shakespeare, at that time, was a big player in rod manufacturing, especially fly rods. After Jim Brewer's shocking

Gary Ellis.

and tragic death in a small-plane crash in the Keys, Ben Hardesty (Shakespeare) appointed Gary as their lead rep. What followed was probably one of the best-ever tarpon outings.

Homosassa Springs, then, was all but undiscovered (early to mid '70's), but leaked reports about its incredible spring population of tarpon made its way back to the Keys through none other than baseball legend and Keys resident, Ted Williams. Hardesty, Ellis, Williams, Shakespeare's VP of Engineering and legendary guides, Freddy Archibald and Ed Wightman took Shakespeare's new rods on a 10-day introduction tour. *"It was incredible. Acres and acres of rolling tarpon and no other fishermen around. We had the whole of it to ourselves and we were surrounded by willing tarpon all day, every day."*

Gary on Ted Williams: *"He was a perfectionist in all things. Ted was like no other person I've ever known. With Ted there was no such thing as a detail too small to contend with. He was, perhaps, a genius, and certainly so when it came to fly fishing."* Ted and Gary, from the Homosassa Springs gathering, would become lifelong friends. It would be Williams who helped Gary launch, in 1988, what are now the famous Mercury/Redbone Series of tournaments.

The Mercury/Redbone tournaments may have their roots in the Keys, but today they are held in venues; around the globe. Incidentally, all Gary's and his wife, Sue's, tournaments were started and dedicated to helping the Cystic Fibrosis Foundation. Nicole, Gary and Sue's daughter, is afflicted with the disease. As a side note: the tournaments have already raised an astounding $2,500,000 for research.

Managing and organizing an increasingly demanding tournament schedule (20), along with consulting assignments, now limits Gary's on-the-water guiding to less than 100 days a year. Gary, like most of us, still has some fly-fishing goals to conquer. Gary and Sue would gladly give up everything for a cystic fibrosis cure. NOTE: See Practical Information chapter for more on the Mercury/Redbone.

CAPTAIN GEORGE HOMMELL, JR., ISLAMORADA

George Hommell, Jr. is a legend in the Keys as both a prominent citizen and a professional fishing guide icon. More importantly, he's liked and admired by all who know him. He's also been very much a part of setting the high mark on the wall for guiding and offshore captaining that has become synonymous with the Keys. If you can name a famous person who likes to fish or fly-fish, George probably knows them personally. As a matter of fact, he has probably fished with them in the Keys, or gone with them to more famous coordinates around the world. He even visited one of them, often, in the Oval Office. George Hommell is very good friends with Lefty Kreh, President George Bush, Anatoly Dobrinyin, Jack

To my friend -
George Hommell -
The Best guide to know.
all The Best -
Lefty Kreh 6/13/96

George Hommell, Jr.

George was never one to miss the entrepreneurial boat. He realized in the mid-1960's that the Keys were gaining popularity with sportsmen from around the globe, but there were few places where people of the fishing predilection could find travel agents catering to their needs, and that the Keys residence themselves needed a travel agent. In 1967, he opened the World Wide Sportsman to accommodate an unmet demand. In 1967, he got a partner, Billy Pate, and later on that relationship helped mature World Wide Sportsman into the best fishing and fly-fishing equipment shop in the Keys. As a side bar to George's business acumen, he was asked by Jack Nicklaus to take over the failing Hall of Fame golfers travel business, which he did and matured it to turnaround status and then, final sale.

George, through the '80's and '90's, remained a busy guide and actively ran his travel and fishing-equipment business (World Wide Sportsman). He served as president of the famous Islamorada Fishing Club, plus maintained membership in world-famous Miami Rod & Reel Club. He ran Cheeca Lodge on two different occasions, as well as serving as the official representative for the IGFA. The latter a post he's held for 30 years.

In 1978, he met a man who would become President of the United States. They became lifelong friends. When George Bush was running for president, George Hommell helped run several East Coast campaigns. George says he enjoyed being part of the political process and, especially, helping his friend. After Bush became president, George (Hommell) was made chairman of the prestigious INTERCOM, an acronym for an agency (Interior Commerce Department) that was designed to take away the shadows of environmental politics and policies, and set right the country's fishery laws and improve the fishery environments. The agency was disbanded, unfortunately, under Clinton's administration.

In 1995, George sold World Wide Sportsman to Johnny Morris' Bass Pro. However, George can be found there just about every day of the week as he serves as General Manager of World Wide Sportsman. Still, George greets everyone warmly and equally, and he'll help you out with anything from the best fly for snook to getting your party ticketed to points around the globe where the fishing is hot.

George says, "Today, the Keys fishing is better than it's been in 20 years, and as good as its ever was . . . and getting better."

LENNY MOFFO, BIG PINE KEY

Captain Lenny Moffo is very outgoing, one of the best guides in the Lower Keys and the consummate perfectionist. His interests and accomplishments are broad based. He has earned a living as an auto body repairman, rancher, outfitter (hunting, fishing and bird shooting), horse trader, blacksmith, cowboy, mate, boat captain, real estate investor, guide, hunting dog trainer, fly tier, fly-shop manager, builder of string instruments, musician

Nicklaus, Malcom Frazer, and past legend, Ted Williams, just to name a few.

He was introduced to fishing in the Catskills. In 1945, after serving three war-time years in the Navy, George decided to come to the Keys. He worked at constructing the Theater of the Sea, doing everything from ditch digging to, eventually, capturing the fish species the theater would feature. In 1949, he had saved enough money to get a small boat and began a side venture called guiding. A profession the Keys would make famous the world over for standards of excellence.

In 1950, during the Korean War, his country called him back to service. This time it was the Air Force where he would serve as a flight engineer on the jumbo C119. By 1951, he was back in the Keys and had decided on guiding as a full-time endeavor. In those early years, he was only booked about 15 days a month. By the 70's, his services were in demand as he'd become a recognized expert on the flats and backcountry venue. Many of his clientele were from the world-famous Miami Rod & Reel Club. His connection with men of recognized accomplishments began. His reputation would spread.

As boat technology improved so did George's range in the Keys. He was now able to trailer his boat anywhere in the Keys and regularly took clients to points as far away as Key West. By the 1980's, he was booked just about solid. He had an earned reputation.

Captain Lenny's favorite target.

and carpenter. He remodeled his Big Pine home by himself and it is quintessentially the signature of his do-it-right persona.

Lenny left his New Jersey roots in 1976 when he was in his early 20's and headed West to Montana. Living in the West had been his boyhood dream, his passion fueled by Curt Gowdy's hit TV show, "American Sportsman," and any publication that had an outdoor twist on the western lifestyle.

After some time in several Montana locations, Lenny finally settled in Coeur d' Alene, Idaho. He had planned on being in Idaho for a lifetime, but during one particularly cold spell in January of 1981 everything changed in a flash. One morning after trekking back to his ranch house from the horse barn in a blizzard, he saw a picture in a magazine of a guy bonefishing in the Keys. He made an on-the-spot decision. It had to be better there than freezing his arse off in northern Idaho. He came to the Lower Keys for a few weeks and by 1988 he was a man of two worlds: fishing and elk hunting outfitter in Idaho and Montana in the summers, and a lone fly-fisherman doing odd jobs in the Lower Keys in the winters.

Lenny, literally, backed into guiding. One day in 1986, while working at a marina docking yachts, his boss asked him if he'd guide two fly-fishermen for the day. Lenny begged off not feeling he was qualified to guide, but his boss pressured him and the fishermen begged. Lenny relented, and he and his first Keys clients conquered several briny swimmers. As it turned out, Lenny's five years

of investigative fly-fishing by himself proved rewarding for his clients. Word travels fast in this fly-fishing community and he began to get booked. The Keys became his home in 1988.

Captain Moffo, oddly, has never advertised in a publication or been much interested in the very popular tournament scene. However, he occasionally enters one of the Redbone/Mercury tournaments held by his friend, Captain Gary Ellis. Lenny is booked over 200 days a year. He has a strong following of very serious players.

Lenny still spends three months of the year in eastern Idaho and western Montana: August, September and October, where he fly-fishes fabled and seldom-seen waters for rainbows, browns, cutbows, and cutthroats, or hunts for elk on horseback in the Rockies and bird shoots for a myriad of feathered treats in the uplands. Captain Lenny Moffo likes his lifestyle (who wouldn't), likes people, pursuing his many interests, his home in the Lower Keys and catching anything that swims.

Most fly-fishermen know Lenny Moffo as a master fly tier. He's probably the most skilled and practical fly tier in the Keys, and his reputation is worldwide. When Lenny ties a fly that's supposed to float, it floats; if it's supposed to sink, it sinks; if it's supposed to ambulate like the creature it imitates, it ambulates naturally; if it's supposed to be weedless, it's weedless; if it's to lie upside down on the bottom, it lies upside down, and every fly tied by Lenny is castable. The latter a trick of more complexity than anyone imagines.

Lenny's six fly-tying videos, *Hooked on Fly Tying*, instruct both the skilled and novice tier without going too fast or too slow. His delivery of information on "how-to" is silky smooth and never leaves the viewer wondering what was meant or how to do any maneuver. Lenny is a consultant to several manufacturers: Gamakatsu, Scientific Angler, Reddington Rods and Yamaha to name a few.

SANDY MORET, ISLAMORADA

Sandy Moret has a bearing that suggest he's the guy you want on your side if an altercation breaks out. But, when you get to know him you're sure of it. He's also very likeable and gentlemanly in the way most southerners are. He's smart, speaks fluent fly-fishing, owns one the best fly shops you'll ever set foot in and runs the best saltwater fly-fishing school in the world. His fly shop, Florida Keys Outfitters, is all about fly-fishing Everyone that works there waxes on the subject in a no-nonsense way, including Sue, his wife and, Drew, his top-guide son.

Sandy came to Miami in the early 70's via Georgia where his family owned a successful beer distribution business. Sandy's preference and schooling were in real estate, but an opportunity to buy out a failing beer distributor in Miami caught his brother's attention. Along with his brother, they moved from Atlanta to Miami to give it a go. By the early 80's, the beer distributorship had a 48% market share, up from its dismal start of 2%. By

1985, he was made an offer not to be refused, sold out and never looked back.

Since childhood he'd been a fisherman and hunter and he decided on pursuing both full time. Sandy, for something to do, attended one of Flip Pallot, Lefty Kreh and Mark Sosin's casting schools, which was held at an obscure site on the Tamiami Trail in South Florida. He noted there was a lot of enthusiasm, and even though it was well attended, it could be improved upon. With some coaxing from some of his angling buddies, he embarked on developing an improved format. By 1989, Sandy had put together his first saltwater fly-fishing school. It would become, hands down, the best in the world. Always a business man, he began to realize the school's attendees wanted more. They wanted to fish, they needed flies and the business grew vertically. In 1994, he opened a full-service fly shop and, again, never looked back.

Sue hard at work.

Sandy has won many fishing tournaments titles, held positions he was either elected or appointed to on the prestigious and influential Everglades Restoration Plan, and remains a keen and outspoken proponent on matters environmental. For those of you who watched ESPN's *Walker Cay Chronicles*, you saw Sandy as a guest angler with his friend Flip Pallot, the shows host, or on the TV show, *Reel Guys*. Sandy has written the foreword to books and his articles on saltwater fly-fishing and wing shooting appear regularly in sporting publications.

Never feel bad for Sandy when it comes to taking a break from the rigors of managing a business as he's on the water laying down a line at least 80 or more days a year. Sandy's favorite pursuit is the flat's ghost itself.

SUE MORET, ISLAMORADA

Sue Moret, Sandy's wife, is very active in the Florida Keys Outfitters and also notable in the Keys fishing scene. While she may look like she just stepped from a commercial shoot modeling clothes, or some exotic travel destination, she is very much an outdoor woman and has enjoyed fishing since childhood. She got hooked on fly-fishing after attending one of Sandy's early fly-fishing schools. She, by her own admission, has had the very best of tutoring through the years, as well as the best guides: Sandy, Flip Pallot, Craig Brewer, Steve Rajeff and the legendary Steve Huff.

While she was helping Sandy with the school some years ago, she noticed that about a third of the attendees were women. Many of them returning to the Keys to fish,

Sandy on a day off.

and stopping in the shop to visit or purchase their current equipment needs. Sue decided it was time for a "women only" bonefish fly tournament and The Women's World Invitational Bonefish Fly Championships was born, which also features a tarpon series. The tournaments are held in Islamorada with 25 to 30 anglers attending each event. It's been a success in every way.

If you're in the Keys with your wife and she is at all curious about fly-fishing, then take her to the Florida Keys Outfitters. Sue will make her feel comfortable, but remember Sue has introduced many, many women to the angling frame of mind so you might end up the babysitter.

Sue Moret, with a group of Keys girlfriends of a similar persuasion, gets out to fly-fish at least 40 days a year and always goes with a guide. Her favorite species to fish for is bonefish and her favorite fly for that occasion is a small Merkin.

Florida Keys Outfitters provides extensive technical advice, has a complete supply of high-end fly rods, reels, fly lines and a very high-quality inventory of flies, many of which are patterns unique to the Keys and seldom seen anywhere else. In addition, the shop is your headquarters for the best guides in the Upper Keys and even if you're heading for the Middle Keys, check in here first. Also, your arrangements for Sandy's world-famous saltwater fly-fishing school are made here.
NOTE: See last chapter, Practical Information.

CAPTAIN TOM ROWLAND, LOWER KEYS AND KEY WEST

Tom is the quintessential new breed guide: young, talented, industrious and a pleasure within which to fish.

Tom grew up in Chattanooga, Tennessee and like most who have chosen the outdoor lifestyle, he had a father that spoke fluent fishing. Tom, however, became intrigued with fly-fishing, and it would possess him. While at the University of Alabama, he spent the summers out West fly-fishing the fabled rivers near Yellowstone, and that matured into professional guiding there for seven years. In 1993, he decided to prospect the Keys. It was a big decision as it would require taking a year off from his Wyoming business connection and an eat-and-sleep-cheap commitment.

Ever astute and meticulous, Tom knew that to be successful in the Keys venue he'd have to learn the waters: the subtle influences of tides, weather, hidden anchorages, observe the seasons, gamefish and baitfish migration habits on and off the flats, as well as the fly patterns that produced the best results. Tom loved every minute of it, and he'd spend over 300 days alone on the waters off Key West. He looked, listened, fly-fished and kept a meticulous log. A dedication only a few commit to. His unusual perseverance attracted the attention of two of the Keys' better-known guides, Captain Simon Becker and Captain Michael Pollock. They would take Tom under their wings; a rare thing in the guiding world where

knowledge is not readily shared, and especially so with the new guy on the block.

With a full schedule still beckoning out West, Tom and his not-so-full stomach, decided he'd have to split his seasons for the next few years, guiding only the winters in Key West. In 1996, the Keys won out as year-round home port and Tom has never looked back.

Captain Tom Rowland represents the best of the new

Captain Tom Rowland.

breed of Florida Keys guides. His vocation is run as any of today's businesses would be with all the current accouterments of communications technology at his fingertips: informative and useful website, immediate e-mail responses, fact-based promotional literature, articles written for the better saltwater publications and participation in a host of high-profile tournaments, which are like executive conventions in the industry. His knowledge, personality and skill as a fish catcher are duly reflected in his bookings. A day with Captain Rowland is as good as it gets.

CAPTAIN JIM SHARPE, BIG PINE KEY

Jim Sharpe is one of, if not, the best offshore fishermen and fly-fishermen in Florida, Caribbean and beyond. There's little he doesn't know. He shares his earned knowledge in his comprehensive book, *Dolphin: The Perfect Game Fish* and in his videos (*How To Dolphin Fish*, *How To Tuna Fish*, *Marlin Fishing The Wall*, and *A Trip To Dry Tortugas*). The book, *Dolphin: the Perfect Game Fish*, is decidedly the best book ever written about the dolphin (common and pompano). Reviews from the scientific and sportfishing community, around the world, confirm the book's stand-alone credibility. However, tucked away in its 160 pages there's more, especially for the fly-fishermen. A huge and unexpected bonus of rarely shared coverage clearly prepares you for all offshore big-game fly fishing—what rods to use, fail-safe rigging from backing to tippets, the best fly patterns and how to present them. If you'd like to know what it takes to be prepared to fly-fish offshore in the Keys for any species, you're well advised to get a copy of *Dolphin: The Perfect Game Fish*. Jim's book also has clean, clear drawings, crisp black-and-white photos, explicit instructions, glossary of terms and index.

A chartered day offshore with Jim means being with one of the best fish catchers in the business. He understands the whole of it, and every part of it, and is respected for it by a long list of who's who fishing clients, such as fish biologists, marine scientists, editors of the major saltwater fishing publications, professional outdoor writers, as well as his captain compatriots from up and down the Keys, and around the world.

Jim, like most Keys professionals of the fishing kind, began a love affair with the subject at the very young age of four under the tutelage of a father who shared out-of-doors passions with a little boy. Jim, like his father, shared his passion for the sea, fishing, the environment and the Keys with his now-grown son and daughter. Both his son and daughter are experts in all facets of fishing and fly-fishing. Christina, in fact, runs the family business fly shop and outfitter service, Sea Boots Outfitters, along with her mother, Barbara. Christina can wax professional with anyone on the merits of any fly pattern, best-bet approach to finding and catching any of the Keys game fish, the casting quality of any fly rod made, the value of any reel on the market or the best leader system and knots to use for any number of possibilities. She's as professional as her dad in every respect and just as likeable. It is she who will put you with the best guides in the Lower Keys.

By the age of 12 Jim had access to his dad's boat, a 32-foot Palm Beach and his first offshore charter opportunity (sailfish) was out of the famous Pier 5 in Miami. From that day forward Jim says he knew he'd be in this business forever. He chartered his own clients, worked as a mate on other boats when school wasn't in session and credits much of his learned skills in those early years to a man he refers to as the best-ever offshore fishing captain, Buddy Carey, who's boat was named *Sea Boots*.

After Jim began working as a Miami firefighter he continued to charter on his off days out of Pier 5 through the 60's. As the quality of offshore Miami fishing declined, his chartering began to increase in Key West, which was fast becoming known as the best marlin fishing water in the world. It soon became apparent that his

Jim with Jim Jr. aboard *Sea Boots*.

future was in the Keys, and in 1976, he moved full time to the Keys. Jim ran two boats by the 70's and both operated out of the Lower Keys and Key West. By the 1980's, Captain Jim Sharpe was the most recognized name in offshore fishing from the Keys to the Caribbean. A title he still holds.

Jim is the president of Florida Keys Fishing Tournaments, Inc., past president of the Key West and Lower Keys Fishing Tournament, and on the board of the Texaco Key West Classic, as well as others. The number of fishing tournament he's won are too numerous to post here. Today, Jim still loves what he does and is as energized as ever about the state of the Keys fishery. *"Make no mistake about it. The Keys waters are still the best place in the world for a hook up and release of a blue marlin."*

NOTE: For books, videos, offshore charters, inshore or backcountry fishing, See last chapter, Practical Information.

RICHARD STANCZYK, ISLAMORADA

You cannot walk away from an afternoon with Richard Stanczyk without a pleasant, lasting impression. Your first and last might be that he could run General Motors or be Jack Welch's replacement at GE. He is engaging, in-charge, open, unusually articulate, knows what he's talking about on a wide variety of subjects, loves the Florida Keys, and catching fish is a passion.

Although Richard maintained a connection to fishing and the water as he matured, it was always interrupted by schooling, which led to the University of Miami where an accounting degree sent him into the world of banking and grayness. At 22 years old he quit the adventure-less world of numbers, the confinement of walls and went into the restaurant & bar business (there's a switch), made some money and sold out. At 26 he wanted back on the water and a boat was a must, but only a good boat would put him back into the business of fishing. A friend, Bob Lewis, who worked at the *Miami Herald* (Lewis invented the 'kite' in offshore fishing) introduced Richard to a man named Mr. Knight. Knight, as most remember, owned the *Miami Herald*, and the boat for sale that Richard coveted. Mr. Knight summoned the prospective buyer to his majestic offices in Miami for an interview. Knight would not sell to just anyone. The price Knight wanted and the price Richard offered were from different planets. A polite, very long and interesting meeting ended with no sale. A few days later Richard was contacted by Knight's office and advised that his bid, miles from the asking price, was acceptable. Mr. Knight wanted Richard to have his boat. For the next five years Richard learned the water and chartered out of the famous Pier 5 in Miami, but business was tough and he had to sell his catches to get by.

Richard switched careers again, this time it would be gold mining in Alaska, not the lonely prospector kind, but real mining. He and his two partners struck gold, literally, and Minnesota Mining bought them out before they turned over a spoonful of dirt. It was back to Florida for Richard, this time to the Keys. He bought a 29-foot offshore boat and had a custom installation put on it, the yet-to-be-discovered 'tower.' As luck would have it, the legendary Jimmy Albright's boat was out of commission and a booked season was at hand. Richard made a deal. He'd let Albright run his boat and Richard would be mate, but there was one caveat to the agreement: Albright had to teach him everything he knew about the Keys waters. In true Keys fashion, a deal was a deal, both men's interests were served, with the added bonus of friendship. In 1977, Albright and Stanczyk won the Islamorada Sailfish Tournament.

In 1978, Bud 'n Mary's came up for sale, a marina with a long-standing history associated with sport fishing and the Florida Keys. Richard thought it would be a perfect business opportunity. He was, however, a day late. It had been sold. Again, serendipity played favorably into his hand. The buy fell apart at the financing table and Richard became the owner of the fabled Bud 'n Mary's Marina in 1978.

Richard's credentials as a fly-fisherman began when he became intrigued with the Keys flats ghost. It turned to passion. He pursued bonefish on his own time, and those times, he says, still remain treasured memories. Richard won the Islamorada Fall Bonefish Fly Fishing Tournament and five other such flats tournament titles. Sun exposure has beaten up his skin and Richard does not get out on the flats as often as he'd like, but if he does, it's a zinc-oxide nose you'll see.

With Bud 'n Mary's landmark for offshore fishing, and with more than a handful of quality fly-fishing captains available, as well as Richard's own reputation growing, more and more editors from as nearby as the *Miami Herald* (Sue Cocking) and the *Sun Sentinel* (Steve Waters) and as far away as ESPN, TNN, the Discovery Channel, *Sports Afield* and *Outdoor Life* 'biggies' came to visit over the years. They would script and film the Keys offshore fishing scene. Richard, as always, the

Richard at his favorite pastime.

willing and generous host. Those introductions and kindnesses, he says, began a relationship with the producers of the Discovery Channel and TNN. The former matured into a four-part series, which would take Richard fly-fishing in Scotland for salmon and trout, and doing similar specials on Keys dolphin, tarpon and bonefish. The TNN connection matured into a sailfishing special with Bass Pro's (World Wide Sportsman), Johnny Morris.

When it comes to reflecting on the Keys fishery, new FKNMS edicts, or even past practices of catching and keeping billfish just for the client's boast, Richard has become decisive and outspoken. *"We can't kill anymore billfish, we've got to reduce commercial takes and we have to let certain species recover, protect them for as long as it takes for full recovery. Without the implementation of realistic limitations our children will face harsh realities. No fish."* Richard is, however, firm and quick to reply when asked about the present state of the Keys fishery *". . . it's better than it's been in two decades and it will continue to improve, count on it."*

NOTE: See last chapter, Practical Information, for more information.

As an aside, Richard's teenage son, Nick, is also an accomplished angler. In a Ft. Lauderdale fishing tournament, when he was 14, Nick caught a near-world-record bull dolphin (51 pounds) on a personally tied fly pattern (see Dolphin Flies). The feat was a full page story in the Ft. Lauderdale, *Sun Sentinel*. The article was written by Steve Waters, the paper's respected outdoor editor.

Robbie's Marina (bayside MM 77.5) is the most popular attraction for its resident, hand-fed tarpon population. You'll find it mentioned in every guide book. However, for a look at what a 300-pound tarpon looks like you'll have to go to Bud 'n Mary's. Try about 4 PM any day of the week. The day's catch is dockside to be made ready for table fare, the fish parts get thrown into the water and the water, literally, boils with the largest and best-fed tarpon in the Keys. It's well worth the stop and you can buy snacks at the marina if you have to wait for the boats to come in.

PREPARING FOR A VISIT TO THE KEYS
WHAT TO BRING

1. Best polarized sunglasses made. Your tint options are: amber, blue, green and blue. Amber seems to work best for most people and is also popular with guides and offshore captains. To further enhance your polarized glasses, consider side guards to further reduce glare. Croakies are a must to keep your glasses on during high-speed runs across the flats or in windy conditions. Additionally, keep optical tissue available to wipe off constant salt build-up. Always wear your glasses when casting.
2. Buy new sunscreen. Leave last year's supply at home. SPF 30 and like-strength lip balm are best. If you have

Tarpon Bust by Diane Rome Peebles.

particularly sensitive skin, check with your dermatologist before coming to the Keys. Apply sunscreen liberally and often during the day. You will not believe how intense the sun can get in the Keys.

3. Clothing: Quality lightweight rain gear, pants and jacket. Forget using a poncho. Wet clothes are uncomfortable and if you're wet you'll be chilled, a quite miserable feeling. Non-slip and non-deck-marking boat shoes. Mark up a guide or offshore captain's boat deck and he'll be rightfully upset. It's hard work to clean off such marks. Hat of your choice with dark underside on bill to further reduce glare. Loose-fitting long-sleeve, collared, vented and quick-dry shirt with pockets. Long, loose fitting, quick-dry pants.

4. A sheathed and belted plier tool with a quality line cutter.

5. File for hook sharpening. A sharp hook is a must.

6. A waterproof aim-and-shoot camera. Keep camera within reach at all times. If you have a somewhat tricky 35mm camera advise the guide or offshore captain how to operate it.

7. Stowage: Get a good waterproof carry-on bag to keep film, bandages, anti-bacterial cream, toilet paper for an emergency, extra hat, sunscreen, bug repellent, wallet, keys and any medicine you might need.

8. It's your responsibility to bring what you want to drink and eat. Leave caffeine drinks and alcohol alone. They all promote dehydration and can produce a headache or worse, malaise. Remember, being outdoors all day in the hot sun is not something you are probably used to. You must be sharp. Try water or sports drinks. Bring more liquids than you think you need and partake often, even when you're not thirsty. Ask your guide what he likes for lunch and pick it up while your getting your own. It's a tradition in the Keys to provide for your guide or offshore captain.

9. At least two rods rigged the way your guide or offshore captain recommended for the day, as well as pre-made-up stretcher, plastic fly box and protective reel covers. Never bring rod tubes, there's no place for them, especially on a flats boat. Your guide will check your rigging and knots. Don't be upset if he changes things. He's the pro, not you. He wants success just as much you, probably more.

10. Back-up fly line, backing, leader material, shock, class tippet material and recommended flies.

CHAPTER IV

WORTH KNOWING ABOUT WHEN FLY-FISHING IN THE KEYS

Where Minutiae Never Meant More.

FISHING LINES AND KNOTS

Ten thousand years ago Florida's indigenous Indians were catching fish by connecting vines, sinews or rawhide together and then tying hand-made lures to terminal lines. Elsewhere, horse hair was used by the Greeks (early AD) and remained in service well into the 18th century where English gentry used it for trout fishing. Fabric threads were also used as fishing line by the Japanese and Chinese (AD). Animal gut came into play in the 17th century, followed by silk in the 19th century along with cotton (flax or Indian grass). All the aforementioned lines used for fishing required knot-making skills. Many were common seafaring knots or simple adaptations thereof.

Synthetics (nylon/monofilaments) were discovered in DuPont's labs in the 1930's followed by advances made by English and German chemical companies. Nylon was immediately recognized as fantastic fishing line and it greatly impacted both commercial and sport fishing. However, this new material created a knot-tying conundrum as many established fishing knots would fail to hold because monofilament was slick. New knots had to be invented and were. Many times just adding extra turns and returns to old knots made the difference between slipping and holding. Some centuries old knots would end up getting new names because of monofilament, undeservedly. Even today many so-called newly named knots are merely slight changes in well-established knots, according to the International Guild of Knot Tyers.

Nylon (monofilament) absorbs water, as much as 10%, but does not lose strength and will reconstitute when dry without any performance loss. Mono-leader material should be replaced at least once a year as age does negatively affect strength. Keys guides and offshore captains prefer leader change-outs far more frequently. Nylon's resistance to oils, alkalis, organic solvents and ultraviolet rays of the sun are excellent, but odor retention, to this day, remains a seldom noticed problem: tobacco, oil product residue and the L-serene factor are odor repellents to fish. The latter only comes from the skin of caucasians. Monofilament comes in a variety of colors, as well as clear.

Dacron is three to four times thicker (same pound test) than mono, and re-tying, or joining broken connections creates a problem when running through guides, especially so at the ring tip. Dacron resists abrasion better than mono and lasts longer with just about the same resistance characteristics to acids and alkalis, as well as oils, organic solvents, sunlight and heat. Knots tied in Dacron hold better than with mono. Dacron has up to 25% less stretch than mono. Newer braided versions, however, reduce knot hold strength by 25%. Dacron can pack down when fighting a large fish and cut into reserve-wound material on the reel spool.

KEVLAR (FLUOROCARBON)

Kevlar (fluorocarbon) is another DuPont discovery (1965). With advances made by others, it was eventually brought to market as a fishing-line fiber. Kevlar is totally immune to rot, moisture and has a greater fiber strand strength than that of an equivalent strand of stainless steel.

WIRE

Nylon-coated (plain or colored) wire will kink and has a memory for the bends, but serves well as bite guards. Single-strand wire, #7 at .018-inch diameter (or smaller) with 69-pound-test strength is still just about the most popular wire material for a bite guard for the fly-fisherman.

Some Essential Knots and Loops for Keys Outings

BIMINI TWIST
A most essential saltwater fishing knot.

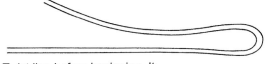

Twist line before beginning. It will add to the shock absorbing quality of the finished knot.

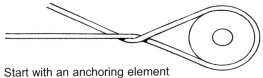

Start with an anchoring element (knee, foot or post) before making line turns.

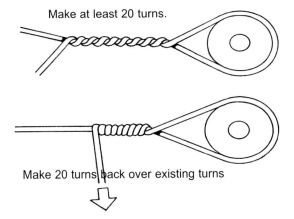

Make at least 20 turns.

Make 20 turns back over existing turns

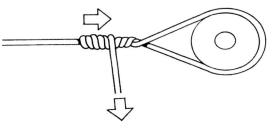

NOTE: Make sure line coils properly on initial, as well as, return turns.

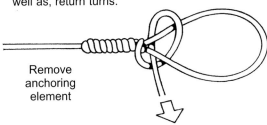

Remove anchoring element

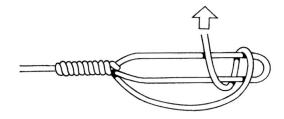

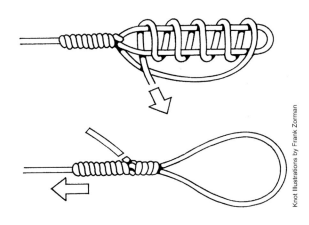

Knot Illustrations by Frank Zorman

BIMINI TWIST NOTES:
Captains and guides all over the world know the Bimini Twist knot. It's considered by many to be the most important knot in all of saltwater fishing & fly fishing.

The Bimini twist is a 100% strength knot and makes anything you attach to it fail-safe at its designated pound test. Never use a Bimini if a delicate presentation is required as it is just too bulky.

The number of turns does not have to be limited to 20 as suggested above. Additional turns produce even more shock-absorbing properties in the Bimini twist.

The origin of the Bimini twist is unknown. Some say that its inventor was a Venezuelan marlin fisherman.

ALBRIGHT KNOT
Used for joining lines of greatly dissimilar diameter or material.

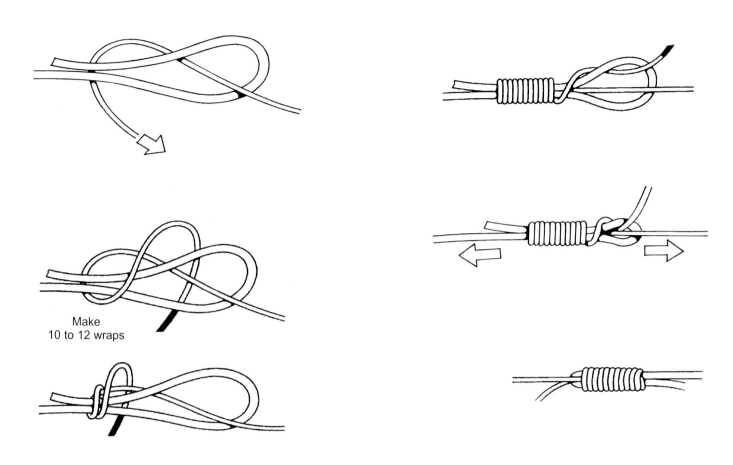

Make
10 to 12 wraps

ALBRIGHT KNOT NOTES:
The Albright knot can be used to join lines of greatly differing materials, monofilament to braided line or single-strand wire, or lines of greatly differing diameters; for example, 20-pound-test monofilament to 80-pound-test monofilament. The Albright is very reliable and needs to be mastered for saltwater fly-fishing. It is, however, rather bulky as it is offset.

  The Albright was developed by legendary Keys guide, Jimmy Albright, and is a staple saltwater knot in the Keys. Since the Albright is used with larger line diameters expect to use pliers to properly seat it. Hand seating even when moistened, will prove difficult if not impossible on large-diameter lines.

SHARPE'S BLOOD KNOT

Terminal line-to-eye hook.

SHARPE'S BLOOD KNOT
Captain Jim Sharpe (Big Pine Key), is one of the most recognized and accomplished fishermen of the deep blue in the Keys. He learned this knot from his father and it has been in service for 80 years without failing, once. It's a simple derivation of the blood knot, hold fast and in-line hook to terminal tackle knot.

NOTE: Pass the tag end through the loop at the eye of the hook from the bottom, only.

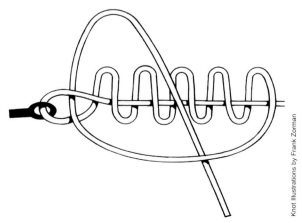

FIGURE-8 KNOT

Metal bite guard used for terminal line to hook.

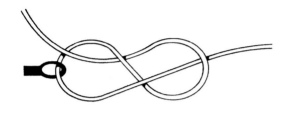

The figure-8 knot is used to tie coated/braided wire to eye of the hook.

HAYWIRE TWIST (METAL BITE GUARD)
used for terminal line to hook.

The haywire twist connects wire to eye of the hook.

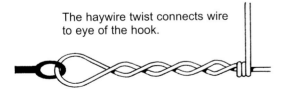

The twists are exaggerated in the drawing for the purpose of clarity.

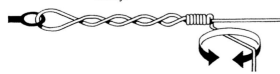

SURGEON'S KNOT

Used for joining lines.

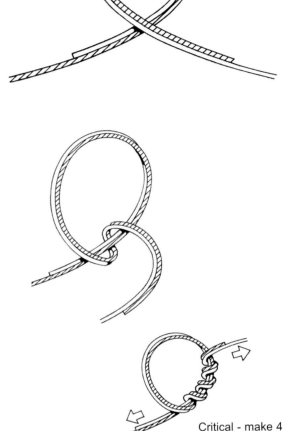

Critical - pull **all** ends taught.

Critical - make 4 turns not 3 or 5.

SURGEON'S KNOT NOTES:
The surgeon's knot can be used to join lines of equal or unequal diameters, as well as similar or dissimilar materials (monofilament to braided wire, for example). It is not recommended using this knot when one line exceeds 60-pound test. Seating the knot by hand with monofilament is very difficult, and using pliers could damage the line.

The surgeon's knot is rated at almost 100% strength knot.

Knot Illustrations by Frank Zorman

DUNCAN LOOP/UNI-KNOT - BLOOD KNOT
Used for joining lines.

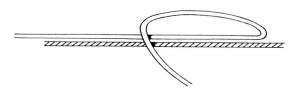

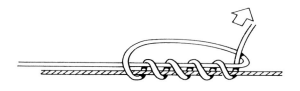

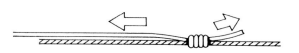

Repeating the knot produces a version of the blood knot.

DUNCAN LOOP/UNI-KNOT
Used for joining terminal line.

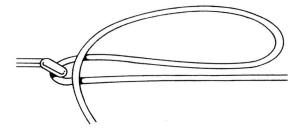

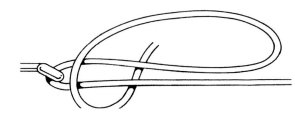

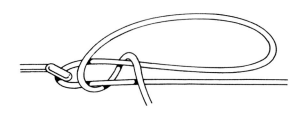

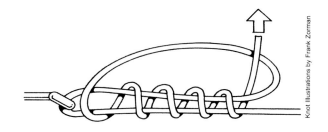

Knot Illustrations by Frank Zorman

DUNCAN LOOP / UNI-KNOT NOTES:
Legendary Keys guide, Norman Duncan, is given credit for inventing this universally accepted and easily varied knot. Vic Dunaway uses the Duncan loop/uni-knot extensively as a replacement for many other knots and loops. Dunaway states it's a 90% to 100% strength knot.

Arbor Knot

Used for backing to reel.

Surgeon's Loop

Used for connecting loops.

Pull all ends taught. Use a tool to pull *both* elements tight.

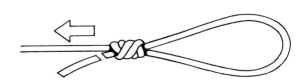

Trilene Knot
Used for terminal line to hook.

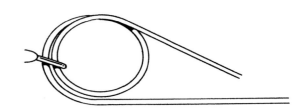

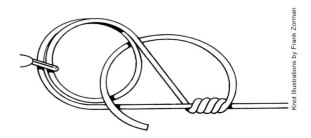

Arbor Knot Notes:
The arbor knot along with the Duncan loop are standards for attaching backing to reel arbor.

Surgeon's Loop Notes:
The surgeon's loop is, of course, a surgeon's knot using a single line.

Trilene Knot Notes:
The trilene is stronger than its variation, the clinch knot, but like the clinch knot it's hard to seat when the monofilament is over 20 pound test and it can sometimes be difficult, if not impossible, to thread the line twice through the hook eye.

Knot Illustrations by Frank Zorman

BLOOD KNOT

Used for joining lines.

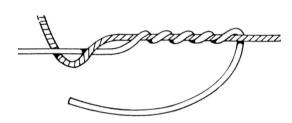

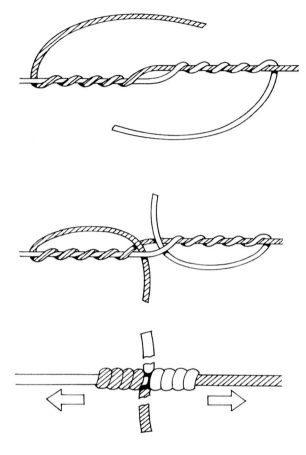

BLOOD KNOT NOTES:
The blood knot becomes difficult to seat when over 20-pound-test monofilament is used, but it is a 100% strength knot and used extensively in saltwater applications. It is also difficult to tie when the line diameters are greatly dissimilar.

IMPROVED CLINCH KNOT

Used for terminal line to hook.

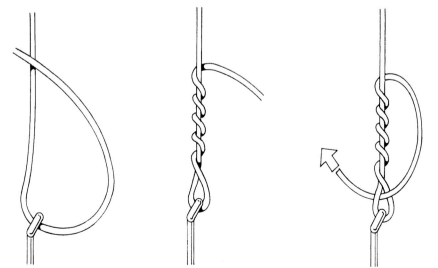

CLINCH KNOT NOTES:
The clinch knot is a 95% strength knot. Best used for monofilament under 20-pound test. For heavy monofilament lines, use 3.5 turns.

HUFFNAGEL KNOT

Used to join light tippet to heavy monofilament.

NON-SLIP MONOFILAMENT KNOT

Used for terminal line to hook.

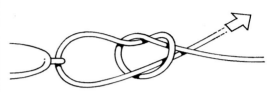

```
10- to 12-pound-test mono  = 5 turns
15- to 40-pound-test mono  = 4 turns (shown)
50- to 60-pound-test mono  = 3 turns
80- to 100-pound-test mono = 2 turns
Braided                    = 6 turns
```

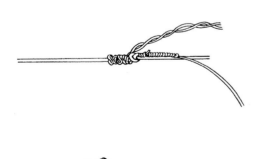

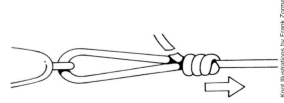

Knot Illustrations by Frank Zorman

HUFFNAGEL KNOT NOTES:
The huffnagel is widely used in the Keys. It connects very light line to very heavy line, and it's a small, lie-straight knot. It's principally used with the Bimini. There are variations of the huffnagel.

NON-SLIP MONOFILAMENT KNOT NOTES:
A true 100% strength and non-slip knot. It's used extensively when natural action of the fly is desirable. It can also be used for small- and large-diameter monofilament lines, and can be tied close to the hook eye to produce lie-straight in-line fly retrieves.

NAIL KNOT

Fly line to leader butt.

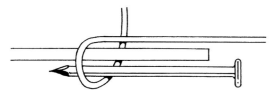

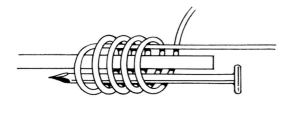

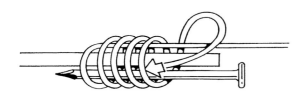

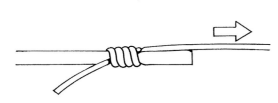

REMINDER: You can use any stiffening device (nail, pencil, paperclip, etc.), but using a straw allows you to run the line back under the wraps (through the straw) much more easily and it also improves the quality of knot.

REMINDER: Proper loop-to-loop connection in saltwater fishing is always a square knot, not a girth hitch.

CAPTAIN JIM SHARPE'S OFFSHORE DOLPHIN LEADER

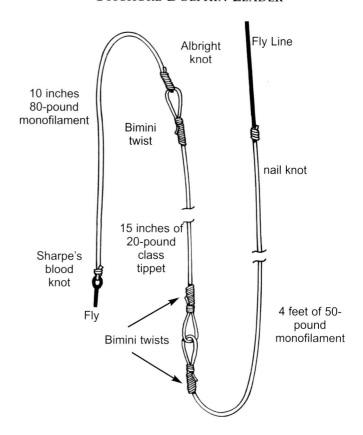

Fly Line

Albright knot

10 inches 80-pound monofilament

Bimini twist

nail knot

15 inches of 20-pound class tippet

Sharpe's blood knot

Fly

Bimini twists

4 feet of 50-pound monofilament

Yes

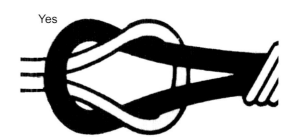

No

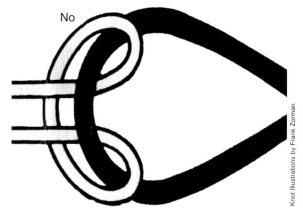

Knot Illustrations by Frank Zorman

TACKLE

NOT EVERY FLY PLAYS

There are many productive fly types in the Keys. All the flies mentioned (after each species, and those illustrated in the flies chapter) catch fish, but they are not the only flies that catch fish in the Keys.

Those who tie flies are familiar with the near-sonic development of saltwater patterns and will notice that the patterns provide a window from which you can view an evolutionary chronology of fly tying. Afficionados of tying saltwater fly patterns, and familiar with fly-fishing in the Keys, will recognize many of the guides and off-shore captains selections as having undergone little or no metamorphosis over the years while other flies will be well defined as new by construction and materials used. The older saltwater fly patterns, tried and true, are, primarily, attractor patterns, and most of the newer flies are pure bait mimics.

ABOUT SALTWATER FLIES

More fly-fishermen and more communication through books, periodicals, TV shows, vendors, fly shops, videos, fishing schools and trade show gatherings have raised salt-water fly patterns to new heights in just the past decade or so. Named flies tied only a few years ago have already been modified to meet local conditions: size, color, body shape and eyes. Subtle tweaks have even earned these merely modified flies new and undeserved names.

SOLVING THE MYSTERY

Fly-tiers and fly fishermen share the desire to solve the same puzzle. Which flies catch which fish when, where and why? Some of the answers are easy, some are dumb-founding. The inexact science of both fishing and tying flies are perfect mysteries that always intrigue us to try again and anew. The allure for many, like the selective memory of a golfer who only chooses to remember the best shot of the day, is the belief that a little more of this or that will bring improved results tomorrow. The fly itself is like the golf club selected for a particular shot from a particular spot on a particular day for a given situation. It either produces confidence, or it does not. Why this is a truism defies logic in both fly-fishing and golf.

FLIES INFINITE

Any qualified fly-fishing guide or offshore captain in the Keys worth his or her salt will have their own flies for each of the 100's of situations, conditions and the dozens of species the Keys experience will present. It is our best advice to always trust your guide's or captain's fly selection. You will be rewarded. You will also find many patterns used in the Keys are from the guides' and offshore captains' own tying benches and many, if not most, never make the front page, a local fly shop display case, or even their next door neighbor's fly box.

BAITFISH, FOOD AND FLIES

Fish strike flies because they mistake them for food (bait-fish), out of a territorial reflex instinct, or even when their stomachs are full because of a competitive reaction when in a schooling profile. Saltwater species eat a very wide variety of foods: other fish, their own young, worms, crustacean, squid and even sea urchins.

SIZE, CONTRAST, SHAPE & COLOR

Saltwater baitfish-like flies (lures) have been used for thousands of years. Today's tiers are able to make almost perfect reproductions of most baits. Baitfish have fairly standard shapes: mullet have fat profiles, menhaden like baitfish have high, flat and thin body profiles, and other baitfish species have tube-like shapes. Baitfish mimics are tied to imitate shape, size and coloration. A good tier will put much emphasis on what the fish sees from above and from below for tidal flats species. Synthetic materials, along with a wide variety of hook shanks, have made tying exact matches of Keys crabs, shrimps, worms, needlefish, eels, squids, and even spiny lobster patterns possible, but sea urchins are still not widely tied or used.

Keys fly-fishing will require very sharp, corrosion-resistant hooks. Inshore hook sizes, generally, size 2 through 5/0, and offshore, up to 5/0 and greater. Many Keys guides and offshore captains prefer coated hooks over stainless hooks. Hook shapes are: straight-back, bendback, keel and the newer 'C' type. The latter reportedly provides better safe releases of fish. However, we could not find any proponents of the 'C'-type hooks amongst the expert fly-fishing guides and captains with whom we spoke.

FLY TYPES

Tube Flies

Tube flies are flies tied on hooks with thin plastic tubes. The leader is threaded through the tube. They offer lots of versatility by using different heads, feathers, bodies etc.

Weedless Flies

Weed-guard flies have looped mono or wire protecting the hook point from hanging up on the bottom, branches and sea grass.

Popper Flies

Surface poppers are not in great demand in the Keys as they are, generally, short-shank hooks. Long-shank hooks are the weapon of choice. Skipping poppers are better suited for Keys waters. These longer-shanked hook-flies have the angle on the face more deeply slanted than surface poppers and, generally, get most use in quiet water and inshore flats. Pencil poppers are just very narrow poppers with slim profiles made to be bait mimics. Sliders are simply, poppers/skippers with the tapered portion facing front.
NOTE: Tube flies, sliders and popper flies are also big-game fish flies.

Shrimp, Crab And Special-Occasion Flies:
Del Brown's Merkin (crab) and Captain Lenny Moffo's version of it could well be all you need when fishing for tarpon, permit and bonefish, redfish and several more flats dwellers. These flies are tied sideways on the hook and properly constructed will match the natural ambulation of a crab (a critical tying element). Generally, these patterns include considerations for fast to slow sinking, as well as size and coloration. The patterns enjoy a fairly wide variety of coastal species attracted to them. On true Merkins, the flies are tied so the hook rides up. Size 4 to 2 will serve you well 95% of the time in the Keys.

Lenny Moffo's shrimp flies are tied with much variation (size, color and shape) as there are several types of shrimps as well as crabs, in the Keys waters. Shrimp flies usually include eyes, carapace, swimming legs and antennae. Several variations of shrimp patterns work. Actually, these shrimp flies, tied larger, work well in deeper water and on bigger species.

In mid-April of 1999, your co-authors were staked up on a sand spit in 5 feet of water just beyond Largo Sound (oceanside). We had only been staked up for 30-minutes and had already failed to hook up with two south-running pod's of tarpon. Within minutes of the last pods departure, Andrew Derr spotted a north-running pod, coming right at us at about 100 yards away. We hunkered down, quietly. Andrew waited and then made a single, on the money 90-foot cast. He hooked up with a tarpon that was the biggest tarpon, by far, either of us had ever seen (from Costa Rica to Boca Grande). It really was, easily, over 200 pounds. Andrew was using a very large (ugly-looking) pale shrimp pattern he'd tied, and his weapon of choice was an under-sized-for-the-occasion 10 weight, but, fortunately, had 20-pound class tippet and 80-pound mono shock. Andrew's fly had made the perfect welcome to the daisy chaining pod of eight or so tarpon (one of the best at-bats you could ask for). A nearly two-hour battle took us inshore twice, once to a point where the tarpon almost beached itself, and was about 70% out of the water, and finally, to almost mid-Hawk channel. We released the tiring brute when barracuda and a shark began surveying. That tarpon deserved a better fate. The largest tarpon we had ever seen had leapt more times than either of us could count, or thought possible, and we had been doused at the boat at least twice. The aerial acrobatics show was something only a few see in a lifetime, and by a tarpon that size, maybe two lifetimes.

Andrew's camera, by the way, was comfortably at rest on the kitchen table and our scale hung idly on the wall in his garage; ugh!

MOE Flies
Mother-of-epoxy (MOE) is molded on the hook shank, with other materials, to suggest crabs and other baits. MOE flies are, generally, reserved for tidal flats species. Bob Popovics made these patterns popular.

Barracuda Flies
Flies with an unusually long tail tied on the hook-shank bend. Heads are reinforced for longer service with an epoxy-like material, and eyes are almost always added, designed to mimic a needlefish.

Clousers
Clousers (Bob Clouser) are, generally, tied with the hook riding up and include weighted barbell eyes. Most Clouser patterns are meant to dive. They are tied in an infinitely wide variety of sizes and color combinations. These patterns are universally effective in the Keys.

Seaducers and Whistlers
Seaducers are large, full-profile flies tied with bucktail, thick collars and lead eyes. A Seaducer has much more material than the Whistler. They both were originally designed to attract bigger game fish. Whistler patterns got their name from the fact that they whistle when cast.

Deceivers
Deceiver patterns are the brainchild of legendary Lefty Kreh. They are highly effective general baitfish imitations that have attracted everything from sailfish to brook trout. Deceivers are tied in as many sizes and colors as one could imagine. The fly has, essentially, epoxy-like head/eyes, long hackle at the hook bend and a body wrap of bucktail with the wing facing toward the shank.

Tarpon Flies (Stu Apte)
Stu Apte's (Florida Keys) patterns remain very productive tarpon flies (Apte, Apte Too and Apte Too Plus). Lenny Moffo's variations on the theme are quite worthy of mention. Apte's and Moffo's traditional tarpon flies are very full at the hook bend, similar to Seaducers and Whistlers. Apte's original version is saddle hackle wing and collar tied at the hook-shank bend with epoxy-like material, running thick to narrow, towards the hook eye. There are, actually, an infinite number of variations on this traditional Keys tarpon fly: color combinations, materials, sizes and use of eyes. Most everyone agrees that the aforementioned tarpon patterns got their DNA from Stu Apte.

Whistlers
A Dan Blanton fly pattern. Quite similar to the Seaducer pattern, but tends to push the water.

Shark Flies
Most Keys shark flies are long-shanked hooks with basic wing-like material tied at the hook bend. Sharks tend to gulp a fly, a wire bite guard will be necessary. Orange seems to be the color of choice in the Keys.

Chum Flies
Chumming, a seemingly disgraceful undertaking for the uninitiated salmon and trout enthusiast, is an absolute

necessity when saltwater fly-fishing in the Keys. The Chum Fly, of course, imitates chum bits. These flies are simply tied and use rabbit-fur strips and other materials that approximate the chum material in size and coloration. Contrast and size are critical.

Needlefish Flies

Needlefish flies are long flies with tight wing patterns tied at the hook's shank. The needlefish-looking head, of course, has epoxy eyes. Generally, an overlooked pattern with more than the usual suspects as suitors.

Offshore Flies

Big-game patterns tend to be bulkier than other types of flies and many are tandem hook flies (4/0 to 7/0). The second hook on a tandem is usually one size smaller and often tied with the hook facing opposite or both at 90-degree angles. Combo tube flies with popper heads incorporate an open-cell foam popper, forward, and fly material to the rear. Typically, the leader is threaded through the tube/popper body and then the fly is attached. The head (usually soft foam), holds up amazingly well and makes plenty of noise, attracting fish of many a religious persuasion. Quick change-outs are built into these flies. Offshore in the Keys, tube flies, poppers and sliders are very much in play. Disturbing the water works very well for several Keys species.

CHEMICALLY- OR LASER-SHARPENED HOOKS

Saltwater fishing in the Keys requires that great attention be paid to hook sharpness. Never take casually the fact that you have to have a sharp hook. Most saltwater species fished for in the Keys have extraordinarily hard mouth plates, bills or razor-like teeth. A dull hook plays out poorly in the Keys. Guides and offshore captains never go there, ever. They tell us it's a profligate undertaking and reserved for the dull witted.

FLY RODS

Saltwater fly-fishing in the Keys necessitates you have more than one arrow in your quiver. In the same Keys outing, and even within minutes, you could easily encounter a 100-pound tarpon and an 8-pound bonefish, or a 200-pound billfish or a 20-pound dolphin. No one rod, reel or rigging is a match for all occasions.

Nine- and nine-and-a-half foot rods get most saltwater fly-fishing jobs done well in the Keys. However, lifting power for Keys billfish, and several other pelagic heavyweights, requires the use of shorter and more powerful rods. A dramatic loss of casting ease can be expected with these shorter rods.

Whippy rods are out in saltwater, werereferring here to rod action which translates to slow action rods that bend well down the rod. Moderate- and fast-action rods are more common in the Keys. Fast action, generally, makes it easier to produce the tightest casting loops and

has better castability in the wind. Lifting/fighting and turning power with new lightweight rods, however, sometimes suffers.

In the Keys, saltwater rods designed to cast 7-weight line to 8-weight line will suffice for fish 5 to 15-pounds, and 9- to 12-weight rods for most fish up to 100-pounds (tarpon and permit). Fish over 50 pounds (offshore), generally, will require shorter 13- to 14-weight rods. A yellowfin tuna or blue marlin, should you be lucky enough to encounter one, would require an 18-weight rod. Always defer to your guides or offshore captain's selections. You will find greatly varying opinions on rod design, as well as other considerations among the Keys guides and offshore captains. Your authors, for example, agree on very little with regard to rods. It's your at-bat, maybe you should pick.

The most common grips for saltwater rods are half wells, full wells, or full wells with a fighting grip. Many big-game fly rods (12-weight and up), for open-water fish over 50-pounds, incorporate a fighting grip. This is a grip forward of, or above, the standard grip. Also, some saltwater rods, starting with some 9/10-wts., have a fixed or attachable extension at the base of the rod. The extension piece aids in fighting and turning a large fish, but will hamper casting.

The best rod guides are all ceramic, but snake guides can work. However, the stripping guide must be ceramic. They range in sizes (12 all the way up to 25). A few guides and offshore captains we met remove the manufacturer's smaller stripping guide (an aesthetic thing) and replace it with a larger size.

BACKING

Backing for saltwater fishing breaks down, basically, to two choices: gel-spun polyethylene or braided Dacron and micron. Stretching and swelling from water absorption are not a hugely different, but a packing problem exists on gel-spun. Gel-spun is much thinner than Dacron and Micron. Equal lengths of 50-pound-test gel-spun line and 30-pound dacron/micron would take up about the same reel space. A rod that once held 200 yards of Dacron now holds, approximately, 500 yards of gel-spun. Gel-spun is gaining favor, but it to has drawbacks. It won't hold color, it can slice your finger to the bone, it can bite through line when not properly stored on the reel, making knots that hold fast remains a real concern, and it is very expensive. On the flip side, and other than holding far more line of equal strength, are the pluses of tremendous abrasion resistance, imperviousness to water absorption and UV degradation. Standard backing on saltwater reels: 20-pounds for 7- to 9- weight rods, 30 pounds for 10- to 12-weight rods, and greater for 13- and above weight rods.

The amount or length of backing, for all practical purposes, would be 150/200 yards for up to 7/8 weights, 200/250 yards for up to 9/10/11-weights, 250/300 for up to 11/12/13-weights, and 300/450 for 14-weights and up to 650 yards for rod weights above that. Reel capacity, ultimately, determines the actual amount of backing you will be able to use.

Note: Manufacturers provide charts that quantify just how much backing/fly line can be accommodated.

FLY LINES

Always get warm weather formulated line for the Keys. For most Florida Keys saltwater flats outings you will only need to use weight forward. These lines produce the best casts as they have the heaviest part in the forward section. There are variations in core material as well as taper. Running line length has, over the years, been modified to meet the needs of different conditions and species. It is in your best interest to consult with your guide and then make your purchase at one of the four fly shops in the Keys. Shooting-head lines (not recommended for flats as they land like a bomb) are a specialty line about 30' long with a thin shooting line that for skilled casters produces even greater casting distances than WF lines. Shooting tapers utilize running line of up to 100' attached to the back of a shooting taper line. This allows running line to become part of the fly line. The use of these lines has greatly improved catch percentages, as well as broadened the species types fly-fishermen can target as they allow, for example, fishing deeper in the water column.

For Keys fishing you can leave level and double tapers lines at home.

Sink rates are another fly-line consideration and these are measured 1 through 10 in IPS (inches per second). A #1 sink rate translates to up to one-and-a-half inches per second (IPS) and a #10 sink-rate number is equal to up to ten-and-a-half IPS. There are new weight standards for fly lines. The first 40-feet is now weighed, not the first 30-feet. These new standards replace the 1960 standards and are relevant to Keys fishing starting, presently, with 7-weight lines and ending at 14-weight lines. For example, a 7-weight line now has 234 grains instead of 185 grains and a 12-weight 443 grains instead of 380 grains. Fly lines can be purchased in a wide variety of colors, as well as clear. When fishing the Keys flats, offshore or line-shy species, these options must be taken into account. Clear or light green are best for avoiding detection, but many guides and offshore captains balk at their use because they are hard to visually track.

LEADERS

NOTE: Never discard monofilament in the water or leave it lying loose in the boat. Keep unwanted monofilament

safely stored and then discard when onshore in an appropriate trash bin.

There are as many leader systems as there are books written about fly-fishing and, perhaps, as many books written about fly-fishing as could leisurely be read in a lifetime. Whoever writes a new one can afford contentment in the knowledge that his is the new picture on leaders, agreeing with no one else's, but likely to be haughtily disagreed with by all those who believe in some other leader system. No matter your allegiance to any leader system it is advisable to use the leader systems preferred by your guide or offshore captain while in the Keys. They've been at it for years, are well past experimenting, and would never recommend a leader system or knot that has failed them in the past. That is bankable.

If you're of the mind-set to rig your own leaders before arriving in the Keys, your most practical approach is to call your guide or offshore captain beforehand and have them advise you on what to pre-rig, and how. However, if you're too busy with life's demands, then the best bet is to contact any of the four fly shops in the Keys and have them pre-rig all your inshore and offshore needs, then just pick up the lot when you arrive. This is decidedly the best and fail-safe way for those with busy schedules.

Leaders are built to aid the angler in allowing the fly line to unroll and deliver the fly, aid in deceiving the fish and attract it to bite, and hold together under stress. Other than most agreeing on the latter, the subject of leader construction can, in some quarters, call for a Jihad. However, the most basic leader constructions that have stood the test of time in the Keys employ the simplest and easiest remembered rules.

LEFTY ON LEADERS

"The saltwater tapered leader is one of the least understood pieces of equipment a fly-fisherman uses. A better understanding would result in few bad casts and infinitely better presentations.

One mistake many fishermen make is using pre-tied or knotless leaders right out of the package, no matter what the conditions. For example, most experienced bonefishermen prefer a leader of at least 12 feet, yet many companies produce only a 10-foot leader—which is OK on a windy day. But when the flats are slick calm, my choice for a bonefish leader is 16 feet. Vary the leader length according to the conditions.

Another myth with tapered leaders that still causes saltwater fly-fishermen problems is that the butt section should be made of stiff or hard mono. Nothing could be further from the truth. A fly line isn't cast the same as other tackle. Instead, the line is unrolled to the target. The leader must also unroll to deliver the fly. If a stiff butt section is used, it won't unroll correctly. A leader that has enough flexible weight to carry the energy of the cast through the leader's end makes the best presentation. Fortunately, this is easily achieved. Simply use the same brand of material throughout to get uniformity. What mono should you use? I suggest buying the best "premium" spinning line of any well-known manufacturer. Their premium brand will be flexible and have good knot strength.

Another key to making a good tapered leader: the butt section should be one-half the length of the total leader. For example, to construct a 10-foot tapered leader for a 9-weight or heavier outfit, the butt section should be 5 feet of 40-pound test. Follow this with a foot of 30-pound test and a foot of 20-pound test, next connect your class tippet of approximately 18 inches. If you want to make a 12-foot leader, start with 6 feet of butt section and lengthen each strand accordingly. Many experienced fly-fishermen will scoff at this formula. However, compare it with your favorite leader on a windy day, and I think you will be convinced of its usefulness."

CAPTAIN STEVE KANTNER ON LEADER RIGS

Steve Kantner, our long-time friend and South Florida's well-publicized Everglades expert, is a fly-fishing guide extraordinaire. Steve's articles regularly appear in Steve Waters' outdoor column in the *Sun Sentinel* as well as several regional sport fishing and national fly-fishing magazines. Steve is also a regular at shallow-water expos. Here's what he has to say about leader rigs/leader boxes.

"Since the cost of a days fishing is considerable, experienced anglers always try to maximize their time by being rigged and ready. This includes being ready to exchange a tattered fly or bite tippet as soon as a hooked fish is broken off or released. In order to expedite changeovers, particularly when pursuing a large fish like tarpon, Keys captains employ a variety of leader-stretching devices to keep flies, tippets, and the necessarily heavy monofilament 'shock tippets' straight and orderly. These so-called 'leader boxes' facilitate the storage of a number of rigs together, since tippets are connected loop to loop, both fly and tippet can be quickly replaced whenever necessary."

KEYS GUIDES AND OFFSHORE CAPTAINS ON LEADERS

There is no consensus amongst the guides and offshore captains in the Keys about tying up leaders, nor is there a consensus about which knots to use. However, you can count on their choices to be worthy of your attention, and you are well advised to tie up your leaders in accordance with your guide or offshore captain's instructions. Your mentor for the day or week does not experiment with your leaders. They have come to a method of constructing leaders the hard way. Every section, choice of line and knot has been thoroughly thought out, and has been battle-field proven.

A leader could be 16 feet long (bonefish on a windless summer morning or evening) or as short as 3 feet for an offshore species on a choppy and murky water day. Some guides use one leader length for all occasions. Alan Finkelman (Islamorada) uses a standard 14-foot leader for all inshore species. His rationale is that he always knows where the fly is and he says that keeps him on target from the very first cast.

CLASS TIPPETS

Class tippets are always monofilament. Typically, 18 to 24 inches or longer. Tippet strength is a matter of choice, roughly, from 8- to 20-pound test in the Keys.

NOTE: The IGFA does not recognize class tippets over 20-pound test (non-metallic) for fly-fishing, nor tippets shorter than 15 inches (no length limit), or a terminal bite/shock tippet longer than 12 inches (including knots). A shock / bite tippet can be any material.

BITE GUARDS

Many Keys species have very sharp teeth or sandpaper-like mouths. Bite guards or shock tippets are respectively required. Bite guards are, generally, heavy monofilament, single-strand wire or coated/braided wire. Shock tippets are almost always heavy monofilament, but some guides/offshore captains will use Kevlar (fluorocarbon). Braided wire is used for real toothy critters (sharks) or billfish, sailfish and marlin.

Pre-made and properly stored leader rigs are a must for saltwater Keys fishing as the need for switching set-ups occurs quickly, and the window of opportunity in all saltwater fly-fishing is always a "right now" kind of thing.

REELS

Assaulting the saltwater scene with less than a quality drag system, and a well-maintained, recently checked out reel, is a disaster waiting to happen. Owning a clunker reel is pure folly in the Keys environment. A quality reel is your only option, and quality reels come in a wide variety of performance specifications.

Reels for saltwater fishing must always be constructed of materials resistant to saltwater corrosion, as well as its working parts: springs, pawls, cogs, drags, handles and feet. All other internal and external parts must also be corrosion resistant (some parts are, unavoidably, made of high-carbon steel). For the top of the line, it's still one piece solid-block, machined aircraft grade T6061 aluminum that sets the standard. Big-game reels usually feature impregnated cork disks that create friction by pressing against the inside of the spool. There are two kinds of designs to consider: one is direct drive and the other is anti-reverse. Direct drive is the choice of guides and offshore captains of the Keys. Direct drive is one that, simply, has the spool attached to the handle and one turn of the handle equals one turn of the spool. With anti-reverse reels, however, only the spool turns when the line is running, which avoids the problem of broken fingers, torn nails, cuts and knuckle bruises so common with direct-drive reels. Unfortunately, anti-reverse reels have a drawback of considerable deficiency, turning the handle to take in line does not necessarily guarantee you are recovering line. You may reel against tension, but not recover an inch of line. The slow process of 1- to 1- take-up was to be solved by multiplier reels, but that has, thus far, failed. Slow (1-to-1) take-up, long thought to be the fly-fisher's lot in life, has been successfully overcome with the advent of large-arbor reels. Now take-up, or line recovery, begins to equal the speed with which a big guy takes line out; a real bonus. Also, large-arbor reels allow for plenty of backing and that, in itself, is very reassuring. Also, many large arbor reels have been skeletonized to reduce weight. Reels also come with selections for left- or right-handed reeling. It is normal to reel with your dominant hand.

EXTRA SPOOLS AND DRAGS

Extra spools provide an opportunity to change your whole set-up without too much delay. The necessity for changing set-ups with regard to reels is a real consideration in saltwater fishing. Switching reels is just as fast as utilizing a spare spool. Drags are common to all reels, but in saltwater fishing a drag system must be clearly of superior design. Drag systems are brakes and there are several considerations for both system design and materials. There are disk, caliper and drum designs used for stopping or slowing spool rotations. Cork, as well as synthetics, are used for brake pad materials.

MAINTENANCE

Not caring for all your equipment in a saltwater environment is profligate. It will cost you sooner than later. Always hose off rods after detaching the ferruled sections, then air dry. Never put a wet rod in a cloth sleeve/tube. Reels: release the drag, unwind at least the fly line, open the spool, soak in warm soapy water, rinse, air dry, rewind and check the drag (store reel with loosened drag). Fly lines are hosed off while rinsing the reel, and unwinding through the backing is not difficult. For floating line add line dressing, lightly. Wash flies and air dry completely. Transparent plastic boxes or leader stretchers (tarpon/billfish) are best. For metal tools use a very light application of oil containing only a whiff of WD40, or equal.

CHAPTER V

GAME FISH OF THE FLORIDA KEYS

Knowing What It Takes To Catch Fish. The Keys Guides' And Offshore Captains' Points Of View.

WELCOME TO WORLD-RECORD GAME-FISH TURF

The Florida Keys, according to the Chamber of Commerce, have had over 500 International Game Fish Association world-record catches come from its waters (several line classes, all tackle, junior, fly rod and several special classes). No other saltwater venue in the world is close to such a claim. World-record gamefish catches that have come from Keys waters, caught on a fly are: amberjack, barracuda, bonefish, cobia, dolphin, gag grouper, jack crevalle, horse-eye jack, jewfish, cero mackerel, king mackerel, Spanish mackerel, permit (every IGFA record was caught in the Keys*), gag grouper, African pompano, rainbow runner, hammerhead shark, tiger shark, mutton snapper, tarpon, tripletail, blackfin tuna and little tunny. At various times throughout the last century, record Keys-caught game fish also included: redfish, snook, blue marlin, sailfish, white marlin, wahoo, seatrout, ladyfish, several snapper species, several grouper species and several shark species, and there's more, lots more.

THINK

Lefty Kreh, or any sane fisherman for that matter, would not head to the Florida Keys, Australia, Panama, Belize, or any world-class saltwater fishing destination, planning on being his own guide or offshore captain. Oddly, however, self guiding and self captaining are a regular occurrence in the Keys, and not so oddly, there are lots of fishermen departing the Keys skunked. All are willing to grumble to all who will listen, "The Keys are not what they used to be." The latter could not be further from the truth. The reason why so many come to the Keys, willing to take on its fishery self-guided, is that the Keys are easily accessible, affordable and there are a plethora of books, articles and "X" marks the spot charts suggesting it is a practical do-it-yourself place. Nothing could be further from reality. Think. When Key West's Captain Jeffrey Cardenas, one the Keys' most notable and accomplished fly-fisherman, goes fishing beyond his natal venue he hires a guide or offshore captain. For example, in one of the Keys-based Redbone/Mercury Tournaments, Jeffery won one of the events with no less than a Grand Slam (bonefish, tarpon and permit caught in the same day). He was not self-guided. His accomplishment was with the help of a fellow professional. If you want to be put on a fish, bottom line, local knowledge is what it's all about.

HIRE A PRO AND COME PREPARED

The professional, expert fly-fishing guiding and offshore captaining population in the Keys is the most skilled and knowledgeable in the world. Anyone not wishing to engage one is wasting both his time and money. Coming to the Keys bent on a do-it-yourself approach, skilled or amateur, will find it to be extraordinarily tough sledding, even impossible, without local knowledge. Another touch of reality is to arrive prepared, able to double haul and get line out, in three or four false casts to at least 50 feet, and do so in breezy conditions.

Remember, your guide or offshore captain wants you to catch fish and he will work hard to make it happen, but if you cannot cast well your chances of catching what you came for becomes self-limiting.

---

* Fittingly enough, Del Brown, the inventor of the 'merkin' crab pattern currently holds the world's record for permit on a fly (41-pounds, 8-ounces), and Sue Cocking, *Miami Herald's* outdoor editor, currently holds the world's record for permit caught by a woman (9-pounds).

Amberjack - Greater
CARANGIDAE, *Seriola dumerili*

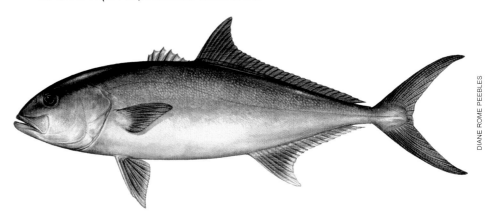

DIANE ROME PEEBLES

IGFA World-Record Catches

Line-Class World Record:
155 pounds, 12-oz.

World Fly Rod Record:
103 pounds, 12oz.

Florida Keys Record - Line Class:
142 pounds.

Florida Keys Record - Fly Rod:
103 pounds, 12oz. (world record)

Quick ID: Pronounced dark stripe runs from snout tip through the eye to the spinous dorsal fin. Largest of all jacks. Distinguished from all other jacks by gill raker count (11 to 16) on the lower limb of the first branchial arch.

CAPTAIN'S NOTES

In the Keys, amberjack are year-round residents, and like all jacks they are aggressive feeders. That fact, coupled with their historic plentifulness, made them an easy take for commercial fishermen, party boats and sport fishermen as well. Too many, it seems, have been culled from the depths and their sustainable levels are in question. In recent years, harvests indicate that both their numbers and size are down. These large jacks are slow to sexually mature. Many highly qualified and respected sportfishing charter captains would like to see the carnage stopped so that the species can make a full recovery, no matter how long it takes.

Generally, amberjack are not a target for the fly-fisherman, more of a found opportunity, but once found and engaged they will provide every thrill all jacks provide: a vicious strike and a tough fight. Smaller amberjack can be found in shallow water in small schools, but the big guys can be loners and found in deep water. Catching an amberjack on a fly rod, of either size, will almost always call for teasing. That requirement calls for chumming, and as everyone knows, that practice can bring a laundry list of other species to the scene. If an amberjack shows amid the chum or live bait, many captains will employ bait and switch, using a hookless popper to entertain the fish. Once aroused to strike, the popper is pulled away, and the fly is offered for the take. When an amberjack is caught it will tend to run to deeper water, but when pulled back up near the surface it may have several of its cousins in tow, which provides a real bonus for other on-board fly-fishermen. Multiple hook-up possibilities is always a nice situation. The amberjack hits hard and, generally, can be counted on to hook itself. After the amberjack slows down from its initial run, it is still a good practice to set the hook, hard, a few more times for insurance.

Historic Densities: Offshore in the spring is best. April is prime because of a current ban in that month, as of this writing, on commercial harvesting. The best amberjack fishing is off Islamorada, south of Key West and in the Gulf of Mexico, north-northwest of Key West. Water temperatures of 65 to 80 degrees F, offshore, deep, near sea mounds, reefs, wrecks and drop-offs of around 60 feet or more are the general locations of amberjack. Smaller species can sometimes be found further inshore.

Feeds On: Mullet, blue runners, several baitfish species, squid and other invertebrate.

ID: The gill raker count is 11 to 16 on the lower limb of the branchial arch. There is a higher count present on juvenile fish. A large specimen will have 6 to 7 small spines on the dorsal fin connected by a membrane. The second dorsal fin will exhibit one spine and 29 to 35 soft rays. A juvenile specimen will have 3 anal spines with the first two detached. An adult will have 3 anal spines, but skin will cover the spines. The anal fins have 19 to 22 soft rays. The keel of the caudal peduncle is fleshy on each side.

Tackle: (For larger species only) 12-weight rod, at least 200 yards of 20-pound Dacron backing, fast-sinking WF fly line, 20-pound-class tippet and 12 inches of 60- to 100-pound mono shock.

Flies: Chum flies, big Deceivers (red, yellow, and blue & white), large streamers, big poppers, large baitfish imitations with fluffy marabou and tandem hook flies (6 to 8 inches).

Barracuda
SPHYRAENIDAE, Sphyaena barracuda

DIANE ROME PEEBLES

Quick ID: Pronounced black blotches on flanks with 18 to 22 dark bars above the lateral line. Overbite lower jaw and very toothy. Long, slender torpedo-like appearance.

CAPTAIN'S NOTES

Barracuda are found year round in the Keys. They are a worthy game fish by any measurement of desirable action on the fly rod. They are not, generally, a targeted species. By gamefish standards, the barracuda is, unfortunately, just plain too ugly for some, and troublesome when brought to the boat. Targeting the barracuda usually requires chumming or live bait teasing. That process will, however, bring other suitors. More than likely sharks, if the flats are opted for.

Fly-fishing for the 'cuda' is uniquely different and a marvelous opportunity for the not-so-great fly-caster. Teasing a sighted 'cuda' requires a cast that puts the fly at about 8 to 10 feet away from the fish, but within its window of vision or hearing. Oddly, the best next move is to pull the fly out of play, immediately. Excitation is the intended ploy. Repeating this teasing process could exceed more than a few attempts before the barracuda reacts. Once the 'cuda' shows agitation, which will be quite obvious, then lay the fly down a few feet closer than your previous put and takes. Let the fly settle for a one or two count, then begin a ridiculously fast and very erratic retrieve. The strike will be explosive and so fast that you will have a tough time replaying the crash in your mind's eye. A timid retrieve will all but assure the fish will lose interest and swim off. The body of a barracuda is extremely slimy, its teeth are built for holding prey, and a bite from its razor-like teeth can also be very toxic. Leave handling to your guide. In some cultures the barracuda is eaten, but it can cause *ciguatera*, a sometimes fatal attack on the nervous system.

Historic Densities: Best temperature ranges 75 to 86 degrees F. Flats or inshore specimens of barracuda are usually young and, as such, smaller than those found offshore around wrecks and reefs. Barracuda, 4 pounds (or less) to 10 pounds (or more), can show up in small schools. Although barracuda are found year round in the Keys, generally, the winter months through early spring produce more appearances on the flats.

Feeds On: True to its predatory instincts, it's a rather non-selective feeder. Needlefish on the flats and smaller reef fish are rather common food sources for 'cuda' in the Keys.

ID: The greater barracuda is easily identified by its body shape and toothy grin. Its coloration also distinguishes it from other species, as well as between the adult specimen and the juvenile. Adult fish have clear markings of irregular dark, black blotches on the flanks, especially near the tail. Barracuda are silvery to silvery gray above and silvery to almost white below. However, coloration can vary depending on habitat and age. The barracuda has 5 spines in the first dorsal and 10 soft rays in the second. There are 75 to 90 scales along the lateral line, the preopercle is rounded and the maxilla extends back to the eyes.

Tackle: (For inshore and flats) 8/9-weight rod, at least 150 yards of 20-pound backing, 12 to 16-pound class tippet and a wire bite guard.

Flies: A barracuda will attack just about any fly, but needlefish patterns (single or double hooks) are a good choice along with big, brightly colored Deceivers and streamers (white, orange and red, all with some flash).

Bonefish
ABULIDAE, Albula vulpes

IGFA World-Record Catches

Line-Class World Record:
19 pounds.

World Fly-Rod Record
15 pounds, 12oz.

Florida Keys Record - Line Class:
15 pounds, 12oz

Florida Keys Record - Fly Rod:
15 pounds, 12oz. (world record)

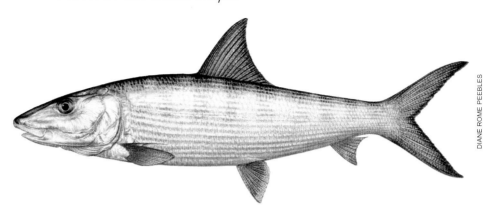

Quick ID: Mouth small, inferior. Snout tip blackish. Body torpedo-like, very silvery to ghost white with barely visible, thin laterally running lines of pale coloration.

CAPTAIN'S NOTES

Polarized glasses are a must for any Keys outing, but guides stress the importance of seeing into the water when bonefishing. It's hard to catch what you do not see. Casting, however, is the name of the game when it comes to bonefishing.

Your menu for dead-calm water is to present the fly about 10 to 12 feet in front of the fish, or double that for quickly moving fish. In moderately calm water you can get in tighter, about 7 or 8 feet, and when the water is choppy even tighter. Always maintain a tight line. Never begin your retrieve as soon as the fly lands. Wait until it settles, and if it has attracted attention, then slowly drag the fly on the bottom in increments of just inches. If your fly has not been seen, then move it in quick twitches of about 2 inches or slightly more, then let the fly settle and repeat. Hook setting will almost always be by hand, but once the hook is set you will have to finger the line onto the reel arbor while keeping slight tension on the line. Let the fish run, never tighten the drag, which should set at about 1 pound of pressure. There are, of course, other scenarios. Your guide will be coaching you through the whole event. Be prepared to pay attention. You will be rewarded.

Bonefish in the Keys are larger than those found in the Bahamas, Belize, Honduras or Los Roques. The largest in the Keys seem to be found in the Upper Keys, with the biggest usually reserved for the Islamorada area waters.

According to Dr. Roy Crabtree (FMRI), an expert on bonefish, permit and tarpon, Keys bonefish can live to a ripe old age of 19 years. Females are slightly larger than males of the same age. The average sexually mature male is 3.6 years old and a female, 3.9 to 4.0 years. Spawning peaks from November to May and occurs outside of the flats. Eggs are found in females every month but July through September. Bonefish begin life looking more like an eel than a fish and undergo a *leptocephalus* larval stage where it grows to about 2.5 inches long before going through a metamorphous stage in which the eel-like larvae shrinks. As it shrinks, fins appear, and after 10 to 12 days a miniature bonefish emerges.

Bonefish are noted for traveling in schools, but in the Keys larger bonefish can be found as a single or in schools of just a few. Bonefish schools can be spotted as several hundred to a dozen or less fish, mudding or tailing. Schools can be slowly moving or in a high-tailing-it mode. The latter seems, principally, to occur in the winter months.

ABOUT TAILING AND MUDDING

The easiest way to identify a feeding bonefish is when it is tailing, which is a shallow-water occurrence that exposes the tips of their tails (or more) above the water line. Sometimes it will appear as though half of their bodies are out of the water in really shallow flats water. Another sign of bonefish feeding is mudding, which takes place in 2 to 4 feet of water. This profile exhibits bottom sediment getting stirred up to create a dusty cloud of mud in the water. When bonefish dig a critter off the bottom they stir up sediment and create what is referred to as a bonefish mud. Rays also create muds, but that condition looks somewhat different than the smaller muds bonefish create. Fresh bonefish muds are thick, dark and more concentrated than those made by rays. Oftentimes you will see a string of muds scaling from fresh ones to fading dispersed ones. The darker, fresh muds help orient the angler to the general direction that bonefish are moving. Both tailing and mudding profiles present the best opportunities to catch a bonefish. NOTE: Permit and redfish also tail and mud, and both conditions can produce excellent and exciting ways to fly-fish for these great game fish.

CAPTAIN DERR AND CAPTAN DIXON'S HERESY

During winter cold flashes in the Keys, bonefish react to the change in water temperature. Many times during these rapid temperature drops anglers may see fast-moving bonefish schools of 100 fish or more. These bonefish, gathering in great big schools, traditionally put on the burners and hightail it up and down the oceanside flats in about waist-deep water. Commonly-held thought was that trying to induce these fast-moving bonefish to feed by conventional presentation of a fly was somewhat fruitless. However, with a little modification of presentation this is now only partly true.

For several years, Captain Paul Dixon, and Captain Andrew Derr, observed bonefish behavior during cold snaps and this was a consistent phenomena. They could even correctly predict when these schools would move through and where. They experimented using fast strips, taking a page out of striper fishing learned on Long Island, NY. The idea here is to get the fly in front of the school so that when they get to the fly you can keep it moving at the same speed and in the same water column as they are moving. The longer the fly is in their faces the better the chance that one of them will take a swipe at it. Hand stripping with the rod held between your knees can help keep an even, steady retrieve equal to the speed of the school moving through. Much to our surprise, delight and far too many times to be a freaky coincidence of luck, this method proved successful with running bonefish in the Keys.

Paul and Andrew's successes were with bright streamer flies, such as the chartreuse Clouser, and bright orange streamers with grizzly hackle. The collective assumption made was that fast-moving bonefish are eating minnows, at least occasionally, while herding up and down the oceanside flats. Further, Paul and Andrew believe that bonefish eat far more baitfish than once thought. Today, some guides in the Keys have been very successful using this striper fishing technique, but with new and very life-like epoxy minnow imitations. Word travels fast amongst guides and offshore captains in the Keys. The heretical approach is now practiced in the Upper Keys by many bonefish guide specialists.

Historic Densities: Bonefish prefer feeding in water temperatures from around 73 to 80 degrees F and are significantly influenced by incoming and outgoing tides. Bonefish become lethargic with regard to feeding when the temperature falls below 70 degrees F, turn on when it climbs back to 73 to 74 degrees F, and will exit the flats for cooler offshore water when the temperature reaches the low 80's F. In the summer months, early morning and late (daylight) evening, given the right tide pushing cooler water onto the flats, produces excellent bonefishing opportunities. The entire Keys, from Biscayne Bay to the Marquesas support populations of bonefish, year round. Biscayne Bay and the Upper Keys have more dense populations and larger bonefish than the Lower Keys, Key West and the Marquesas. Bonefish are, however, caught in good numbers in all of the latter venue, year round.

Feeds On: Shrimps, crabs, mollusks, clams, small squid, sea worms, urchin and small fish of the flats.

ID: Inferior mouth and tip of snout are black. Sides and belly are bright silver and parts of the snout and fins are a yellowish, dusky color. The backs of some bonefish in the Keys appear black to gray/green, a not uncommon adaptation of surroundings.

Tackle: An 8-weight rod is probably the best choice with, up to, moderately weighted flies, but on a calm summer morning a 7-weight would be fine with light flies. However, on a windy winter day and heavier flies, a 9-

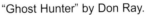

"Ghost Hunter" by Don Ray.

weight is a good choice. For backing, at least 150 yards of 20-pound Dacron. WFF bonefish taper for fly line. NOTE: Clear line and light green line have the advantage of not being easily seen by the fish, but the same is true for the fisherman, and tracking your fly is vitally important. There are ways to mark your fly line to help overcome losing sight of the leader/fly. However, many guides prefer colored line. Your leader can be 9 to 10 feet on a choppy day or 16 feet on a calm day. On class tippet there is no need to go below 8-pound test or above 16-pound test.

Flies: Clousers #1 to #4 (tan & white, green & yellow, chartreuse, chartreuse & white and pink), Lenny Moffo's version of Del Brown's Merkin (#1 to #4) in natural colors (Merkins and a few Clousers may be all you need), Fur Shrimp (tan & grizzly), Bonefish Slider,

"Bonefish Run" by Diane Rome Peebles.

Borski's (Swimming Shrimp and Chernobyl Crab in natural colors), Dorsey's Kwan fly, Bill Curtis' All-Round (white & light green #4) and #2 to #4 bright orange streamers with grizzly hackle.

Cobia
RACHYCENTRIDAE, Rachycentron canadum

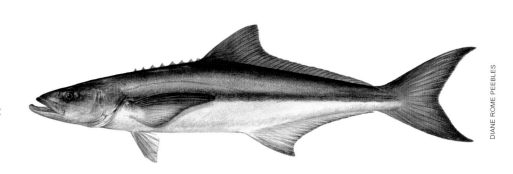

DIANE ROME PEEBLES

Quick ID: Pronounced dark stripe on mid-side. Head low and depressed. First dorsal fin very low profile with 8 separate short spines. Looks very similar to a remora without suckers.

CAPTAIN'S NOTES

Teasing cobia up from nearshore waters produces the easiest opportunity for the fly-fisherman. A cobia caught on the flats is more difficult. The latter usually comes up when cobia are spotted following a ray's wake, which stirs up the flats' bottom sediment, dislodging crabs and other morsels.

When teasing with chum or live grunts any number of other species can show, but if cobia surface it will be necessary to keep them interested, and bait and switch is just what the doctor ordered. This time-honored practice employs a hookless popper cast amid the chum/bait. When the cobia arrives on the surface, the popper is used to further agitate the fish. When this is obvious, the popper is yanked out of play just before the strike, and the angler replaces it with a fly. The latter demands a coordinated effort and a lot of work for the captain. Being ready, and able to get an accurate (short) cast off immediately is a must when the opportunity presents itself. In this situation cobia offer opportunities for other on-board anglers as it will bring up some of its brethren. If caught near piling or buoy markers, the cobia will make an immediate run for cover, and a stout rod will be required to keep it away from entangling your line.

For most fly-fishermen, the preferred at-bat for a cobia is on the flats, and the best case scenario is when it is following a ray. Your guide will position the boat and arm you with need-to-know information and instructions. Follow them to the letter. Generally, you will cast just behind the ray and into its sediment cloud so that the following cobia gets to encounter your fly.

Flats-traveling cobia, usually, will tend to be smaller than those found offshore. No matter the size, when a cobia hits, it is an extremely hard strike, and once hooked cobia make long, determined, head-shaking runs, but only occasionally leap, and those are not acrobatic.

Historic Densities: Cobia prefer water temperatures from about 68 to 86 degrees F. They are fond of buoys, anchored boats, piling and flotsam, offshore markers, and pilings, but can show up off sea mounds, near reefs, entrances to channels, under any floating debris, or in the company of sharks (offshore). They are also considered pelagic; and as such, have seasonal arrangements with Keys waters. However, they are found in Key West waters just about all year round. In the winter months, there are more dense populations in Key West, but they will start to show throughout the Keys into spring. Cobia become more available in the Keys as you head south. More reliable appearances beginning after Long Key in the Florida Bay/Gulf of Mexico side of the channel. They become even more likely in the Lower Keys, with Key West a principal location. However, it should be noted that several IGFA (International Game Fish Association) world records (different pound-test classes) include catches in Florida Bay, as well as the Upper Keys (Islamorada). The world record is from Key West waters.

Feeds On: Crabs (its colloquial name in Australia is 'crab eater'), smaller fish and squid. Not a persnickety feeder, but more an opportunistic predator.

ID: Looks like a remora without suckers. The first dorsal fin has 8 to 10 short spines, which are not connected by membrane and can be depressed. The second dorsal fin has only 1 spine with 27 to 33 soft rays. Its markings are rather unmistakable, with its back a unique and deep chocolate color. The sides are much lighter and have alternating horizontal stripes of brown and silver to bronze colorations. The aforementioned markings are more pronounced in juvenile specimens.

Tackle: Same as tarpon, 10- to 12-weight rods. Backing, 300 yards of 30-pound Dacron. Fly line, WF intermediate to fast sinking. Class tippet, 14- to 20-pound test. Shock, 40- to 80-pound mono.

Flies: Chum flies, sar-mul-mac (Don Blanton), 2/0 cobia diver in red & white (Randy Morgan), Clouser's Half and Half, Seaducer, Whistler, Deep Candy Bendback in tan & white (Bob Popovics), and imitations of mullet, crab (Lenny Moffo's version of Del Brown's Merkin) and squid. All in various hook sizes.

"Dangerous Distraction" by Diane Rome Peebles.

Dolphinfish

CORYPHAENIDAE, *Coryphaena hippurus* and *equiselis*

IGFA World-Record Catches
(*hippurus*)

Line-Class World Record:
88 pounds.

World Fly-Rod Record:
58 pounds.

Florida Keys Record - Line Class:
77 pounds, 120oz.

Florida Keys Record - Fly Rod:
27 pounds, 8oz.

male hippurus

DIANE ROME PEEBLES

Quick ID: Brilliant coloration of bluish-green with many yellow spots. Male has a step forehead, as shown in Diane Rome Peebles' illustration.

CAPTAIN'S NOTES

NOTE: Captain Jim Sharpe, Big Pine Key, FL, is an authority on the 'dolphinfish' (*hippurus* and *equiselis*). His book, *Dolphin: The Perfect Game Fish*, is recognized, worldwide, by marine academics and professional sport fishing captains as an authoritative work. As a side bar, he's even developed an easy-to-use slide-rule-type wheel that predicts, with an amazing accuracy, the show-up probabilities for the dolphin in multiple wind and prevailing weather conditions throughout the calendar year. It's called the *Dolphin Crystal Ball* (Practical Information chapter - Sea Boots).

In the winter, dolphin are available in Key West, if the winds are right. Key West is about the northern limit of the dolphin, generally, at that time of year. In April, the wind changes and the *Florida Current, which has been running fast, subsides, and lots of the dolphin's favorite time-of-the-year food source, flying fish, become more available. The dolphin's satisfaction with an abundantly

"Dolphin Working The Weeds" by Don Ray.

available food source can produce lots of rejected flies. NOTE: Dolphin, oddly, are unwilling to compete with early-morning feeders: bonito, skipjack, blackfin tuna and sailfish. Dolphin wait until the latter have gone deep, around mid-day. At this point, your captain is looking for frigate birds, as the bird relies on dolphin to force the flying fish airborne where they can be picked off. Capturing that sight is to witness an art form of mutual predation in motion and, alone, it is worth the price of admission. A hooked dolphin, kept about 30 yards from the boat, will keep its cousins swimming about close by, and that phenomena affords other on-board anglers the chance for their hook-ups. Once the fish is boated, however, the cousins disappear. It is a good practice to keep one bent rod in the water while working a school of dolphinfish.

This is where larger (15 to 30 pound and up) dolphin leave the northerly flow of the Gulf Stream (20 odd miles offshore), and feed closer to shore, and can be seen tailing.

As the summer progresses, so does the dolphin fishing. Waves of changes effect the dolphin during the seasons as baits, weather, wind, and currents will change their feeding behavior and coordinates. Turtles, flotsam, sea birds, sargassum weedlines, trade winds and the movements of eddies are but a few of those influences.

The most productive way to fly-fish for dolphin falls into just two categories according to Captain Jim Sharpe. First, is 'trolling and teasing' and the second is 'dead boat casting.' Each plays out to perfection if all conditions are right. Teasing is common throughout the saltwater sport-fishing world for both conventional tackle fishermen and

The Florida Current is a current of water running counter to, and inshore from the Gulf Stream. The shoreward edge of the Florida Current is in about 300 feet of water and the outward limits is about 500 feet.

fly-fishermen. The procedure works on everything from sailfish to marlin (any pelagic), or flats species that can be teased up to the surface, or into a state of aggression.

TROLLING AND TEASING

For dolphin, feeding on flying fish or in open water, the best approach is trolling with hookless teasers (baits or lures). The angler positions himself at the corner of the transom, then pulls out enough line to reach in front of the teasers. When the dolphin are up, the angler must be ready to snap-cast when the teaser is pulled. A simultaneous event. To execute a snap-cast, strip about one and a half rod-lengths of line beyond the tip-top of the rod. Hold the fly in your off-hand, then back cast. The loading of the rod will pull the fly from your hand. The snap-cast is intended to land in front of and to the near side of the dolphin. If you make an unsatisfactory presentation, then use a waterhaul retrieve and employ a double-haul cast for the return placement. Once the fly is in play, strip at about 6-inch increments. When the dolphin strikes, pull down on the line with your off-hand and lift the rod with the other hand until all the free line is on the reel. As the dolphin runs, take care in getting the line neatly, and without a snag, back onto the reel. The captain will be advising you all the way and will have put the boat into neutral to meet IGFA requirements.

NOTE: When the dolphin takes the fly, or appears to, do not try to set the hook immediately. Wait until it turns, then set the hook. Too quick on the trigger hand loses more fish than several other possible screw-ups. When the dolphin runs, let it. Do not touch the drag.

DEAD-BOAT CASTING

The captain maneuvers the boat around flotsam or floating objects and into a still position at 90 degrees to the wind. The latter lets you cast with no back or forward casting resistance. All of the procedures of 'trolling and teasing' are in play, but in this situation you can cast from the cockpit or bow and place the fly right on the dolphin's nose.

The captain and mate will have been there and done all of the above many times before. Your best posture is to pay attention and follow instructions to the letter. Your reward will be on the hook.

Historic Densities: Common dolphin (*hippurus*) begin to show up when the water temperature reaches 69.8 degrees F and pompano dolphin (*equiselis*) at 72.5 degrees F. When daytime offshore feeding is good it will be from around 11AM to 2PM; and, when building tides precede bright moonlight nights of a full moon, and several days before the new moon. Also, during the

"Competition" by Don Ray.

same time period, when coastal tidal rips occur inside of 400-feet of water. Another good time is from around 4PM to 6PM. Spring migrations of dolphin are northerly and southerly in the fall. Weedlines, debris, turtles, position of the Gulf Stream, time of the year, wind, weather and the presence of frigate birds or sea birds are some of the alerts that dolphin might be about. Peak is, generally, April through July.

Feeds On: Dolphin feed in the top 100 feet of water, but are also willing surface hunters. Dolphin feed on flying fish, mullet, any small fish, invertebrate, quite readily on its own young and even birds. As it is capable of swimming at 50MPH, not too many baitfish have a chance. A dolphin can also swim, because of its shape, on its side, which enables it to pick off juvenile fish seeking refuge in any kind of floating debris.

ID: Dolphin, common and pompano, are differentiated by the widest point of their bodies. Common dolphin (*hippurus*) is widest at the head and pompano (*equiselis*) at mid-body. Pompano dolphin are rarely over 8 pounds. Common dolphin have a 55 to 66 soft ray count on the dorsal fin, 25 to 31 soft rays, a concave anal fin, and 31 vertebrae. The pompano dolphin has 52 to 59 soft rays on the dorsal fin, a convex anal fin, 23 to 29 soft rays, and 33 vertebrae. There are no spines on the fins of either species.

> **TIDBITS**
>
> Casting Tip - Maxim
>
> The fly will land in the same line your rod tip is pointing at the termination of your cast.

Coloration is stunning. In-water an irredescent bluish to blue/green with gold or blue gold flanks peppered with blue, black and gold spots, and silvery white to a rich hue of blue on the belly. Dorsally, rich blue, and anally golden and silvery. All other fins are gold tipped. When a dolphin is removed from the water it loses color faster than you can say, wow (grayish yellow).

Tackle: For schoolies (small) a 7/8-weight rod, 20-pound-test Dacron backing, WFF fly line, 8- to 12-pound-test class tippet and 30-pound-test shock. Medium-size dolphin (10 to 25 pounds) a 10-weight rod, 20-pound test dacron backing, WFF fly line, 10- to 16-pound-test class tippet and 50-pound-test shock. For large dolphin, a 12-weight rod, backing should be 30-pound test with at least 250 yards of line, class tippet at 16- to 20-pound test and shock of 80-pound test.

NOTE: Dolphin grow rapidly (1 pound to 32 pounds in 7.5 months. Marineland study on common dolphin as reported by *The Miami Herald* in 1961)) and sexually mature early. The maximum life span of a dolphin is about 3 to 4 years, but only about 2% of the population reaches 3 years old. A 16-pound female dolphin lays about 250,000 to 3,000,000 eggs in each of an average of 3 spawnings a year. Eggs develop in 60 days.

Flies: Big dolphin: Lenny Moffo's blue and white Big Boy (4/0), Nick Stancyzk's dolphin imitation, big Deceivers (2/0 to 4/0) and Bob Popovics' (Bob's Banger). Medium dolphin: poppers, tarpon flies, Clousers and Blados' Crease Fly. Small dolphin: Epoxy Minnows and small tarpon flies, Deceivers and Clousers.

Sunny days use bright colors with some flash; and darker flies on low light days, or in the evening.

About Don Ray

Mastering the painting of game fish with such taxonomic detail involves much on-location study, and his love of fishing only aids a part of that research. Hours and hours of in-water research are necessary to produce his stand-alone treatments of each species. Don, consistently, captures natural environments, the effects of light on the surface of the water and the fishes innate locomotion profiles. The final effects of his work are always incredible. A tribute to not only his skills as a painter but to his attention to detail.

Don Ray's attention to detail and taxonomic correctness have earned him more first place awards than we can mention, but a few noteworthy ones are: State of Florida Lobster Stamp competition (1990, '91 and '93), State of Florida Snook Stamp competition (1992 and '95), Coastal Conservation Society Stamp and Print competition (1994 and '99), Texas Saltwater Fishing Stamp and Print competition (1996 and '97), and the highly coveted, Award of Excellence, awarded by The Society of Animal Artists.

Don Ray spent most of his life developing a reputation as a painter of freshwater and saltwater fish, and his efforts now rank him as one of, if not the best, in the field. His paintings appear regularly in and on the most popular wildlife magazines, periodicals and catalogs, such as: *Field & Stream*, *Outdoor Life*, *Florida Sportsman*, *Ontario Out Of Doors*, *Game Fish* (France), Cabela's, Penn Reels, National Wildlife, IGFA's Annual World Record Game Fish Book cover and many, many more.

NOTE: For information on purchasing originals, prints, or commissioned works, contact Don Ray at 407-388-2477, or write: Don Ray Studio, 1124 Landsdowne Dr., Sebastian, FL 32958.

"Frequent Flyers"
by Don Ray.

Drum - Redfish
SCIAENIDAE, *Sciaenops ocellatus*

IGFA World-Record Catches

Line Class World Record:
94 pounds, 2-oz.

World Fly-Rod Record:
43 pounds.

Florida Keys Record - Line Class:
52 pounds, 5oz.

Florida Record - Fly Rod:
43 pounds. (world record)

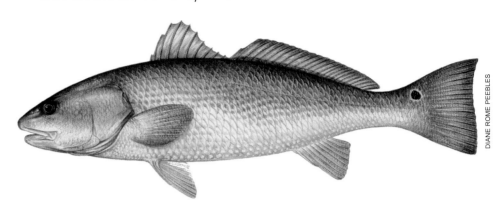

DIANE ROME PEEBLES

Quick ID: Overall coppery brown coloration. Some approach the color of a newly minted penny, especially in the winter. Square tail. Very distinctive black spot, or spots, on the base of the caudal fin.

CAPTAIN'S NOTES

Note: Until a few years ago, redfish seemed a territorial hostage of the Upper Keys backcountry, but they are now showing up all the way down to the Lower Keys. However, home-court is still the Upper Keys.

In the mid-1980's, an overweight Louisiana chef made delicious and famous blackened anything that swam, but it was the red drum that was mostly under siege. In just a few years, their stocks were almost decimated by commercial takes and weekender fishermen caught up in the craze. As abnormal as it might seem, fisheries managers, from Florida to Texas, were able to convince their state legislators and federal agencies that an apocalypse was at hand. Conservation measures were put in place rather quickly, money became available for research, and a renascence of grand proportions for redfish was created. Redfish recovery has been remarkable. The whole effort and success remains a poster-child lesson in the value of conservation and a responsive government. Today, there are size and bag limits. Redfish have no commercial value and they are even protected in federal waters. Additionally, the ground swell of catch-and-release behavior has, finally, touched almost every sport fisherman's soul.

The ghost-like cruising signature of a redfish on the seagrass flats is a "V" wake, the residual of its broad caudal fin. The event can be seen from great distances, especially, on calm water days. They can also be spotted by your guide, paused in a white hole amid the seagrass, discolored water created by their own schooling, or tailing and mudding (see tailing and mudding - bonefish). They can also be productively fished by blind casting in channels. A good choice for that occasion is weighted-eye flies. When blind casting you may hookup with other species (tarpon or snook). Blind casting with weighted-eye flies, Clouser-like patterns, a jigging retrieve (up and down) in relatively short pulls works well. Many guides prefer challenging reds during low tide rather than high, as it concentrates them in shallower water. Redfish are fished using the same techniques as employed for bonefish and permit, with exceptions of note. When your guide spots a redfish, and puts you on point; he will instruct you to cast in front of the fish, about 8 to 10 feet; or in as tight as just over a foot, if it's tailing/mudding. In the former scenario, let the fly settle, then twitch it a few inches at a time to gain an up and down jigging bounce. If the red is tailing or mudding wait to move the fly until the fish is almost on top of it. Your guide will be instructing you all the way. Pay attention. Reds are usually less finicky about flies than bones or permit, not as spooky, and their eyesight is not as keen. However, it is still stealth of approach, a quiet and quality presentation that counts for a lot, and how you wiggle the worm is always of paramount importance. You can also catch reds on the surface with a popper; or any derivation thereof, but its mouth is built low on its head for grubbing on the bottom, and more than a few exciting moments end because of missed hook ups. You can also expect to spook some fish with a popper.

NOTE: Hand setting the hook is the most likely in every redfish hook up (sight fishing or blind casting) so you will have to carefully feed the line back onto the reel arbor with your off-hand while the fish is bolting. As a matter of importance, in-boat line maintenance and back onto the reel management of fly line cannot be stressed enough. There are lots of lost fish because no attention was paid to drag setting beforehand, nor was care taken of loose line on the boat deck, or feeding it properly back onto the reel arbor.

Historic Densities: Redfish are primarily found in Upper Keys backcountry, from South Biscayne Bay to Florida Bay, and all the way into the Everglades, with the best of it starting several miles north into Florida Bay. However, do not be surprised if you catch smaller reds in a canal or boat basin. April to November is good to excellent; and the months of September, October and November are considered the best for redfish. Preferred temperatures are from around 58 to 86 degrees F. Redfish are found around mangrove islands and on the edges of drop offs near mangrove, and near shorelines inside bays. Early morning and late evening are the most intense feeding times for reds. Redfish do not migrate and rarely leave their natal waters. In the cooler weather, redfish will move to deeper water, but will return as soon as the water warms. Redfish, in the heavyweight class, weighing in at 30-plus pounds are most often found in offshore waters. A hooked red will make a rather attention-getting run when it realizes something is wrong and, usually (on the flats), it may stop its run, more than once, to rub its industrial-strength lips on the bottom to rid the fly, similar to a bone or permit.

Feeds On: Crabs, shrimps, smaller mullets, menhaden, worms, clams and a bevy of marine insects.

ID: Coloration of coppery brown on a background of silvery gray, square tail (truncate/concave) and a distinctive spot, or spots, on caudal fin. The first dorsal fin has 9 to 10 spines and the second dorsal fin has 23 to 26 soft rays. The anal fin has 2 spines and 8 soft rays. There are 40 to 45 scales along the lateral line and 8 to 9 gill rakers on the lower limb of the first gill arch.

Spawning can occur from July to December in nearshore shelf waters or inshore. In the Keys, redfish spawning is usually peak as the days become shorter and the water cooler. Males reach sexually maturity at about a year and females at age 2 to 3. A female can yield 2.1 million eggs per spawning cycle. Growth is rapid through the 4th to 5th year, but then slows. Red drum can live over fifty years, weigh in at over 50 pounds (offshore), and can inhabit brackish water as well as tolerate freshwater environments.

Tackle: In the Keys, an 8-weight or 9-weight rod. Backing at least 150-yards. Class tippet at 8- to 12-pound test and a (grubbing) shock of at least 30-pound test.

Flies: A rather wide range of patterns can attract redfish, but preferred food imitations are very productive. A Moffo tied Merkin-like pattern, for example, in various sizes and profiles (ambulation) could be a single favorite for many a Keys guide. Also, Borski-like shrimp patterns. Clousers, Seaducers, Deceivers, Chico Fernandez's natural color Bend Backs, and Joe Cave's Gold Wobbler, as well as poppers. Weedless is just about a must, and a little chartreuse never hurt a thing.

"Red and Blue" by Don Ray.

Jack Crevalle
CARANGIDAE, Caranx hippos

IGFA World-Record Catches

Line Class World Record:
57 pounds, 14-oz.

World Fly-Rod Record:
44 pounds.

Florida Keys Record - Line Class:
23 pounds, 12-oz.

Florida Keys Record - Fly Rod:
37 pounds, 8oz.

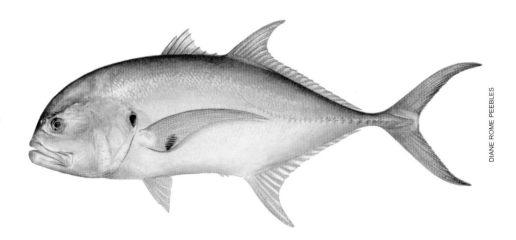

DIANE ROME PEEBLES

Quick ID: Coloration of sides silvery and greenish / bluish above. Distinct black spot or blotch on pectoral fin and one on the operculum. NOTE: Juvenile crevalle have about 5 broad bands on body and one on head.

CAPTAIN'S NOTES

Jack crevalle are not usually set out for as a primary target, but rather an encountered opportunity. Crevalle, once they are in play, provide all the action a sport fisherman could ask for: a pounding strike and a flat anatomical profile that ensures plenty of resistance, and a forked tail that produces powerful runs. They are also one of the best at-bats for the novice fly-fisherman. Presentation can be quite a bit less than brilliant and a jack crevalle will tend to self-hook when attacking your fly. Your captain will generally spot crevalle from a distance with the aid of birds circling and diving into churned baits. Once identified as jack crevalle, your captain can approach the school without the normal stealth required of many of the other Keys game fish as they are not as motor or boat shy, line shy, leader shy, nor do they ask for fly-pattern credentials. Larger specimens will be offshore and smaller inshore.

Chumming with live or dead baits can also bring jack crevalle up, but as with all chumming there is a likelihood of other species responding. The tried-and-true tease, casting a hookless popper into the fray, then pulling it out of the water just before a strike, keeps fish in an aggressive mode until the fly is cast to the frenzied fish. A fast steady retrieve is required, offshore or inshore.

Historic Densities: Jack crevalle are, primarily, a schooling species. Moderate to very large, fast moving schools in the 10- to 25-pound range, are found in the prime months of April and May along the entire Florida Keys reef line. Jacks can, in fact, be found all summer long, but favor offshore wrecks. In the winter months they can be encountered on the Gulf of Mexico side of Key West.

Jacks can tolerate a wide latitude of salinities, which allows them to attack baits far away from their normal turf, as estuaries of the Everglades to canals around the Keys. Preferred temperature ranges are 70 to 86 degrees F. NOTE: Jack crevalle, in open waters, circle their prey, force them into a tight pack, and then attack from all sides. Inshore, they herd baits against a seawall or shoreline, and then attack.

Feeds On: Mullet, smaller fish of many a species as well as invertebrate and shrimp.

ID: Distinct black spot or blotch on pectoral fin and one on the operculum. Silvery sides and blue/green above. The straight line portion of the lateral line has 26 to 35 scutes and the curved portion of the lateral line is over 60 to as much as 100% of the straight portion. There are 19 to 26 gill rakers on the lower limb of the first branchial arch. They are also easily distinguished from their nearest relative, horse-eye jack, by having some scales on its almost bare chest. The horse-eyes save all scales on their chest. Juveniles jack crevalle are different (see Quick ID).

Tackle: 8/9-weight rods for inshore, or smaller specimens, and 10-weight rods for the reef-line version. Minimum of 150 yards of 20-pound Dacron backing. Fly line; WF intermediate to fast sinking, and floating for poppers. Class tippet 12- to 16-pound test. Flies: Poppers, Deceivers and Clousers in just about any color in sizes from as small as #2 to as large as 2/0.

TIDBITS

Jack crevalle, amberjack and cobia all favorably react to a fly or popper that lands like a bomb right next to them.

Jack, Horse-eye
CARANGIDAE, Caranx latus

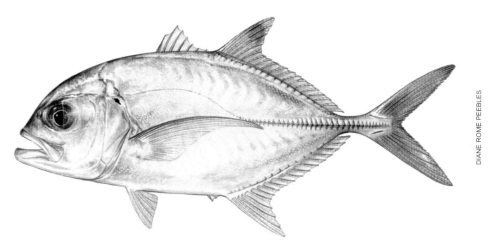

IGFA World-Record Catches

Line Class World Record:
29 pounds, 8-oz.

World Fly-Rod Record:
18 pounds.

Florida Keys Record - Line Class:
23 pounds, 12-oz. (world record line class)

Florida Keys Record - Fly Rod:
14 pounds, 8-oz. (world record line class)

Quick ID: Very similar to crevalle, but front of head not as steep and eyes are much larger. Also, black spot on opercle small or poorly defined and there is no dark blotch on pectoral fin. Scutes are blackish. In adults the chest is scaly.

CAPTAIN'S NOTES

NOTE: The horse-eye jack is not as plentiful as it used to be. In the past, large schools could be encountered at the light changes of morning and evening.

If you are fortunate to come upon horse-eye it will be in the very early morning or at night, and they will be on the surface in an extremely large, fast-moving school. Horse-eye will track a chum line and pop up unexpectedly. They are fished for in the same manner as schooling crevalle, but their aggressiveness will not match that of the crevalle, and they may be more selective with regard to your fly. Using a pattern similar to the bait they are pursuing, usually mullet is productive. Like all jacks, the horse-eye will put up a worthy fight. The horse-eye jack is also smaller than the crevalle. This species is a found opportunity, and not at all

a species one targets in the Keys.

Historic Densities: July through November. Water temperature from 70's to mid-80's. Tracking a chum line, chasing baits around sea mounds, blue holes and even inshore around deep channels.

Feeds On: Mullet and other marine baitfish.

ID: See quick ID. Caudal fin is yellowish. There are 20 to 22 soft rays in the dorsal fin and 14 to 18 gill rakers on the lower limb of the first arch.

Tackle: Rods 8- to 9-weight. Backing at least 150 yards of 20-pound Dacron. Fly line, WF to sinking. Class tippet, 12-pound test and a wire bite guard. Toothy critter.

Flies: Deceivers, Clousers and poppers or bait/chum mimics. All #2 to 2/0 with flash.

"Kings and Jacks" by
Diane Rome Peebles

Mackerel, Cero
SCOMBRIDAE, Scomberomorus regalis

Line Class World Record:
17 pounds, 2-oz.

World Fly-Rod Record:
11 pounds, 1oz.

Florida Keys Record - Line Class:
17 pounds, 2-oz. (world record)

Florida Keys Record - Fly Rod:
7 pounds, 12oz. (world record line class)

DIANE ROME PEEBLES

Quick ID: Distinguished from the Spanish mackerel, its look-alike cousin, by rows of short, yellowish-brown, brassy streaks on its sides.

NOTE: Glenda Kelley, IGFA's fish biologist, and pro golfer, Greg Norman are both line-class world-record holders. Glenda with a Key West catch on a fly rod (5 pounds), and Norman, a Bahama's fly-rod catch (8 pounds, 8oz.). Most of the world records for cero on a fly have occurred in the Keys, and all of those were in Key West.

CAPTAIN'S NOTES

Cero mackerel usually prefer feeding deeper in the water column than is practical for pursuit by fly fishermen. Bringing them to the surface is the required ploy. Your captain achieves the latter by creating a chum line of live pilchards, ballyhoo and/or glass minnows. Other species can, of course, show up (Spanish mackerel and king mackerel). However, once the cero are up, a good cast amid or near them is likely to bring a hook-up. Your captain will position the boat to best advantage casting and you will not be limited to casting from the cockpit. Demands on your casting skills will not be the paramount issue, so the cero is a nice opportunity for the relatively novice fly-fisherman. However, all the attendant elements of fly-fishing are still in play, getting a reasonable cast off and managing fly line back onto the reel, for example. Also, your window of opportunity may be short, so be ready and pay attention to the captain's instructions. Cero mackerel are epipelagic and coastal, and they tend to travel in small groups or as a solitary fish.

Historic Densities: Preferred temperature ranges are the 70 through 80 degrees F. The Florida Keys are their home port and the best geography for hooking up with them. They usually start showing up in good numbers in the fall and peak through the winter months. They are more abundant down the Keys, and peak in Key West. There they can be caught much earlier in the season (July) and much later in the season (April). For feeding, their routine pattern is to utilize the waters inside the outer reef tracts on patches in about 12- to 30-foot depths. Feeds On: Small schooling baitfish, squid and shrimp.

ID: See quick ID. Evenly sloping and downward lateral line. The first dorsal fin is blackish and has 17 to 18 spines, and there are 15 to 18 gill rakers on the first arch.
Tackle: Rods 8- to 9-weight. Backing at least 150 yards of 20-pound Dacron. Fly line, WF to sinking. Class tippet, 12-pound test.
Flies: Yellow is the color of choice with small Deceivers, Clousers, glass minnows and pencil poppers #2 through #4 work well.

TIDBITS

Casting Tip - Heavy Fly Line

Shooting head, sinking and lead core lines require slowing down (delaying) both the back and forward casts, which produces a desirable bigger loop in the line. Practice makes perfect.

Mackerel, King
SCOMBRIDAE, *Scomberomorus cavalla*

IGFA World-Record Catches

Line-Class World Record:
93 pounds.

World Fly-Rod Record:
55-pounds.

Florida Keys Record - Line Class:
75 pounds.

Florida Keys Record - Fly Rod:
55 pounds. (world record)

DIANE ROME PEEBLES

Quick ID: Adults have no distinctive markings (juvenile fish have round dark spots of yellowish-gold, but fade at death). Dark bluish above and silvery-whitish below.

NOTE: In 1910, serendipitously, Zane Grey and his brother, Roemer (RC), found themselves in the Florida Keys (Long Key) for an unplanned fishing holiday. For the next dozen or so years, the Greys would return and put the Long Key Fishing Club into the history books. Zane's writings about their Keys fishing experiences would announce to the world that the Keys were a bountiful fishery. Early on, it was the king mackerel that was the target of preference for Keys sport fishermen. Today, every fly-rod world record for king mackerel caught was done so in Florida Keys waters.

CAPTAIN'S NOTES

King mackerel prefer feeding in the 20- to 60-foot water column, which necessitates chumming them up with live or dead baits. Once up on the surface, kings can provide long-lasting action, which can include an initial and remarkable sky-rocketing jumps, followed by plenty of resistance—all you could ask for in a fish-on situation. Casting amid or near the action, created by chumming, does not require tremendous casting skills, but the rod weight needed, an often weighty fly, can complicate things for the beginner. Your retrieve will be fast and steady. Pay close attention to your captain's instructions, and as always, properly finger the line back onto the reel. Careless mistakes are not comedic events. Your drag will have been set before the action starts. Do not play with the drag while the fish is running.

Historic Densities: Kings can be found just about all year round in a good year. Principal months of high-volume king mackerel traffic in the Keys is, however, reserved for the winter months of late December through March, but in a fairly good year the big boys can hang around until late spring and/or show up earlier than expected. Smaller kings can show in October. However, like any best-bet calendar reference in the Keys, it can be off on either side by months as there are so many water cocktail mixes and

weather possibilities, that influence a whole chain of favorable marine conditions. Preferred water temperatures are from around 70 to 76 degrees. Adult kings are pelagic, schooling and are, generally, found around wrecks, sea mounds, the reef tract, and inward of them. Very large kings may be found as loners. Kings will show up way down the Keys with a higher concentration starting around Islamorada and, generally, increasing in population all the way to Key West.

NOTE: All but 3 of 10 listed world-record catches (different line classes) are Key West caught. There are two populations of kings in the Keys, and they will mix in the winter, one with a Gulf of Mexico origin and the other from the Atlantic Ocean.

Feeds On: Mullet, shrimp, squid and a myriad of small and seasonally available schooling baitfish.

ID: See quick ID. The anterior third of a king is never black as it is in both the cero and Spanish mackerels. The lateral line of a king is distinctive. It drops quickly to below the second dorsal fin, then undulates. There are 15 to 16 dorsal fin spines, and 6 to 9 gill rakes on the 1st arch. Males can live to a ripe old age of 7 years and females to 14 years. Most kings in the Keys are about 7 to 8 years old and the most common size is around 20 pounds. NOTE: Young kings will swim with Spanish mackerel and are sometimes misidentified by novices since they are close look-a-likes.

Tackle: Rods can be anywhere from 8/9-weights for smaller specimens to hefty 12-weights for large kings. For larger specimens, backing should be at least 200 yards of 20-pound test. Fly line, sinking or sink-tip. Floating line for poppers, and class tippets anywhere from 16- to 20-pound test. A wire bite guard will be necessary, very toothy fish.

Flies: Sar-Mul-Mac, Seaducer, Sea Habit, Tres Generation, Deceivers, Clousers, Glass Minnows and Pencil Poppers. Jose Wejebe's Spanish fly a favorite of many. Bait imitations about 4-inches long are excellent.

Mackerel, Spanish
SCOMBRIDAE, Scomberomorus maculatis

DIANE ROME PEEBLES

IGFA World-Record Catches

Line-Class World Record:
13 pounds.

World Fly-Rod Record:
8 pounds, 11oz.

Florida Keys Record - Line Class:
12 pounds.

Florida Keys Record - Fly Rod:
6 pounds, 12oz. (world record line class)

Quick ID: Distinguished by large, dark brassy spots.

NOTE: An inshore netting ban has increased stocks dramatically.

CAPTAIN'S NOTES

In the Keys, Spanish mackerel are, primarily, a winter time game fish. They can show up in any kind of weather, and they are also very democratic in their choices of bodies of water: Gulf of Mexico, Atlantic Ocean and Florida Bay, and offshore to inside the reef tract. Additionally, Spanish mackerel can tolerate brackish water. Spanish mackerel are not a target species, but when they are about, no guide or offshore captain will turn his nose up at a nice chance for some light-tackle action. Many times the opportunity to fly-fish for them will come when chumming or even dragging live baits for other species. The preferred water column for Spanish mackerel is about 20 to 35 feet, but they willingly surface to feed and, of course, will be in much shallower water if they are in Florida Bay. When they are up on the surface use a quick retrieve with frequent jerks to keep their interest. This mackerel is also a good species on which the novice fly fisherman can hone his skills. They are not generally shy nor persnickety about presentation or flies.

Historic Densities: Throughout most bodies of water in the Keys, from December to March, with a good latitude of forgiveness on either end, along with random arrivals and departures. A good bet for their whereabouts is always the Marathon area and nearby Florida Bay. They are prone to being in waters that range from 68 to 78 degrees F.

Feeds On: Menhaden and a wide variety of small, schooling baitfish.

ID: See quick ID. Lateral line slopes downward and evenly. The first dorsal fin has 17 to 18 spines and is blackish. The gill raker count on the first arch is 13 to 15. Spanish mackerel, unlike the king and cero, have no scales on its pectoral fins.

Tackle: A 7- or 8-weight rod is all you will need. Backing of 150 yards is more than enough at 20-pound test. WFF to intermediate fly line is fine, and 8- to 12-pound-test class tippet is sufficient. A wire bite guard is necessary. Toothy critter.

Flies: Highly visible, bright yellow #2 to #6 Deceivers, Clousers, Glass Minnows and Pencil Poppers. Also, Bob Popovic's Surf Candy.

Comparison and Probable Max Weights for the Keys

Cero: max 10 pounds   **King: max 60 pounds**   **Spanish: max 7 pounds**

Marlin, Blue
ISTIOPHORIDAE, *Mackaira nigricans*

DIANE ROME PEEBLES

Quick ID: Lateral line is complex and forms a network on flank. Front lobes of first dorsal fin and anal fins are pointed. The dorsal lobe is less high than body length.

*NOTE: Above record is for the State of Florida, not the Florida Keys, and is not an IGFA record. In the 1990's, the state relinquished record keeping to the IGFA. The IGFA did not recognize the above catch.

From the prologue of James W. Hall's
Blackwater Sound:

"The marlin was the color of the ocean at twenty fathoms, an iridescent blue, with eerie light smoldering within its silky flesh as if electrons had become unstable by the cold friction of the sea. A ghostly phosphorescence, a gleaming flash, its large eyes unlinking as it slipped into a seam in the current, then raced toward the luminous surface where a school of tuna was picking at the tiny larvae and crustaceans snagged on a weed line.

The marlin attacked from the rear of the school. An ambush. It accelerated from thirty knots to double that in only a few yards. A fusion of grace, efficiency, and building power. For a creature with the bulk of a bull, the marlin was as sleek as any missile and blazed through the water at a speed not even the most powerful torpedo could attain. When it crashed into the school, it stunned each fish with its three-foot bill, then swallowed it headfirst."

NOTE: Jim is a Key Largo resident, an avid fisherman and author of several bestselling mystery novels that take place in the Keys.

CAPTAIN'S NOTES

NOTE: The Keys have not posted a fly-rod-caught marlin qualifying to be in the IGFA record book, but that might not be so unusual. Offshore captains in the Keys have, for well over a decade, been reluctant to kill any billfish (see The Billfish Foundation). Also, many skilled anglers rig their fly rods outside the IFGA's tough requirements and, thus, are automatically out of the record loop. Namely,

they will avoid the IGFA shock tippet requirement, which stipulates that it cannot exceed 12-inches (including knots). A bill, even on a small marlin, or any billfish, will exceed 12 inches and creates a huge handicap that ups the chances of a break-off to near certain. To some anglers of the fly-fishing persuasion, talking about the restrictive rigging policy placed on fly-fishermen by the IGFA is a problem similar to the elephant in the living room nobody wants to mention. The conundrum arises out of the simple fact that the IGFA is powerful, a friend and ally of all sport fishermen. They are also the only game in town when it comes to rules and regulations regarding record catches, which keeps the playing field even for all those who are record oriented. It should also be pointed out that catching a marlin on any tackle is a feat, and especially so on a fly rod, no matter the rigging. Only two records, out of a possible 14 mentions, are in the IGFA world-record book for blue marlin caught on a fly.

The blue marlin, regardless of one's religious persuasion towards tackle, has to be one of the fantasy catches for just about every fisherman, leading all to know there is a bit of Hemingway's *Santiago* in all of us. There are several expert offshore fly-fishing captains in the Keys who can take you to the blue marlin promise land (see last chapter). The marlin gig is one that is made up of lots of details, lots of on-the-water time and considerable expense. The reward, a hook-up with a blue marlin. Well worth the sum of its parts.

Fishing for marlin is all about trolling while employing well-practiced techniques to create a tease or disturbance that encourages the mighty blue to visit. Outriggers, with swimming baits and an assortment of teasers on conventional tackle are, generally, out at various distances from the boat. NOTE: You can expect other species to find this all very interesting, and could put

"Chasing the Carrot" by Don Ray.

sailfish, wahoo, several varieties of tuna or other species in the bite mood.

When, however, a marlin is sighted, the show really begins and all aboard become players: you, your fishing buddy, the mate and the captain. Beforehand, your captain will have given you the game plan, profiled several scenarios and instructed you on what to do when any of them come into play. Pay attention even if you have been there, done that many times before. Only a fool does not heed professional advice, especially if he's paying for it. Assuming you have the first at-bat and are right handed, you will be assigned the left side (port) of the cockpit to avoid fly-line entanglement with the outriggers. To be rigged and ready, your setting-up will begin by stripping off a predetermined amount of line (about 40 feet) into a bucket, which will collect line and avoid snagging any number of protruding objects, not the least of which would be your feet. Your fishing buddy will have become a spectator or be assigned a line to retrieve. The mate and captain will be very busy when a fish is up, reeling in the outriggers and flat lines, and maneuvering the boat. A single remaining bait (teaser) will be left in the water to keep the marlin's interest. It will be yanked clear when

it's about 40 feet away from the transom, and the marlin is on it. The latter is the tricky part of this fish-catching equation, and requires considerable skill. The captain will tell you when you are to cast, which will be simultaneous to the teaser being pulled completely out of the water. Your cast has to land near the marlin, and 6 feet or so on either side of the fish works well. It's got to see your fly. The captain will have, of course, stopped the boat when you cast, which lets you work the fly and also complies with IGFA catch regulations. If all goes well, the marlin will take your fly, which will be quite obvious. You'll set the hook on cue from the captain, utilizing decisive pulls (2 or 3), not jerks. Some captains prefer setting the hook as the fish turns. Others take a page out of conventional fishing techniques and let the fish run until all line is back on the arbor, then set the hook. If the fish runs right, you pull to the left, or vice versa. The drag will have been preset and the captain will have checked it. You will find it to be very soft. Leave it alone. When the marlin runs, let it, but always try to keep your line managed so as not to involve the bill. When the aerial show begins do not pull on the rod, just point it at the water in the same line with the fish. When the marlin seems to be catching its breath, which will seem like never, start pump-retrieving line as fast as you can. Be sure you're winding line back so that it is relatively evenly spaced on the arbor. The captain will be passing out instructions while he does what few can do, backing down on the fish and keeping the boat positioned to give you the best possible advantage. No small feat. When you seem to have won and gotten the marlin near the boat, you will be surprised to find that you have not won. A marlin will, with renewed vigor, bolt several more times when it's close to the boat. The mate will handle the landing of the marlin, tagging and safe release. Your well-deserved photo-op can be managed by your buddy.

Historic Densities: The "wall" and the "hooters"are no secret. The 'wall' is a piece of ocean bottom geography with well-known coordinates. These sea landscape anomalies feature an 1,800-foot dropoff some 20 miles south of Key West. The 'hooters' are just 12 or so miles further south. The Gulf Stream rushes by both pieces of real estate at a good 4- to 5-knot speed with the added peculiarity of canyons or cracks creating huge upwellings. The attraction for marlin is as high as it is for tunas, sailfish, wahoo, dolphin and others. The Islamorada "Hump" is also a very likely suspect for showing marlin. The entire Gulf Stream, provides great marlin fishing potential throughout the length of the Florida Keys year round. The Keys can produce better marlin fishing in the spring with the best month usually April, but it can last into fall. However, marlin density down Key West way increases to excellent late in the fall around the 'wall' and 'hooters.' Preferred water temperature ranges are from 70 to about 80 degrees F. Blue marlin are pelagic and very migratory. A marlin, after long aerial shows and tremendous runs, can favor deep diving, and that profile adds measurably to the difficulty of landing one.

Feeds On: Marlin favor tunas, and blackfin tunas are prime targets since they are abundantly available in the Keys. Marlin also feed non-selectively on dolphin, mackerels, mullet, flying fish and cephalopods.

ID: Distinguishing features for adults are their bills, coloration, size, and lateral lines. Coloration is cobalt blue on the back, the lower flanks are silvery white, and the underbelly is white. A male will max out at about 300 pounds and females are much, much larger. The lateral line of a blue marlin branches into a network of iridescent, lavender hexagons. The dorsal fin is large, high and pointed (toward the anterior). The anal fin is also large and pointed. The tail is large and lunate. NOTE: There is an open debate about whether the Pacific blue marlin and the Atlantic blue marlin are the same species. Currently, the debate has not been conclusive and a consensus remains outstanding. However, the Pacific blue and Atlantic blue both remain named *Makairia nigricans* (IGFA). Some ichthyologists call the Pacific blue, *Makairia mazara*.

Tackle: New developments, perhaps more utilized in the Keys, calls for up to 18-weights. Under-gunning with lower-weight rods leads to an inability to control (turn and lift) a large marlin and leads to too long a fight, which is detrimental to survival of the fish. Backing has to be in the 600-yard range for 30-pound Dacron. Here is a good application for gel-spun, which could accommodate over 1,000 yards of backing. Class tippet of 20-pound test is prudent as is a mono shock with a minimum of 80-pound test.

Flies: Billy Pate's tandem-hook streamers and poppers at 6 to 8 inches long. Removable head tube-like flies that have tandem hooks (6- to 8-inch-long-patterns) are good bait mimics. Color choices are bright for sunny days and darker for cloudy days. Other favorite color patterns in the Keys include: purple & white, green & yellow, blue & white, black & white, and pink & white. Heads should closely match dominant feather color.

Marlin, White
ISTIOPHORIDAE, Tetrapturus albidus

IGFA World-Record Catches

Line Class World Record:
181 pounds, 14oz.

*World Fly Rod Record:
109 pounds, 5oz.

Florida Record - Line Class:
142 pounds.

Florida Keys Record - Fly Rod:
Open

DIANE ROME PEEBLES

Quick ID: The lateral line is a single canal and arches above the pectoral fin, then runs straight to the caudal fin. Also, the first dorsal and the first anal fins usually have many dark spots.
NOTE: The Keys own Billy Pate and his former wife, Jodi Pate, hold four of the world's eight fly-rod records for white marlin.

CAPTAIN'S NOTES

NOTE: Since 1960, longliners have pummeled white marlin, driving stocks down to an alarming 86% below normal levels, worldwide.

Because of the above, encountering a white marlin in the Keys is rather rare, but they are caught every year. White marlin are fished for in the same manner as sailfish and marlin. Generally, white marlin will take a fly more readily than other billfish. When they are onto a fly, they will surface bound after it from some distance and that, alone, is a heart-pumping treat worth the price of admission. When hooked, they tend to stay on the surface and sustain a very acrobatic mode longer, for example, than sailfish.

Historic Densities: White marlin tend to show with the dolphin and, thus, are more likely an opportunity target from April to July. Their water temperature preference is from around 70 to 85 degrees F.

Feeds On: Dolphin and non-selectively on other schooling fish and cephalopods.

ID: See quick ID. The white marlin is more green in tint and in a lighter hue than the blue marlin. Its fins are also more rounded than a blue marlin. Conspicuous hump between the eyes to the first dorsal fin. From 38 to 43 dorsal spines, but the predominant number is 40 to 43.

Tackle: A 12- to 14-weight rod, 300 yards of 30-pound backing and intermediate to sinking fly line. Class tippet from 16- to 20-pound test and 50 to 80-pound mono shock.

Flies: Bright-colored, 5-inch-long soft-head poppers with single hooks. Mackerel, dolphin, mullet and other bait imitations. Billy Pate's streamers and poppers.

TIDBITS

Billfish Flies

The original fly patterns for billfish were developed in the Keys back in the early 1970's when Webster "Doc" Robinson broke new ground by landing the first sailfish on a fly. Billy Pate soon followed with his versions. Harry Kime from the West Coast made famous his pattern, Tutie-Fruitie, which utilized foam. Lee Wulff had his variation on the theme, but started tying with double hooks, making the flies look like baits and employing many color combinations. Other improvements were made by Joe Butorac, Cam Sigler and Otto Beck. Surface commotion created by these poppers and streamers are what interested the fish. Now, soft-head bait mimics with tandem hooks interest and catch far more fish than the original cork and foam.

Permit
CARANGIDAE, Trachinotus falcatus

IGFA World-Record Catches

Line-Class World Record:
56 pounds, 2oz.

World Fly-Rod Record:
41 pounds. 8oz.

Florida Keys Record - Line Class:
46 pounds, 4oz.

Florida Keys Record - Fly Rod:
41 pounds, 8oz. (world record)

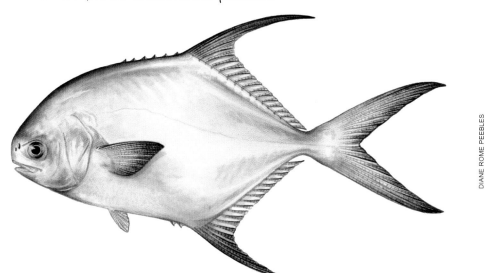

DIANE ROME PEEBLES

Quick ID: Differentiating Florida pompano from permit, a near look-alike, is not a problem in the Keys. The Florida pompano would be a rarity in the Keys as it's usually a surf-caught fish. The shear size of an adult permit would also easily distinguish it from being a Florida Pompano.

NOTE: Every world-record catch listed by the IGFA was caught in Florida and primarily in the Keys. The Florida Keys are considered by everyone in the know to be mecca for permit fishing. Every fly-rod record for permit was caught in the Florida Keys.

CAPTAIN'S NOTES

NOTE: Del Brown, developer of the extremely versatile Merkin fly pattern (never leave home without one), has devoted most of his sportfishing life in pursuit of, and understanding of, the permit, and he has caught more of them on a fly than anyone in the world. He is Mr. Permit.

Anyone who is recognized for having caught a permit on the flats using a fly rod speaks volumes to his fellow anglers. The permit is, for almost every saltwater flats fly fishing enthusiast, the ultimate game fish. To catch one requires the angler perform every known skill related to fly-fishing, which in the case of fishing in the Keys also means being smart enough to hire a top guide. Without the latter, good luck. As a side bar: Lefty Kreh and Del Brown, who could out-fish most, wouldn't consider an outing for permit in the Keys without the aid of a local, professional guide.

Being skilled at casting is of paramount importance when going after permit on a fly. You must be able to handle at least a 10-weight rod, cast at least 50 feet in a stiff breeze, present the fly properly after a maximum of three or four false casts, hit the target and be able to assimilate and follow the running instructional commentary of your guide. The latter starting when permit are spotted and ending when the fish is duly caught. In the Keys, permit can be teased off wrecks,

> **TIDBITS**
>
> Gulf Stream
>
> The Gulf Stream moves more water a day than all the rivers of the world combined.

found near deep channels and passes, and inshore on the flats. It's the sighted flats fishing for permit that holds the grail rights. Using crabs are best in any scenario as they are the preferred dining experience for permit. Catching a permit by teasing it off a wreck is a marvelous fly-rod experience, and not so easy, but again, it fails to measure up to the pure sight-fishing experience on the flats.

Picking a fly for permit is not a tough assignment as it will always include a Merkin. Actually, the Merkin may be all you need, or at least just variations of it in size, dressing-out (eyes and legs) and ambulation design. Also, the use of eyes (various weights), as well as different hook sizes, accommodates water-depth considerations. Casting to a flats-based permit has all the earmarks of bonefishing with a few exceptions, such as, the distance you want the fly to land from the fish. For permit, a cast that presents the fly about 2 or 3 feet in front of the targeted fish usually works best. Additionally, and different from bonefishing, you do not twitch the fly when it settles. You just wait for a strike. In the best of situations the permit will take the fly before it settles, and that will almost be simultaneous to its entering the water. If your fly is rejected, do not immediately pick-up, but wait until the fish is well past, then cast behind it to draw attention. The latter case scenario is not, however, the best at-bat. The presence of rays, which permit will follow in hopes of a stirred-up meal from the bottom, is another good way to spot them, via a detectable wake. Also, birds can sometimes aid in finding them on the flats as their overhead flight can spook them into bolting and leaving a wake, from which they settle down quickly. NOTE: Permit have a near-concrete mouth, and during their run often stop to try and rub off the offending hook on coral outcroppings or hardbottom real estate of the flats.

After you hook a permit, and it finally decides to run, let it, and do not mess with the drag. Your hook setting will more than likely be by hand and you'll have to finger the outstanding line back onto the reel arbor, carefully. These are delicate moments and frantic behavior spells trouble. Your guide will have prepped you on the drill; rehearse it more than often in your head. Your first at-bat may be your best, or only, one. Permit will travel in schools of hundreds, groups of 6 (more or less), in pairs, and even as single fish. Generally, a lone fish will be big.

"Prowling Permit" by Don Ray

Historic Densities: Permit are found in the Florida Keys throughout the entire year, but Key West, the Marqeusas and the Lower Keys are more prolific venue.

Permit are found on the flats, off wrecks, in deep channels, on the edges of channels and in white holes. Following the passage of cold fronts in the breezy winter months of February can trigger good opportunities, especially in the Lower Keys. A cool, windy winter day is not at all bad, and the strong currents of spring tides also create good opportunities for permit. The preferred water temperature ranges for permit are from 68 to 85 degrees F.

Feeds On: Permit feed almost exclusively on crustaceans.
ID: See quick ID. The coloration of a permit is silvery, overall, and its back is a bluish/gray. The fins are a dusky color and the anterior of the ventral fins, and the anterior margin of the anal fin can often be tinged with orange. Sometimes there is a triangular patch, yellowish, just prior to the anal fin. The second dorsal fin has only 1 spine with 17 to 21 soft rays. The body is laterally compressed and there are tell-tale second and third ribs that are thick and prominent in larger specimens (over 10 pounds).

According to Roy Crabtree (FMRI), permit will spawn in the Keys from late spring through early summer (March to July) and that takes place, generally, over wrecks and natural reefs in depths of 3 to 60 feet. Females reach sexual maturity at approximately 3.3 years and males at 2.3 years. Growth is quite rapid until about age 5, then slows. A permit can live to the ripe old age of 24 years, but the predominant age group in the Keys is 4 to 6 years old.
Tackle: Overall, a good choice would be a 9/10-weight. With the latter, you're over-gunned on a small permit, and a little under-armed for a very large permit. Backing, 200 yards of 16- to 20-pound test. Fly line, WFF to intermediate for flats and inshore, and sinking for teased-up,

offshore permit. Class tippet of 14- to 16-pound test works fine. Flies: Del Brown's Merkin (#1 and #2 and 1/0), MOE Shrimp flies (#1 and #2), Borski's Chernobyl Crab, Swimming Shrimp and Slider (#1 and #2 to 1/0), and any Lenny Moffo tied permit patterns.

"The Opportunist" by Diane Rome Peebles

Pompano, African
CARANGIDAE, Alectis ciliaris

IGFA World-Record Catches

Line-Class World Record:
50 pounds.

World Fly Rod Record:
33 pounds, 8oz.

Florida Keys Record - Line Class:
48 pounds, 2oz.

Florida Keys Record - Fly Rod:
31 pounds, 4oz. (world record line class)

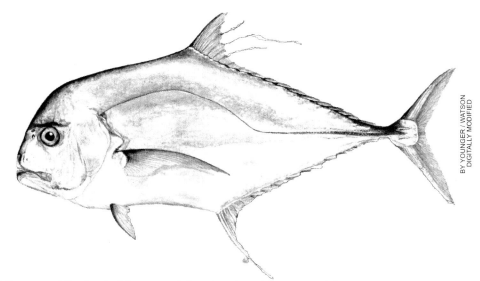

BY YOUNGER / WATSON
DIGITALLY MODIFIED

Quick ID: Four to six elongated, thread-like rays at the front of the second dorsal and anal fins, especially noticeable in young specimens where the rays exceed the length of the fish. Front portion of head steep and rounded.
NOTE: Every IGFA world record for the African pompano caught on a fly comes from South Florida, and 40% of those are from Keys waters.

CAPTAIN'S NOTES

This large, meat-eating jack is generally not a targeted game fish, but rather an opportunity fish. It can be teased up from its wreck-dwelling preference with live baits, such as pilchards, pinfish and blue runners. However, other visitors can be expected to show when live bait teasing.
Historic Densities: A deepwater-dwelling species with a preference for wrecks from the Upper Keys to Key West. Found year round, but primary months are December through March.
Feeds On: Small fishes.
ID: See quick ID. Deeply compressed body. Spinous dorsal fin is usually not visible in adult specimens. Rear half of body is triangular. The lateral line distinctively arches over the pectoral fins, then straightens and runs to the base of the caudal fin. Large specimens are light bluish-green above and silvery on the balance of its body. Dark blotches sometimes evident on the operculum, dorsal side of the caudal peduncle, and on the anterior portion of the second dorsal and anal fins.
Tackle: A 9/10-weight rod. Backing at least 150 yards and intermediate sinking fly line. Class tippet of 16-pound test. Some captains will use a mono shock of 40- to 60-pound test.
Flies: Large Deceivers.

TIDBITS

Offshore Tides and Currents

Tides influence offshore currents by forming rips (water flowing over a shoal, for example), and upwellings (structure, hump or irregularity that interrupts the current and drives cooler water to the surface). Detected currents can predict where fish will be. Most fish stay on the edge of a current, behind an obstruction or near the bottom where water flow speeds are less, which allows the fish to conserve energy while keeping its position. The latter vantage points provide an opportunity to prey on anything that swims or drifts by. Currents also produce barriers between various physical characteristics of water, principally, water temperature, salinity and distinctive color line changes. These are important elements as they determine where fish will feed.

Driven by tides, offshore currents will have peaks and valleys of velocity within the daily tidal cycle, as well as 28-day cycle. Captains in the Keys know their coordinates and keep reliable records with regard to cycles. They can predict when the fishing will be good, better or best and, for which species and where. They can also factor in the influences of season, weather, and a myriad of other environmental factors.

Sailfish, Atlantic
ISTIOPHORIDAE, Istiophorus platypterus

DIANE ROME PEEBLES

Quick ID: Pronounced, large, high, colorful and spotted dorsal fin.

CAPTAIN'S NOTES

NOTE: Sailfish in the Atlantic are now believed to be much larger than previously thought, more than 8 feet in length and weighing over 125 pounds. In reality, however, an over-100-pound sailfish caught in the Keys, or anywhere on the Americas side of Atlantic Ocean, is more than rare these days. Over-harvesting by long-liners has decimated all billfish stocks worldwide.

Sailfish are found in both the Atlantic and Pacific oceans and different scientific names have been assigned. Pacific, *albicans* and Atlantic, *platypterus*. Current ichthyology and marine biology thinking is that the fish may be the same species. The Pacific Ocean version, however, tending to grow significantly larger, up to 10 feet.

Records from the Long Key Fishing Camp (LKFC), 1910 through 1934 (Long Key, Florida), indicate that sailfish in those days were more plentiful and much larger, on average, than found in the Keys today.

Zane Grey made the LKFC and the Keys fishery famous, and he also announced to the world that sailfish, as well as tarpon and bonefish, were worthy game fish; not a nuisance by-catch as previously thought.

Sailfish belong to the pelagic family of billfishes called, Istiophoridae, which currently has three other members: blue marlin (*Makaira nigricans*), white marlin (*Tetrapturus albidus*) and longbill spearfish (Tetrapturus pfluegeri). The standard for classifying these billfish as one family is based principally on internal characteristics.

Teasing with live balao or larger ballyhoo can be very effective in the Keys. A chum line will also work, but like all open-water angling with a chum line, as well as live-bait trolling, can bring up suitors of any description. Today, most Keys captains prefer using a fly that resembles a preferred bait of the sail in coloration and size. It keeps the sail's attention far better. Fishing for sailfish is the same as it is for blue marlin and white marlin. Your most probable at-bat coming when trolling for any number of fish, but dolphin seem to lead to most opportunities (see

blue marlin for best rehearsal). Sailfish are prized as a game fish given their predilection for acrobatic leaps. When caught, sailfish usually stay near or on the surface, which adds to the angling enjoyment. Sailfish do, however, tire relatively quickly and will sound. NOTE: Acoustic tagging and tracking experiments by Keys offshore captains cooperating with TBF (The Billfish Foundation) and other scientific study groups suggest that a caught and then released sailfish has an excellent survival rate. Recapture rate is, unfortunately, very low. Estimated at .04% worldwide, according to Dr. Eric Prince, U. of Miami, Rosenstiel School of Atmospheric Science and Oceanography. Dangerously lowered stocks, the nature of sailfish to be loners and highly migratory are a few of his given reasons.

A sailfish is about the fastest swimmer in the ocean. It has been clocked at 68 MPH, so don't be too amazed at the speed with which it leaves the scene when hooked. The last stage of the fight is critical. When the sailfish nears the boat it will get renewed energy and one swipe with its bill and the ball game is over. The captain and

---

TIDBITS

The first ever recorded billfish (sailfish) landed with a fly rod is attributed to Lee Cuddy, a member of the world-famous Miami Rod & Reel Club. He caught a sailfish (47-pounds) offshore Miami in June of 1964. His feat was followed shortly thereafter with other billfish catches on a fly rod by: Doc Robertson, also of the Miami Rod & Reel Club, Lee Wulff, Stu Apte, Harry Kime, Lefty Kreh, Ted Williams, Billy Pate, Flip Pallot and two women, Dolores Williams and Laura Pate. The former were the respective wives of Ted Williams and Billy Pate.
Jack Samson's, *Billfish on a Fly*.

"Dropping Back" by Don Ray.

mate will have been there, done that many times before so pay attention to instructions. The captain will tell you exactly what to do. Follow his instructions to the letter, and then get out of the way.

Today, the Florida Keys are still considered one of the best sailfish destinations in the world. Oddly, however, is the fact that no sailfish caught on a fly rod in the Keys is part of current IGFA records.

Historic Densities: Sailfish prefer to live in warm waters with, approximately, 79 degrees F the most favored water temperature in the Keys. The water temperature range for sailfish is 77 to 82 degrees F. Sailfish are highly migratory, many times lone pelagic travellers, but sometimes found in small groups. Sails in the Keys will feed in mid-water, on the surface, near the edge of the Florida Reef Tract, over sea mounds and in currents and eddies of both the Straits of Florida and Gulf Stream. A sailfish could be caught in any month in the Keys. Best sailfishing in the Keys is generally along the reef line from Upper Keys to Key West (Upper Keys best late

---

TIDBITS

Casting Tip: The Double Haul. Increasing Line Speed Begets More Yardage.

You will never be able to increase, substantially, the length of your cast by simply speeding up the cast with your casting hand. It will produce, more than occasionally, a much shorter cast that collapses. No matter how hard you try to speed up the cast with your dominant hand to gain distance, nothing like the intended result will ever happen. Substantially increasing the length of a cast only comes about from increasing line speed. That requires use of the off-hand performing the double haul. It is, decidedly, tricky for lifelong freshwater fly-fishermen, because a new memory has to be created. Starting out with the right approach makes it all a lot easier. With a good, manageable dominant hand cast, just increase the line speed via the hauls on both the back and forward casts with the off-hand. Do not let yourself get in the habit of using more than two or three false casts. To greatly improve distance you only increase the line speed while performing the two hauls (forward and back). You'll find that each new, correctly performed cast will increase your distance capabilities. The results will amaze you, and so will the distance you get. Once you are automatic with increasing line speed via the double haul the whole casting motion will become less tiring, your accuracy will improve as will the quality of your presentation of the fly. Bottom line, you'll catch a lot more fish—guaranteed.

November through February, and Lower Keys/Key West best in March through May). In late November, or very early December, more aggressive juveniles can start arriving, primarily in the Upper Keys, and they will even react well to dead bait. In the Lower Keys, sailfish are considered 'hot,' March through May, and are found at the color line change of the Gulf Stream. In March/April, and November/December sails will average 35-pounds in the Keys, but much larger sailfish are taken every year, with 7-footers not at all uncommon. When sailfishing is 'on' in the Keys, the sailfish will tend to be of the larger class.

Feeds On: Tunas, mackerels, jacks, ballyhoo, balao, pilchard and mullet, and other schooling fish that swim near the ocean's surface and/or mid-water. They are not highly selective feeders and consume wide varieties of fish as well as cephalopods (squids). Sailfish are large eyed, see well at a distance, and hunt for prey utilizing their sight, along with hearing (inner ear and through the lateral line). Standard feeding profile for sailfish is to swim into baitfish, stun or kill with their bill or caudal fin, and then return quickly to feed. Sailfish have been observed by divers. They've been watched corralling baits by circling with their high first dorsal fin (sail) fully extended, which creates a wall that traps the prey.

ID: Common to all Istiophoridae are prolonged upper jaws (bill), which have no teeth, just sandpaper-like denticles. No doubt a Darwinian invention designed to hold prey. Also, Istiophoridae are, collectively, dark bluish above, pale white below and have pale bluish-gray vertically spotted bars on the sides, which are seen only in life. Colors and most markings disappear with remarkable alacrity at death.

Sailfish, *platypterus*, are easily identified by the prominent 1st dorsal fin (sail), which has iridescent qualities of slate to cobalt blue with miscellaneously scattered black spots. In addition, sailfish can be externally identified by, according to C. Robert Robbins (Rosenstiel School of Marine and Atmospheric Science at the U. of Miami) and G. Carlton Ray (Department of Environmental Science at the U. of Virginia), ". . . lateral line in a single canal along mid-side. Anus is close to anal-fin base. Front lobe of dorsal fin high (deeper than body at that point) and pointed or squared off. Rear part of dorsal fin high, sail-like, much higher than spines at front. 1st dorsal 1st anal fins spotted. Profile has a distinct hump from area between eyes to 1st dorsal fin. Front lobe of anal fin pointed and low; fin height less than body depth at that point. Pectoral fin small, shorter than pelvic fin. Usually, 42 to 45 dorsal-fin spines." (*Atlantic Coast Fishes*, Peterson Field Guides, 1986). Sailfish spawn in the Keys during the summer,

but can begin in April and extend into late fall. The female sailfish, larger than the male, can lay as many as 4,500,000 eggs that hatch 36 hours later. Growth is rapid in this species, within months a juvenile sailfish can weigh 6 pounds and be over 4 feet long. In its first year, a sailfish could grow to be 6 feet long.

Tackle: A 12-weight is about minimum, but a 14-weight is a better choice. Backing, at least 300 yards. of 30-pound test Dacron (gel-spun just about doubling your backing if you choose it). For fly line, some captains suggest underlining the rod weight, which will effectively reduce in-water drag, a very big deal. It will not diminish strength or castability. Use WF fast-sinking line and cut off the back end so that only 25- or 30 feet of the front remains (these days you can buy line in that configuration), which further reduces in-water drag. Mono replaces the last 70 or 75 feet of fly line. Most captains use 100 feet of 50-pound mono, which connects to the backing and fly line. The mono also reduces the problem of being cut badly by conventional backing.

Flies: Tandem-hook Cam Sigler big-game flies. Anything that looks like a balao or ballyhoo, mackerel, squid, mullet or a dorado. Billy Pate's tandem-hook streamers & poppers. Paul Bunchuk's tandem-hook streamers that convert to poppers (removable heads). Purple/white, green/yellow, blue/white, black/green, pink/white. Heads should match predominant feather color. Smaller flies work best in the Keys. A 5/0 hook works fine with front hook smaller (nearest the eye). Best advice for flies and leaders will come from your captain.

Seatrout, Spotted
SCIAENIDAE, Cynoscion regalis

IGFA World-Record Catches

Line Class World Record:
17 pounds, 7oz.

World Fly Rod Record:
12 pounds, 7oz.

Florida Record - Line Class:
17 pounds, 7oz. (world record)

Florida Record - Fly Rod:
12 pounds, 7oz. (world record)

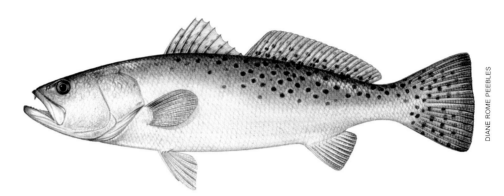

DIANE ROME PEEBLES

Quick ID: Two large, recurvate teeth protruding from the upper jaw. Round black spots on back, upper flanks and throughout the tail. NOTE: Most IGFA records were caught in Florida, but none are from the Keys. The Keys, however, support a large population of spotted seatrout.

CAPTAIN'S NOTES

What is unique about the Florida Keys spotted seatrout is that there is a genetically isolated version. Also, they are not migratory on a large scale and do not mix with other migratory stocks of Florida seatrout. Marine scientists believe that female fidelity to natal waters appears to play a large role in the genetic isolation. A useful by-product of this isolation is that it provides an indicator of what role commercial fishing plays in reducing stocks. A netting ban on the spotted seatrout proved a point. Spotted seatrout stocks in the Florida Keys are now increasing. Trout are now showing up in some of their old haunts: Blackwater Sound, Barnes Sound and Card Sound in the Upper Keys.

Backcountry in the Keys, primarily the Upper Keys, are home to the best seatrout fishing. In the Keys seatrout are found in waters that hold both snook and redfish. The approach to fishing for seatrout, however, differs. Backcountry guides in the Keys will drift Florida Bay's seagrass beds and the angler will blind cast until a hook-up is made. Some guides will then prefer to anchor as a school is, obviously, about. The angler is then directed to use a 360-degree horizon for his casting reference. Another technique is to tease the trout into action by casting (spinning rod) with a hookless popper, designed to make a lot of noise on entry and retrieve. Seatrout respond well to noise. Seatrout are another game fish in the Keys that are a great at-bat for the novice fly-fisherman as it rarely calls for extremely long, delicate and accurate casting. However, all the proper fly-fishing mechanics are still incumbent upon the novice. Setting the hook with seatrout is a consideration because its mouth is soft. Horsing a trout will often lead to losing it. When the seatrout fishing is on, it can provide hours of enjoyment.

Historic Densities: Principally, Florida Bay, the sounds of the Upper Keys and portions of the eastern section of the Gulf of Mexico. Water temperature preferences are from about 65 to 77 degrees with a rather wide latitude on either end. The good months are April through August, but the best months are September through March. Most trout schools will be found in water depths of around 10 feet, on mud or grass flats and the edges of tidal currents. During cold snaps they will move to deeper holes, lagoons, drop-offs and even shallow-water wrecks. Spawning takes place in the spring, summer and fall within the near Everglades estuaries, but primarily in nearshore waters of Florida Bay. NOTE: The Keys version of seatrout rarely strays further than 5 to 10 miles from its natal boundary. A female, the larger of the sexes, will lay 10,000 to 1,000,000 eggs. The young mature in very nearshore bay waters (50 yards or so). In the fall, when they are mature enough, they will move to the traditional seatrout waters of the bay. Seatrout are sexually mature at age 1 when the male is about 10 inches long and the female around 11 inches. Some marine science studies indicate seatrout can live for 15 years, other studies suggest 9 years as the lifetime limit. However, a seatrout over 5 years old in the Keys is rare.

Feeds On: Shrimp are a favorite. Find any variety of shrimp in Florida Bay and you'll probably encounter seatrout. Small mullet, pinfish and all common baitfish are also on the seatrout menu. They will also devour their young.

ID: See quick ID. The seatrout has 10 spines on the first dorsal fin and 1 spine with 24 to 27 soft rays on the second dorsal fin.

Tackle: 6- to 8-weight rods are adequate for spotted seatrout in the Keys. Backing of 150 yards of 20-pound test and class tippet of 8- to 12-pound test are also adequate. A 30-pound-test bite guard of mono or flourocarbon is called for because spotted seatrout are toothy.

Flies: Clousers, Deceivers, streamers, Seaducers and poppers. The use of flash, red & yellow, black, and red & white are good combinations in sizes from #2 to 1/0. Weed guards are more than prudent.

Sharks

Class ELASMOBRANCHIOMORPHI - Cartilaginous Fish

CAPTAIN'S NOTES

The families of sharks that can be found in Keys waters are many. We profile only a small sampling of shark species that are possible catches for a fly-fisherman in the Florida Keys.

The Keys are just about mecca for shark fishing with a fly rod. There is ample proof. Most of the articles about shark fishing in shallow water using a fly rod, or light-tackle equipment, are and continue to be authored by the Keys guides and offshore captains. In addition, many of the world records for sharks, caught on a fly, come from Key waters. Fortunately, the breed of fishermen the guides are raising have been trained to practice catch and release.

NOTE: There are far, far fewer sharks then there were just 25 years ago. They have been unfairly vilified, caught and killed for the boast of it, and longliners have slaughtered them for food and fin. Recovery, if the slaughter stops now, is estimated to be 35 years away, or more. Noteworthy, however, is that most sharks do not sexually mature until reaching an age of 12 to 20 years old. Also, the gestation period is rather lengthy for a fish, and offspring, in some species, can be limited to just a few pups.

In the Keys, shallow-water fly-fishing for sharks is a year-round opportunity, but the best shallow water shark activity takes place in the winter through early spring, January to March. While a laundry list of shark suspects are possible in the Keys, a few of the best bets are: blacktip, hammerhead, lemon and tiger (the blacktip is not listed by the IGFA as a fly-rod game fish). There are other possibilities, of course. Fly-fishing for sharks presents a whole new set of rules, including: equipment considerations, pursuing, presenting the fly, hooking, playing and bringing it to the boat and, then releasing it. Captain Bob (TR) Trosset, Big Coppitt Key, has fished for sharks in shallow water with light tackle or fly rod for years. He has contributed several articles on the subject. A summary of one of his conclusions is as follows: your three fly pattern color selections should be orange, orange or orange. The rest of it is not as simple.

Captain Trosset, Fordyce and several other guides, have come up with solutions and techniques for pursuing sharks in shallow water. One of the best ways to begin, according to TR, is to set up a chum line in 6 or 7 feet of water when the wind is against an outgoing tide, which helps present a more compact odor drift. An outgoing tide will act as a funnel. Sharks, intuitively, position themselves to take advantage of the currents funnelled offerings. A live bait teaser, and the put-and-take technique, can also work wonders. Both of the latter inducements, however, can be of interest to barracuda and other species. Once a shark is interested, and within the limits of the anglers casting range, cast the fly so it can be retrieved alongside the body (same water column) and into view. The fly track has to be kept within the shark's window of vision. Cast only to a shark that is heading toward you.

NOTE: A fly cast dead in front of it will not be seen. Do not bother to cast if a shark is swimming away from you. Most of the time conditions are not perfect, so casting at an angle that will allow you to place the fly alongside the shark is more probable. When the shark takes the fly you must try to keep the hook on the same side that you are on. A crossed-over line is never a safe bet, but with a shark it is a situation that is not likely to last long. All sharks have coarse, sandpaper-like skin and their fins are cutting-edge sharp. Some sharks are more acrobatic than others. A blacktip shark, for example, is probably the most game fish-like in its reaction to being hooked. It will leap many times and perform similarly to an angry tarpon.

Almost all sharks will tend to do two things differently from most other game fish caught on the flats, or in shallow water; one, they will arrive out of nowhere and, at once, make you keenly aware of their power and prehistoric predatory capabilities; two, when they decide to leave the scene after recognizing the dilemma of being hooked, it will be with knuckle-busting speed, and any attempt to halt their initial run will approach impossible, even for a blacktip that weighs-in at 40 pounds.

Your guide will pre-set the drag for you. Don't touch it until he advises differently. Setting the hook on a shark has to be hard, and managing line back on the reel can be especially troublesome as sharks are unpredictable. They can sit for a time after being well hooked, make an instantaneous run, or even charge the boat. They'll do just about anything one can think of. Alert and attentive are good mental postures when a shark is hooked. Always pay attention to your guide, he wants you to succeed.

NOTE: In the late 1950's, Captain Norman Duncan, Upper Keys, began targeting sharks as a game fish, and a lot of his pioneering findings became seeds for new angling discoveries.

Shark, Blacktip

CARCHARHINIDAE, *Carcharhinus limbatus*

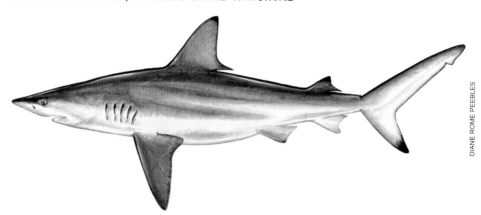

The IGFA does not currently recognize the blacktip shark as a line-class or fly-rod game fish. The All Tackle IGFA record is 270 pounds. 9oz. (Kenya). A flats-caught blacktip is, generally, under 100 pounds. In the Keys they will more than likely be 40 pounds or less.

Quick ID: Distinct white stripe on flank. Conspicuous black tips on inside of pectoral fin, dorsal and anal fins. The lower lobe of the caudal fin is also distinctively black on young specimens, but faded on older specimens. Snout V shaped and long. A blacktip can grow to 8-plus-feet, but on flats in the Keys most blacktips are smaller (4 to 6 feet). Adult coloration is a dark, bluish-gray above and whitish below. Young specimens are paler in color tones. The blacktip and thresher shark are commonly mistaken, one for the other.

Shark, Scalloped Hammerhead

SPHYRNIDAE, *Sphyrna lewini*

IGFA World-Record Catches

Line Class World Record:
991 pounds

World Fly Rod Record:
154 pounds

Florida Keys Record - Line Class:
463 pounds

Florida Keys Record - Fly Rod:
154 pounds. (world record)

NOTE: 1. The IGFA only recognizes the genus *Sphyrna*, to which all 8 species of hammerhead belong (family Sphyrnidae). Individually named species of hammerheads are not recognized for record-keeping purposes, except for All Tackle catches.
NOTE: 2. Every world-record for a hammerhead caught on a fly is from the Florida Keys (6).
Quick ID: Eyes are at the ends of their flat, hammer-like lateral protrusions. The front portion of the head (hammer) is convex. The first dorsal fin is high. Hammerheads use their odd frontal lobes as scanners. Tiny lampullae of Lorenzi (within its head) act as electroreceptors, enabling them to detect food on the bottom, such as rays, a favored meal.

Shark, Tiger
CARCHARHINIDAE, *Galeocerdo cuvieri*

IGFA World-Record Catches

Line Class World Record:
1,780 pounds

World Fly-Rod Record:
220 pounds

Florida Keys Record - Line Class:
255 pounds 8oz.

Florida Keys Record - Fly Rod:
220 pounds (world record)

NOTE: The tiger shark has recurvate teeth, upper and lower, and they are deeply notched and serrated. A bite from a tiger shark can cause a massive, life-threatening wound. While a tiger shark can appear sluggish, it can quickly reach great speed. Its ferocity of aggressiveness during an attack is an awesome sight. All tiger shark world records, caught on a fly, were caught in the Keys.
Quick ID: The shape of a tiger is distinctive as well as its short pointed snout. It also has a median keel that runs along the caudal peduncle. A tiger has its first two gill slits directly above the pectoral fin. The tiger and leopard spots are more pronounced in juvenile species than adults. Coloration in an adult is bluish-gray to brownish-gray. Darker on the back than flanks. Belly is whitish.

Other shark species that can be caught in shallow water in the Keys are: lemon, mako, sand, spinner, dusky, bull, blacknose, nurse, silky and bonnethead.
Tackle: Rods, 14-weight and up. NOTE: Juvenile blacktip or bonnethead could safely be handled with a much, much lower-weight rod. For larger sharks, backing should be at least 300 yards of 30-pound test (a good application for gel-spun). Class tippet, 20-pound test and #7 wire as a bite guard.
NOTE: TR uses 58-pound-test braided Steelon, exclusively. Flies: Large (5-inch, plus or minus) Deceivers, tarpon patterns and streamers (5/0 hook). According to TR, orange is the best color, and few argue with that.

Blacknose Shark - *Carcharhinus arcronotus* (to 5 feet)

Bonnethead Shark - *Sphyrna tiburo* (to 5 feet)

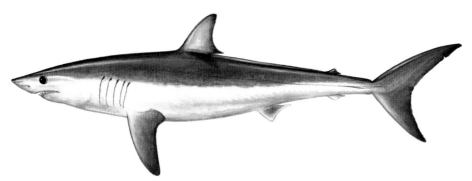

Shortfin Mako Shark - *Isurus oxirinchus* (to 12 feet)

Sandbar Shark - *Carcharhinus plumbeus* (to 10 feet)

DIANE ROME PEEBLES

TIDBITS

Sharks

Sharks are among the world's most successful groups of animals. They have inhabited the seas for more than 400 million years. For more than 100 million years, they have remained nearly unchanged.

1. A shark can produce a bite of 36,000 pounds per square inch.
2. Sharks have the same five senses we have, plus electrosensitivity. The latter is an incredible electrical field response mechanism, and along with sound sensors, sharks can detect vibrations from incredible distances.
3. Sharks are not color blind. Their eyes are equipped to distinguish colors, and they have lenses that are up to seven times more powerful than a human's. Some shark species can detect a light that is as much as ten times dimmer than the dimmest light the average person can see.
4. Sharks have no bones, only cartilage. There are 400 species of sharks that are skeletally entirely of cartilage. No shark has a swim bladder, and if it stops swimming it will sink to the bottom. Almost all sharks have to keep swimming to breathe.
5. A large shark, in a feeding frenzy, can shred a truck tire; no problem.
6. Contrary to popular opinion, sharks do not have an extraordinary sense of smell.
7. Like higher animals, sharks reproduce by internal fertilization {40% of shark species are egg layers, and 60% are live-bearers (aplacental or placental viviparous)}. When the pups food source is exhausted, the young shark (pup) hatches and swims free to fend for itself.
  Gestation can take a year or longer and a litter usually has from four to ten pup's depending on the species.
8. A shark's teeth are in parallel rows, and tooth loss and replacement is continuous throughout life. Studies by Mote Marine scientists have shown that, on average, a small nurse shark, for example, will, replace an entire front row of teeth every ten days in summer, and every one to two months in winter one tooth at a time. In the winter they feed less, and their metabolism slows down.

Snapper, Mutton

LUTJANIDAE, *Lutjanus analis*

IGFA World-Record Catches

Line-Class World Record
28-pounds, 3oz

World Fly Rod Record
17 pounds

Florida Keys Record - Line Class
26 pounds, 4oz

Florida Keys Record - Fly Rod
17 pounds (world record)

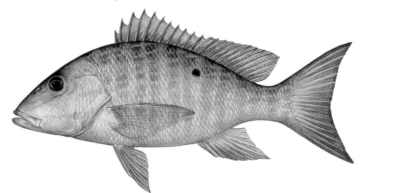

DIANE ROME PEEBLES

Quick ID: Distinguishing small black spot on flank along with blue stripes on head, back and flanks. Iris of eyes are bronze to red. The anal fin is decidedly pointed. Coloration can vary, but mainly orangish to red-yellow.
NOTE: Sixty six percent of all the world records, caught on a fly, were taken from Keys waters. Del Brown, inventor of the Merkin and holder of the world-record permit on a fly, holds the record for mutton snapper on a fly.

CAPTAIN'S NOTES

NOTE: Mutton snapper stocks are down due to overharvesting.

There are about 15 types of snappers found in Keys waters, but it's the mangrove, mutton and yellowtail that are better possibilities for fly-fishermen. Mangrove snapper are found in the mangrove fringes of the backcountry and, along with the yellowtail, they can also be found offshore around hard bottom-areas, patch reefs, wrecks, and coral reefs. Yellowtail can readily show while chumming, offshore or inshore, and are truly non-selective feeders.

Captain George Hommell, Jr., legendary Islamorada Keys guide, says that one of his favorite things is an evening on the flats, fishing for mutton snapper. Although evening is a preferred feeding time for most snappers, the mutton feeds during all times of day. They tend to substrate feed (crustacean) from mid-day to evening, and in mid-water early morning and late in the evening. Unlike most snappers, mutton prefer the flats, and often on traditional permit turf (also found on the reef tract). On the flats, mutton are usually encountered as a solitary fish, or in small schools of just a few fish. They can also be found trailing the muds of rays, or tailing and mudding in the traditional permit/bonefish/redfish profile. Mutton are just as skittish as any flats species so put your fly about 10 feet in front of an approaching mutton and employ bonefishing techniques. You can be a little bolder on stripping, 5 or 6 inches at a time, and let the fly settle before each new strip. When the mutton strikes, wait for it to turn before setting the hook. Over-anxiousness will often yield disappointment.
Historic Densities: Key West waters have produced most of the IGFA record catches, but mutton are caught all the way into the Biscayne Bay portions of the Keys. The best mutton fishing begins in the spring (late February through April) and then again in the fall.
Feeds On: Crustaceans and small fishes.
ID: Often confused with several other snapper species (red and lane). One difference is that the lane snapper's anal fin and rear edge of its dorsal fin are squarish to round, not

pointed. A large adult mutton is more reddish, similar to a red snapper, but the spot on the mutton's flanks will telltale it. The mutton has a lunate tail, and the dorsal fins have 10 spines and 14 rays.
Tackle: A 9/10-weight rod covers just about all occasions. Backing at 200 yards of 20 pound-test Dacron and WFF fly line. Class tippet of 10 to 14-pound test.
Flies: On the flats, when the mutton is in a bottom-feeding profile, use Del Brown's Merkin and Shrimp patterns. When feeding in mid-water, use small bait imitations.
NOTE 1: The Center for Marine Science, University of North Carolina, Wilmington, NC, and PIER's president, Dr. Michael Domeier, conducted independent studies on the mutton snapper. Dr. Domeier's 1991 study documented what commercial fishermen have known since the late 1970's, Riley's Hump (Dry Totugas) was 'spawning central' to the Florida's population of mutton snapper. He surveyed the Tortugas site and went on to publish a scientific paper describing what he observed. Mutton snapper spawn on cue a few hours after sunset on the day of the full moon in May and *". . . prefer to spawn in huge groups at very precise locations and times of the year. The predictability of the spawning aggregation has made them an easy target for fishermen, who catch them with rod and reel, handlines, longlines and fish traps."* After mutton spawn, millions of fertilized eggs float to the surface, hatch in about 24 hours and the larvae drift in the current. If all works well, they wind up on the grass flats of the Keys in about 3 weeks as a juvenile snapper. Some eggs drifted to as far away as Palm Coast, FL, 500 miles from the Tortugas.
NOTE 2: The mutton snapper population in the Keys, and throughout Florida, was greatly lessened for many years after 1979, when its aggregating spawning site was discovered (the spawning season is currently closed). Riley's Hump, as a side bar, is also responsible for 75% of all commercial catches in the Keys. It's no wonder there were loud objections to the Tortugas 2000 Proposal, which calls for temporary closure to rebuild stocks. The future of sport fishing in the Keys being all the better for it.

Snook

CENTROPOMIDAE, Centropomus undecimalis

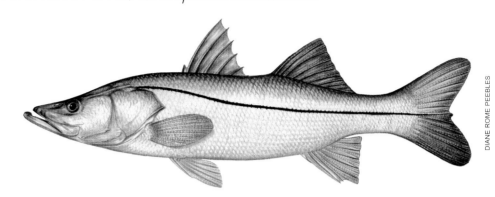

DIANE ROME PEEBLES

IGFA World-Record Catches

Line-Class World Record:
57 pounds, 12oz.

World Fly Rod Record:
30 pounds, 4oz.

*Florida Record - Line Class:
44 pounds, 3oz.

*Florida Record - Fly Rod:
30 pounds, 4oz. (world record)

Quick ID: A very distinct black lateral line that extends to the edge of the caudal fin. The lower jaw protrudes.
NOTE: Currently there are no world records for snook caught in the Keys. *Records above are for Florida. At one time, legendary Keys guide, Captain Bill Curtis held the world record for snook caught on a fly rod (27 pounds/Flamingo).

CAPTAIN'S NOTES

There are three other species of snook, all are found in Keys waters: *pectanatus* (tarpon snook), *ensiferus* (swordspine snook) and parallelus (fat snook). Two of the latter, swordspine and tarpon, are also IGFA world records caught in Florida waters. All of the latter species are much smaller than *undecimalis*. Snook (*undecimalis*) are a favorite of many guides as it offers every opportunity and element of tact that fly-fishing is noted for: stealth of approach, excellent casting skills for both sighted- and blind-casting situations, and discovering likely haunts. The fish itself has a potent strike, puts up a good fight and requires skill in managing it when caught as it is generally near hook break-off objects, such as mangrove roots. Getting a snook interested will usually require a long cast and a quality presentation. Your cast for a sighted fish must be in front of it, about 6 to 8 feet. An immediate retrieve seems best, but some guides prefer a 1 or 2 count before retrieving, especially when a snook is in deeper water. In any case, a steady and relatively fast retrieve is agreed upon.

"Snook In The Mangrove" by Don Ray.

Snook are generally limited to the Upper Keys, principally, the backcountry, and in the fresh water or brackish estuaries of the Everglades.
NOTE: Snook season is closed during June, July and August, and again from mid-December through January. It is perfectly legal to catch a snook during the closed seasons, but it is quite illegal to keep it. Keys guides will not intentionally fish for snook during closed

seasons. Additionally, there are bag limits and size limits in play when the season is open. Currently, nothing below 26 inches or above 34 inches can be kept. Snook are quite sensitive to cold water and will seek deeper water before it gets into the mid-60's. At the latter temperatures they become lethargic. Being in water below 60 degrees F for any extended period of time will kill many fish. Most snook are born males and later change to females. Females, as in most species of fish, are larger.

Guides look for snook in white holes (sand patches amid a field of sea grass), in cuts between mangrove islands, up against mangroves where they park parallel to the bank (roots), and adjacent to sand bars around mangrove islands. Big lunkers are often pulled out of deep channels, and a dock is not a bad option at night. After a cold snap in the winter, and when the water starts to warm, the best guides will know of lagoons internal to the mangrove, or in the Everglades, that will harbor a pool full of hungry snook. These found Vahalla's can result in a day to remember. The action could last for the whole day (a similar situation, particularly in the Marquesas, is true for tarpon looking for a day in the sun).

Tides are always a factor when snook fishing. The best snook fishing in the summer is at night during the first two or three hours of an outgoing tide, when mosquitoes rule the world. The best fishing for snook in cooler months is the same tide, but during the day. Natural aggregations of snook occur prior to and during spawning. Bridges, pilings and estuaries of the Everglades are prime locations.

Historic Densities: As sited above, and in positions within its ambush style that afford the best near-strike potential. A snook will not venture into a prolonged attack and will return to its favored haunt within an hour, should you have spooked it. Preferred water temperature ranges in the Keys are from 70 to 86 degrees F. Snook are perfectionists at not expending more energy than the morsel it chases offers in metabolic return.

Peak spawning takes place in the Keys, generally, June through July, but can last late into October. A large female can lay 1,000,000 to 1,500,000 gamets (eggs) over a 1- to 3-day period. Previous belief was that spawning was a celestially-inspired event (new or full moon phases). Current thinking is that eggs are released late in the afternoon or early evening with no regard to moon phases or tide. Water temperature is believed to be a big influence, which could explain the wide latitude in the spawning calendar. Major inlets are considered prime spawning locations.

NOTE: The Keys-bred snook is not a likely migrator, but its cousins from as far away as Jupiter, FL, are likely winter visitors.

Feeds On: Non-selectively, but within the limits of its fishery in the Keys, pinfish, needlefish, shrimps, mullet and a variety of other baitfishes.

ID: See quick ID. Golden-brownish to darker on back, fading to lighter, and then a whitish-silvery belly. Both

"Tide Watch" by Diane Rome Peebles.

dorsal fins are separated by a noticeable gap. The third anal fin has a very large spur. There are no physical differences between male and female snook. NOTE: Snook are, predominantly, born males, but change later in life to a female. No doubt a Darwian inspiration designed to ensure the species' survival. Hermaphroditism (sex reversal) is not that unusual in fish.

Tackle: For most Keys snook an 8- to 10-weight rod will covers all bases. Backing at a minimum of 150 yards of 20-pound-test Dacron and fly line of weight forward to sinking. Class tippets can be an arguable point, but in the Keys, 8- up to 16-pound test finds few objections. Many guides use a 40-pound-test shock.

Flies: Tying flies for snook offer an opportunity for invention since snook eat such a wide variety of offerings, even within their Keys confines: pinfish, mullet, menhaden, shrimp and a whole host of other baits. Patterns that guides prefer for adult fish are not, of course, limited to these tried and true, but weedless is a definite must: Clousers, seaducers, sliders, Muddlers, Deceivers and top-water Dallberg Diver's. Also, Chico's Bendback, Joe Cave's, Gold Wobbler, and the Ratlin Minnow are also good on-board choices.

NOTE: For information on purchasing originals, prints or commissioned works, contact:
Diane Rome Peebles
Box 12855
St. Petersburg, FL 33733
813-321-5951

Tarpon
ELOPIDAE, Megalops atlanticus

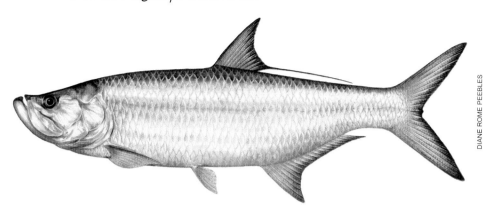

DIANE ROME PEEBLES

Quick ID: Very silvery body covered with large scales. Lower jaw juts out in a pronounced way. The dorsal fins have 12 to 16 spineless soft rays. Long ray at the rear of dorsal fin.

CAPTAIN'S NOTES

NOTE: Pick up a copy of John Coles's book, *Tarpon Quest* (Lyons & Burford, 1991). In 106 pages, Cole eloquently captures the world of the tarpon itself, all the attendant details of how they are caught and how, in the same prose, one can screw up. Cole also captures the enormity of any occasion in which an angler is so privileged as to find himself in the singular specialness of the Florida Keys environment. John Cole's mentor on the quest, as well as the reader's, is a young Key West captain, the now-famous Jeffrey Cardenas.

Tarpon can be found year round in the Keys. The slower months (normally November through January) hold resident populations of large adult specimens, as well as, smaller juvenile tarpon. They are found from the Marquesas, in deep channels throughout the Keys, well into the backcountry of Florida Bay, and the Everglades. Fishing in earnest for the silver king, however, begins when thousands of tarpon arrive, anywhere from late January to early March, and kick-off the world-renowned "spring Run." Hooking up with one of these spring-run behemoths increases, dramatically, if you have engaged a top guide, and you can cast well. That latter requirement would include making the grade in distance (50 feet or better), with accuracy and ability to reach your target using only 3 or 4 false casts. While it is true that the lesser skilled with a fly rod can and do catch tarpon, a little reality is noteworthy. In addition, you should at least be cerebrally familiar with some of the tarpon-fishing scenarios so that when your guide begins delivering precise instructions, in the heat of the battle, you are on familiar ground.

The spring run in the Keys produces some of the best big-tarpon fishing opportunities in the world. The phenomena lasts a minimum of three months and usually peaks in April and May. The event has been going on for thousands of years. It was a quiet and unnoticed affair until Zane Grey decided, in the pre-flapper years of the twentieth century, that the scaly, prehistoric and acrobatic tarpon was a worthy opponent. Tarpon arrive by the thousands during the spring run and the Keys provide all the hosting essentials: a place to put on the feed bag, spawn, and a coordinate from which to choose an Atlantic Ocean or Gulf of Mexico run continuance. During the run in the Keys, the population of tarpon swells, from the Marquesas all the way to Biscayne Bay, including the oceanside flats, bay and gulfside flats, and the many channels that dissect the Keys. During the run, tarpon tend to aggregate in pods, roughly of 6 to 12 fish (more or less). In this profile anglers will spot them in skinnier water (4 to 10 feet), affording good sight-fishing opportunities. In skinny water your guide will also spot tarpon high tailing it (similar to bonefish), cruising, rolling (gulping air), leaving a trail of surface bubbles, daisy chaining (a presumed pre-spawn activity), and even leaping into the air (10 feet) or bounding porpoise-like (20 feet) across open water just for the fun of it. Daisy chaining offers just about the best, classic at-bat, followed by tarpon running the Marquesas channels and flats, entering or exiting the deeper channels throughout the Keys, and running the oceanside flats, east to west, and west to east.

NOTE: In the early stages of the run, tarpon will populate the bay/gulfside of the Keys, and oceanside later (May is prime). As the run nears its end, usually in late June or even early July, many 'run' tarpon will have chosen the Keys as their new home, and, along with a large resident population, begin to hunker down in the channels or make their way into the backcountry. Key West, and the Marquesas especially, will hold a large population of big tarpon well into the summer. As the water heats up under the long summer sun, tarpon will start opting to out more frequently in the cool of early morning, evening and into the night.

RUNNING PODS

Casting to an oncoming pod of tarpon requires the fly be presented reasonably in front of it, so that the pod encounters the fly, and in the same water column in which they are swimming. NOTE: Tarpon will not descend to take a fly. A good cast of 100 feet will always be better than a shorter cast of 30 feet. A longer cast offers less detection of you and the boat, and allows the fly a chance to settle into the preferred water column, and allows the 'food' mimic to be in the water longer. A shorter cast, obviously, increases the possibility of detection. For tarpon fishing, the fly retrieve begins with stripping in long, steady and deliberate pulls that make the fly ride up and down. When a tarpon is convincingly taking the fly, cease your retrieve, wait until it turns (silvery flash), or closes its mouth, before setting the hook. Remember, tarpon gulp a fly. They do not bite it. Your best bet is to wait for your guide's, "hit it" directive. Most guides agree that setting the hook on a tarpon is an all-out, quick set, and the pull is parallel to the horizon. A second and third setting is always a good idea. If, however, you time your hook-setting just as the fish runs, you'll probably end up breaking it off. When a tarpon decides it has been duped, which can be faster than a nano-second or seem like never, it will haul-ass and begin its aerial show. When the fish runs, let it. Never tighten the drag while any fish is running, or try to further imbed the hook. When it jumps, bow the rod tip straight down and out towards the fish; never pull. Setting the hook will be done, in all probability, with your off-hand, and you will have to clear the slack line back through the stripping guide while the fish is running; not easy to do. Shoes, laces, legs, reel handle, pliers, reel seat and anything on the deck are magnets for loose fly line. One snag or spaghetti knot and your at-bat is quite over. When you start to gain line on a tarpon, be sure to thwart its efforts to gulp air. Gulping air supercharges its batteries and unnecessarily extends the fight. A tarpon of any size will get renewed energy when it sees the boat, so it is rarely over when the fish seems conquered. Pay close attention to your guide's instructions at all times. He will help you through casting, hooking, catching and playing it to the boat. Many tarpon are lost because of the following mistakes: line is not taut and straight at the take (you cannot set a hook with snaked line), not heeding the guide's instructions, setting the hook too fast, setting the hook too softly, or not bowing the rod when the fish jumps.

DAISY CHAIN

Fishing a "daisy chain" is a great opportunity, if it all happens within the limits of your casting range. The rules of engagement are as explained above with the exception of your cast. If the tarpon are circling counter-clockwise, present the fly to the left and beyond the front-most fish. For clockwise circling. A fly presented on the opposite side will tend to spook them. When pods are running in deeper water, fly presented to the lead fish could spook it, and alarm the other fish. NOTE: The fly must always be made to appear as though fleeing, not approaching, which would be unnatural.

DEEP WATER

Blind casting into deep holes or channels can be very productive, especially so if you have engaged a top guide, he'll know the most favorable locations. Here you'll need sinking line and fly patterns that push a lot of water on the retrieve (Whistlers, for example).

"Tarpon Bust" by Diane Rome Peebles.

Historic Densities: Spring run as described above. In the fall it starts again when tarpon make the return trip south. Water temperature preferences are around 74 to 88 degrees F.

Feeds On: Shrimps, crabs, mullet and a wide variety of small fishes.

ID: See quick ID. NOTE: *Tarpum*, as native American Indians (FL) called them, are labeled, ichthyologically, in the order of bony fishes (30 such orders), in the super-order, Teleosti, suborder, Elopidae, family Megalopidae, and of the single genus, *Megalops atlanticus*. Tarpon are coastal inhabitants of North and South America and have a range that extends over 80 degrees of latitude, and east of the Caribbean, all the way to the African coast (Sierra Leone, for example).

Evidence, supported by fossilization, puts the tarpon in a special place: taxonomically unchanged for millions of years. Built-in survival mechanisms are the entire explanation. According to Dr. Roy Crabtree, a marine scientist of considerable note (discoveries relative to bonefish, permit and tarpon), has concluded, to date, that the tarpon is unique amongst its brethren. A tarpon begins life offshore and in its initial leptocephalus stage its appearance is dragon-like, and not even remotely similar to the look of a tarpon. In 6 to 8 weeks the microscopic dragon will have grown to an inch-and-a-half, then begins a metamorphosis in which it shrinks in order to grow. In about three months, the metamorphosis is complete and an inch-long tarpon emerges. These wee tarpon will have started life as many as hundreds of miles offshore, drifted shorewards, and then into the backwaters. In the backwaters is where its unique ability to gulp air comes into play. A tarpon avoids normal predation because it can tolerate waters that are highly saline, fresh, brackish, extremely murky and in a wide range of temperatures.

Tackle: For large tarpon a 12-weight rod (for smaller tarpon a 9/10-weight or less). Backing should be at least 250 yards of 30-pound test Dacron. Class tippets, anywhere from 12- to 20-pound test, and for larger tarpon, 80- to 100-pound-test shock (fluorocarbon seems best).

Flies: Hook sizes 2/0 to 5/0 with 3/0 more common and patterns that are about 2 to 3 inches long. Patterns: Deceivers, Stu Apte-like flies, John Emory's Cockroach, Rabbit Fur, and Whistlers. Also Merkin Crab patterns, and shrimp and baitfish imitations. Primary colors are natural for imitations and for feathery patterns: black, orange, yellow, white, red and grizzly, and some flash can help. NOTE: Baitfish imitations that mimic wide profile species are becoming prevalent, and some guides are starting to use circle hooks.

"Marquesa Keys Tarpon" by Don Ray

Tripletail
LOBOTIDAE, Lobotes surinamensis

DIANE ROME PEEBLES

IGFA World-Record Catches

Line-Class World Record:
40 pounds 13oz.

World Fly Rod Record:
20 pounds

*Florida Record - Line Class:
40 pounds, 13oz. (world record)

Florida Keys Record - Fly Rod:
20 pounds (world record)

Quick ID: Distinctively mottled head and body with tan to very dark brown spotting. Two dark streaks behind eye. NOTE: * Florida record, not Keys record.

CAPTAIN'S NOTES

Tripletail are not a target game fish, anywhere, but they are an excellent fly-fishing opportunity in the Keys. They can be found offshore, but in the Keys they are primarily caught in the western half of Florida Bay (Flamingo) and into the Gulf of Mexico. The tripletail has a unique approach to finding its prey. It, literally, lays on its side, motionless and adrift, usually near debris, weedlines, buoys, channel markers, boards and the like. They'll wait for small fish to think of it as cover, then pounce with surprising speed. Good casting skill is called for when trying to entice a tripletail to the bite; too close an approach (boat) will spook it. A cast that can utilize a current drift to the fish works very well. A cast on top of it will spook it. Once hooked (set the hook hard), the tripletail will surprise any angler with the power of its departure. Generally, it will surface run and jump somewhat porpoise-like, but not acrobatically. The fight will not be long, but will get your attention.

Historic Densities: The western part of Florida Bay and into the Gulf of Mexico. They can be found most of the year with summer putting them in the more western waters of the Keys. November is a good Keys month for tripletail (Florida Bay).

ID: See quick ID. Broad, dark bar (brown) from its eye to across the cheek, and another extending from the upper corner of the eye to the beginning of the dorsal fin. Profile, flat. NOTE: Very sharp gill covers.

Feeds On: All varieties of shrimps and small fishes.

Tackle: A 9-weight covers all occasions. Backing of at least 100 yards of 20-pound test, and WFF or sink-tip. Class tippet of 10-pound test is adequate.

Flies: Streamers, Clousers and Deceivers work well (1/0 to 2/0).

Tuna, Blackfin
SCOMBRIDAE, Thunnus atlanticus

IGFA World-Record Catches

Line-Class World Record:
45 pounds, 8oz.

World Fly-Rod Record:
34 pounds, 3oz.

Florida Keys Record - Line Class:
45 pounds, 8oz. (world record)

Florida Keys Record - Fly Rod:
34 pounds; 3oz. (world record)

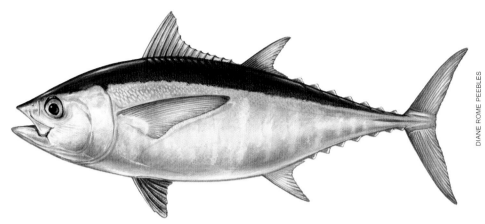

DIANE ROME PEEBLES

Quick ID: Dark black back. Eye large. A broad brownish stripe that runs on the upper sides. Unusually long pectoral fins.

CAPTAIN'S NOTES

The blackfin is a target game fish in the Keys. Almost every IGFA record for this fish comes from the Keys waters. Oddly, it's also a leader-shy fish, even when it's in an aggressive school-feeding profile. A 12-foot leader will be more successful than the usual, short (5-foot or less) open-water leader. Blackfin prefer feeding below the surface, but will naturally come to the surface to chase baits. Trolling with live baits or teaser lures can bring blackfin up, but as is the case with all chumming and teasing, a host of other species can get very interested. When there are a lot of blackfin around, then there's a good chance there are blue marlin below them, be prepared. Good casting capabilities are needed for blackfin. They are a bit spooky. Getting the boat in tight on a school of blackfin will, generally, alarm them. Sometimes, your captain will have to create a down-current chum line of fish parts to help bring blackfin into casting range.

NOTE: Tunas are warm blooded and burn lots of energy when they are hooked. Also, they have no swim bladder, and if exhausted to an inability to swim, they will sink and die. Keys captains prefer you use heavier-weight rods and class tippets than generally prescribed for fish of similar size. The purpose of using a more powerful rod and stronger tippet is to enable catching and releasing, without exhausting a tuna to its death.

> ### TIDBITS
>
> Casting Tip - Heresy
>
> Try using a short punch or jab on both the back and forward casts to get good, tight loops. Do not depend on a lot of wrist.

Historic Densities: Offshore and well beyond the Keys reef tracts. Blackfin are around all year, but by mid-December through May they are a "hot-to-trot" go-to species in the Florida Keys. Blackfin spawn in Keys waters April through November.

ID: See quick ID. All finlets and second dorsal fin are dusky in color with white margin trim. Usually there are 21 to 23 gill rakers on the first arch. Light-colored bars with alternating spots on flanks.

Feeds On: Variety of small, schooling baitfish, and squid as well as shrimp.

Tackle: A 12-weight rod, 200 hundred yards of 20-pound-test dacron backing, fly line floating to sinking, and 14- to 16-pound test class tippet.

Flies: Pilchard imitations, Deceivers, Clouser with weighted eyes, Sar-Mul-Mac and Jose Wejebe's Spanish fly (white & blue).

"Blackfin" by Don Ray

Tunny, Little
SCOMBRIDAE, Euthynnus alletteratus

IGFA World Record Catches

Line-Class World Record:
35 pounds, 2oz.

World Fly-Rod Record:
19 pounds

Florida Keys Record - Line Class:
16 pounds, 8oz.

Florida Keys Record - Fly Rod:
19 pounds (world record)

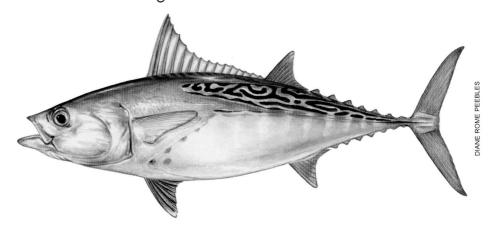

DIANE ROME PEEBLES

Quick ID: Wavy, dark, diagonal bars on rear half of back with 4 to 5 dark spots just below the pectoral fin. NOTE: Key West's, Phil Caputo, a Pulitzer Prize-winning author, holds the world's record for little tunny caught on a fly rod.

CAPTAIN'S NOTES

The little tunny is the most abundant tuna in the Atlantic Ocean. They are not leader or boat shy, nor do they require a great casting skill for a take. Large schools can be seen from a long distance away as they'll boil the surface and attract lots of birds. Little tunny venture nearshore to around the reef line.

Historic Densities: Huge schools from February to September.

ID: See quick ID. Used to be called bonito or false albacore, but got singular classification in 1970. Dusky finlets and its scales are limited to the corselet. Its upper side, worm-like markings are the most distinguishing markings, and separates it from its bonito cousin.

Feeds On: Small fishes, squid and shrimp. Tackle: A 9-weight with backing of 200 yards of 20-pound test. Fly line, WFF to intermediate sinking. Class tippet of 10- to 12-pound test. Flies: Deceivers, large and small, as well as, streamers, bait imitations (glass minnows).

Goliath Grouper (formerly called Jewfish)
SERRANIDAE, Epinephelus itajara

IGFA World-Record Catches

Line-Class World Record:
680 pounds

World Fly-Rod Record:
356 pounds

Florida Keys Record - Line Class:
369 pounds (world record line class)

Florida Keys Record - Fly Rod:
356 pounds (world record)

DIANE ROME PEEBLES

Quick ID: Large adult have an olive cast. Pale to dark brown on head and body with 4 to 5 irregular, broad and darker brown bands. Totally rounded caudal fin.
NOTE: The goliath grouper was renamed. It was previously called jewfish.

CAPTAIN'S NOTES

The goliath grouper is the largest of the groupers. It is also endangered and protected. The chances of a hook-up via the fly rod are slim. It's a deeper-dwelling fish, and it's been over-fished. The goliath, like many groupers, sexually mature late in life (even a large specimen may not be mature enough to procreate). Culling one out of the spawning loop has a dramatic impact on the overall population. Groupers, such as the goliath, are hermaphrodites, able to change sex (to females) when adults. The goliath can be found anywhere from pilings around the main Keys bridges, deep holes or well into the backcountry. Many Keys guides will not intentionally allow you to cast to a goliath grouper.

Gag Grouper
SERRANIDAE, Mycteroperca microlepis

IGFA World-Record Catches

Line Class World Record:
68 pounds, 14oz.

World Fly Rod Record:
7 pounds, 8oz.

Florida Keys Record - Line Class:
55 pounds

Florida Keys Record - Fly Rod:
7 pounds, 8oz. (world record)

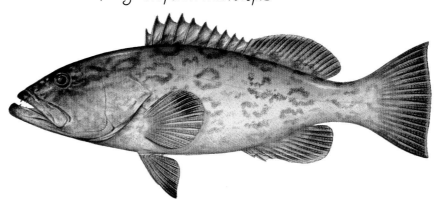

DIANE ROME PEEBLES

Quick ID: Random groupings of dark, worm-like, marbled blotches. Overall pale to dark gray, to olive gray. Anal, pelvic and caudal fins are blackish with a bluish outer edge. NOTE: Every world record for the gag grouper, caught on a fly rod, came from Keys waters.

CAPTAIN'S NOTES

A large gag grouper would be a rare find when fly-fishing. They are normally a deep hole, reef or otherwise deep-water fish. Smaller specimens are far more likely in shallower waters.

TIDBITS

Casting Tip - Let the rod do the work

The more the rod flexes in the back and forward casts, the more power (less tiring). Let the rod do the work.

Ladyfish
ELOPIDAE, Elops saurus

DIANE ROME PEEBLES

IGFA World-Record Catches

Line-Class World Record:
6 pounds

World Fly-Rod Record:
5 pounds, 4oz.

Florida Keys Record - Line Class:
6 pounds (world record)

Florida Keys Record - Fly Rod:
5 pounds, 4oz. (world record)

Quick ID: Similar to a juvenile tarpon, but its length limit is about 39 inches. Small scales. Most ladyfish in the Keys are in the 1- to 3-pound class.

CAPTAIN'S NOTES

Ladyfish are a backcountry species and predominantly an Upper Keys (backcountry) game fish. They are not targeted, but when your guide spots them, they are worth your while as they are as acrobatic as their tarpon cousins. Your guide will usually see them from a distance chasing baitfish. Once engaged, they can provide hours of light-rod (5-weight) action. Use small tarpon flies.

Tuna, Skipjack
SCOMBRIDAE, Katsuwonus pelamis

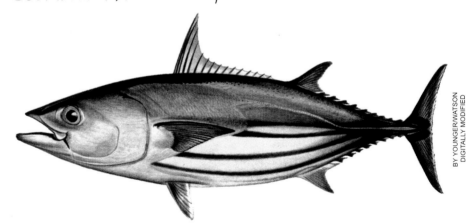

BY YOUNGER/WATSON
DIGITALLY MODIFIED

IGFA World-Record Catches

Line-Class World Record:
41 pounds, 12oz.

World Fly-Rod Record:
16 pounds, 1oz.

Florida Keys Record - Line Class:
N/A

Florida Keys Record - Fly Rod:
N/A

Quick ID: Clearly distinguished from all other similar species by the absence of markings on the back and 4 to 6 prominent black stripes on a silvery belly.

CAPTAIN'S NOTES

Skipjack tuna are very much a part of the Keys gamefish population, but currently there are no catches that qualify as an IGFA record. Lots of skipjack are around all summer in deep water around wrecks and reefs. The population increases in August, September (prime) and October. They will run with blackfin and yellowfin tunas. Tend to form large schools. Fish the same as for blackfin, including flies.

Tuna, Yellowfin
SCOMBRIDAE, *Thunnus albacares*

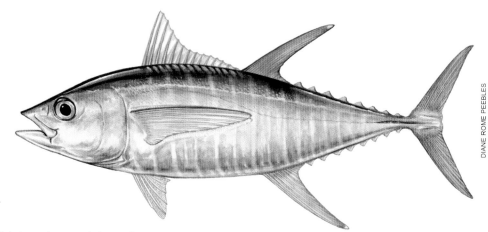

DIANE ROME PEEBLES

Quick ID: Golden stripe on sides. All finlets and second dorsal fin are yellow.

CAPTAIN'S NOTES

Yellowfin tuna are caught every year in the Keys, but some years are better than others, according to Captain Jim Sharpe, Sea Boots Outfitters & Charters, Big Pine Key, FL. The primary months are mid-December through January, and any time bonito and blackfin are running. A fly-fishing client of Jim's recently had a yellowfin on in the 200-pound-plus category, but it was eaten by a shark less than 50 feet from the boat. Several yellowfin, well over 200 pounds, are caught every year. Teasing with live pilchards seems to produce the best results. The yellowfin is not, however, a targeted species in the Keys. Yellowfin prefer the 120- to 140-fathom water column. Rods in the 14- to 18-weight lifting class are necessary. Being able to turn this big fish is critical.

"Approaching Front" by Don Ray

Rainbow Runner

CARANGIDAE, Elagatis bipinnulata

IGFA World-Record Catches

Line-Class World Record:
33-pounds. 10-oz

World Fly-Rod Record:
14 pounds

Florida Keys Record - Line Class:
17 pounds

Florida Keys Record - Fly Rod:
8 pounds, 10oz (world record line class)

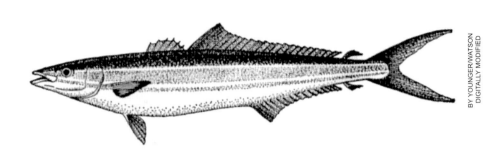

Quick ID: Slender and long in profile, resembling a cobia. However, at first in-water sighting they can easily be mistaken for dolphin due to coloration. Greenish-blue above with stripes on its sides. Dark blue stripe running from mouth to caudal fin with a narrower pale blue stripe running below the eyes and just below the darker blue stripe. Whitish to yellowish below. NOTE: Lefty Kreh, Steve Abel (Abel Reels) and Stu Apte (Keys legendary guide) all hold world records (line class). Kreh's and Abel's on a fly and Apte's on conventional tackle.

CAPTAIN'S NOTES

Rainbow runners are fast, surface-busting and schooling. They act very much like a dolphin in their surface-feeding profile. This jack is not a targeted species, but when they pop up they can provide long-lasting light-rod enjoyment. In the spring they will chase baits well inshore. Fished for like any jack. When hooked, you can expect a jack-like fight, but with unique, long-surface runs. Flies: (see crevalle and horseye).

Snapper, Gray (mangrove)

LUTJANGIDAE, Lutjanus griseus

IGFA World Record Catches

The IGFA does not currently recognize the gray snapper (mangrove) as a line-class game fish, nor as a fly-rod game fish. All Tackle is recognized, (17pounds./Florida).

Quick ID: No distinct patterns, but dark reddish or copper tone. One dark stripe running from snout tip through the eye, angled toward the dorsal fin. A young, small specimen will have a bluish line running along the snout, ending below the eye.

CAPTAIN'S NOTES

Fly-fished for in the same manner as mutton snapper. A large specimen would be 10 pounds, but likely catches in the Keys would be under 5 pounds.

Bet You Didn't Know

Following are a few additional IGFA world records caught in the Florida Keys:

1. Red hind (*Epinephelus guttatus*) 6lb. 1oz. - Dry Tortugas
2. Yellow jack (*Caranx bartholomaei*) 23lb. 8oz. - Key Largo
3. Yellowfin mojarra (*Gerres cinereus*) 1lb. 3oz. - Marathon
4. Green moray (*Gymnothorax funebris*) 33lb. 8oz. - Marathon
5. Spotted moray (*Gymnothorax moringa*) 5lb. 8oz. - Marathon
6. Caribbean reef shark (*Carcharhinus perezi*) 154lb. - Molasses Reef
7. Nurse shark (*Ginglymostoma cirratum*) 210lb. - Bahia Honda Channel
8. Schoolmaster snapper (*Lutjanus apodus*) 13lb. 4oz. - North Key Largo
9. Roughtail stingray (*Dasyatis centroura*) 405lb. - Islamorada
10. Sand tilefish (*Malacanthus plumieri*) 2lb. 4oz. - Key Largo
11. Gag grouper (*Mycteroperca microlepis*) 7lb. 8oz. - Key West (fly rod)

Many, many other world-record catches come from Keys waters; line class for both conventional and fly rod, women, juniors, and several special IGFA club categories.

For absolutely everything you might want to know about the Keys species records, and more, contact:

International Game Fish Association
(954-927-2628 or fax 954-924-4299)
www.igfa.org / e-mail: igfahq@aol.com

Baitfish

A few of the many species of baitfish found swimming in the Keys waters.

The rainbow runner and blue runner are primarily baits for larger fish (along with many others), but when encountered, these two underappreciated species can produce some great lightweight rod action. The rainbow runner is actually considered a game fish in many parts of the world, and the Keys have produced world records for both line class, conventional tackle and fly rod; respectively, 17 pounds. and 8 pounds 10 oz. The all-tackle world record for the rainbow runner is 37 pounds 9 oz. (Mexico), and the all-tackle record for the blue runner is 11 pounds 2 oz. (Alabama).

Baitfish have many commercial uses: fish meal, fish oil, pet food and fertilizer. The Florida Keys waters host about half (2 dozen) of the world's known baitfish species of which there are 50. In 1980, according to FMRI, the commercial baitfish harvest in Florida waters was a severely depleting 37,000,000 pounds. Presently, catch-limit regulations keep the harvesting down to around 10,000,000 pounds a year (State of Florida). The increase in sport fishing has created demands for fresh and live baits, which also keeps the pressure on baitfish populations. Baitfish are an incredibly valuable source of food for sub-adult Keys game fish, from as far away as the open ocean to as near as the estuaries of the backcountry.

Baitfish nicknames have always been regionally developed and that makes properly identifying baitfish difficult. For example, there are five species of 'halfbeaks' (balao and ballyhoo, for example) and 12 species of flying fishes. Most all of the latter can be found in the Keys waters. In the Keys, a few varieties of menhaden are called pilchards.

FISH NOTES

Over millions of years, fish species developed many unique sensory organs, anatomical anomalies and survival techniques, all helping to preserve their progeny, and thus, species. All of this is well in-tune with Darwinism. Many specialties of survival are unique only to a single species, or family of fish. Survival skills for game fish found in the Keys are many. Here are a few: lateral line for detecting and placing objects as well as orientation to the earth's gravitational pull (balance), hearing (through an inner ear), and in some species (tarpon), in

---

TIDBITS

Current research indicates that a fish played out to dead-tired will most likely die when released. Not good, unless you plan on having it for tablefare.

Fish catching just for the boast of it (killing) is now bad form and runs against the conservation grain. If your fish is not scheduled for tablefare, then it should be safely released back into its natural environment.

Today, a good taxidermist can produce a more life-like replica of your trophy from a simple girth and length (fork) measurement. They also look better than skin mounts and last almost indefinitely.

Remember the fish you release today will live to clone many more just like itself. The Florida Keys fly-fishing guides and offshore captains all practice catch and release. Your cooperation is appreciated.

Ballyhoo - to 16 inches in length.

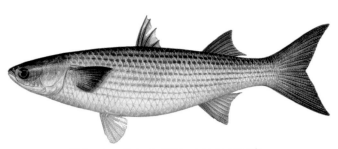

Striped mullet - to 20 inches in length.

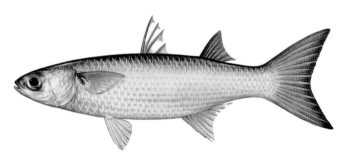

Blue runner - to 4 pounds in size.

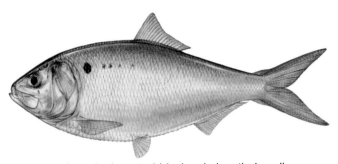

Gulf menhaden - to 14 inches in length. Locally (Keys) called 'pilchards,' 'razor bellies' and 'sandy keys.'

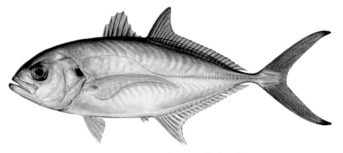

Fantail mullet - to 18 inches in length.

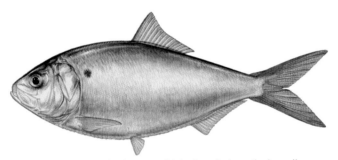

Yellowfin menhaden - to 14 inches in length. Locally (Keys) called 'pilchards,' 'razor bellies' and 'sandy keys.'

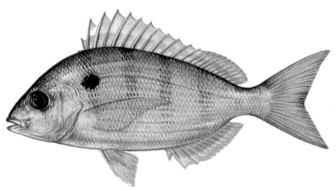

Pinfish - to 14 inches in length, but more normal is 8 inches.

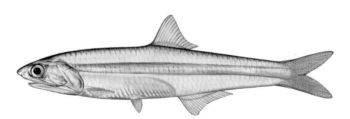

Striped anchovy - to 6 inches in length.

conjunction with their swim bladder. In some species, hearing is used to communicate with like species. Nares (nostrils) detect odors so efficiently that many fish species can distinguish elements within a chemical compound. Internal thermometers, whether cold blooded or not, keep almost all species in thermoclines primary to their life's needs. Taste, which is a function of a fish's lips and mouth, distinguishes between salty, bitter, sweet, acidic, and, unlike humanoids, lets them know whether it's good for them or not.

NOTE: Large predatory fish found in the Keys, and many schooling baitfish, have large eyes. Marine scientists have discovered that predatory fish will, predominantly, focus on their prey's eyes at the moment preceding the final attack, and that a darting fly/lure increases interest. Paradoxically, when a tarpon is about to strike (gulp a fly), it's best to rest and let the gulper gulp.

Interestingly, many baitfish have the ability to camouflage their eyes by changing coloration, this is particularly true of reef-dwelling species.

GAMEFISH BEST-BET CALENDAR
AN AVERAGE YEAR IN THE FLORIDA KEYS

Any prime-time calendar is open to much debate, if not pure criticism. Year to year can be different with regard to show up and departure times for many species. In some instances more than a month either way. In addition, species not mentioned as suspects on anyone's best-bet calendar can turn up in any venue or month and become new targets in any given year. For example, not too many years ago no one in the Lower Keys thought of catching a redfish on the flats because they were not there. Today, redfish are in the Lower Keys on the flats as well as on near-shore wrecks where reds of 40 pounds and up have been taken.

The Keys' fishing turf runs from lower Biscayne Bay to beyond the Marquesas; Florida Bay to the Everglades, well into the western and northern portions of the Gulf of Mexico, the southern shores of the respective Keys to well beyond the Florida Reef Tract and many miles into the Gulf Stream. All of the latter comprises several thousand square miles of vastly differing waters, and an unbelievable number of true gamefish species. The Keys, as a fishery, should not be underestimated, they remain one of the world's best sportfishing destinations.

Whether you've come for marlin, bonefish, redfish, wahoo, tarpon, or any number of other offshore or inshore species, you'll need a guide or offshore captain who knows his stuff. You can come to the Keys any time of the year and find plenty of fish if you are with a good guide or offshore captain. A guide or offshore captain will know where to look, know what's possible and what's not. Further, you can be assured he will not consult our best-bet calendar or anyone else's. Any best-bet calendar is merely a rough estimate based on generalities.

The game fish of the Keys, or elsewhere in the world, react to many things: weather, wind direction, sunlight, water temperature, bait availability, their own biological clock needs, the biological clocks of other species, water clarity and a myriad of sub-category possibilities. Therefore, you must shower a bit of salt on our best-bet calendar, as well as all others.

FLATS

Flats in the Florida Keys, as elsewhere in the world, are large areas of salt water with decidedly skinny water of just inches to a few feet. In the unique coordinates of the Keys, there are thousands of shoreline miles of flats on both the bayside (Florida Bay and Gulf of Mexico) and oceanside (Atlantic Ocean). The flats run from Biscayne Bay to the Marquesas Keys. They are interrupted after Key West with open water, but restart in the Key West National Wildlife Refuge after which there's more open water and then flats again on the only atoll in the Atlantic Ocean, the Marquesas Keys. The entire shorelines of all 1,700 islands that make up the Florida Keys are surrounded by flats. Many have internal lagoons and some are large enough to have named bays. All these islands interrupt tidal flows, have channels and nuances of bottom geography that can produce varied tidal flow speeds. All of which complicate the fish-catching equation. Also, there are the tide differences of the Gulf of Mexico (one high and one low) and the Atlantic Ocean (two highs and two lows). Where the latter mix makes reading the effects on fishing all but impossible, except for the skilled guides.

The flats real estate in the Keys sustains life for hundreds of organisms per square yard, and some grow up to be 100-pound tarpon or 15-pound bonefish. The health of the flats fishery is one of the dip-sticks by which the entire Keys eco-system is measured.

BACKCOUNTRY - EVERGLADES

Backcountry goes from Key Largo to Key West and it is all bayside, or gulf side. North Key Largo backcountry is the most westerly and southern portions of Biscayne Bay, but

---

TIDBITS
ACTIVISTS
Many animal activists are appalled by the pain fishermen cause a fish. Unfortunately, they support their programmed prejudices with false information. Only thick-skinned fish, like those sport-fished for in the Keys, have nerve endings, but it is limited to their skin. The message to the brain when hooked by an angler or bitten by another fish is, however, unrelated to pain. In fact, all fish lack a region in their brain capable of generating the impulse of pain. Far worse for a fish is to overplay it or mishandle it. Its worst enemy remains over-fishing and pollution.

A BONE'S EYE VIEW
Bonefish have eyelids, but are not so fully developed as to do anything more than restrict the amount of light entering the retina. Some fish have pigments in their eyes, which allows them to modify the light entering the retina.

FAKERS
Baitfish will form schools that are so tightly packed marine scientists believe they can appear to would-be predators as one, seriously large fish.

HARD LIFE
Most baitfish only live a year or two and die of natural causes or, in the usual Darwinian way, by getting picked off when weakening.

FRISKY FELLAS
Almost all baitfish spawn many times a year. In the Keys waters, spring and summer are prime. The exception is the gulf menhaden, which spawns in estuaries in the fall and winter. Menhaden also cross breed.

GYPSIES ALL
Baitfish travel, generally, north to south, inshore to offshore and move, as a rule, about seven miles a day.

NIGHTLIFE IN THE KEYS
Baitfish are also prone to being night feeders, staying deeper, generally, during the day and coming closer to the surface at night.

---

includes Card Sound, Barnes Sound, Blackwater Sound, Little Blackwater Sound, Long Sound and Manatee Bay. All of the latter are accessible from Florida Bay. Local guides divide backcountry real estate into "near" backcountry and "far" backcountry, and the line of disembarkation is always a point of interpretation. "Near" backcountry being pretty much most of the mangrove islands, but not all, that stretch into Florida Bay and the Gulf of Mexico. "Far" backcountry, all seem to agree, is near the Everglades, the Everglades shoreline from east and west of Flamingo, as well as the more open water of Florida Bay and Gulf of Mexico. The freshwater outflow into Florida Bay, the influence of the Gulf of Mexico tides, and the tides of the Atlantic Ocean make these backcountry waters a cauldron of sea life, and as complex a tide puzzle as exists in the world. Master it and you are a guide. A word of caution for do-it-yourself folks: The backcountry is more than complicated and can be treacherous. An unscheduled overnight tide stuck in the mud, is not a fun thing to do, especially if it's a windless night. The mosquitoes can make a grown man cry.

OFFSHORE

Keys big-game fishing begins in the deep water off Biscayne Bay National Park and generally ends around the Dry Tortugas. Big-game fishing is also a part of the Gulf of Mexico. In our best-bet calendar we are not specific to species found just inside, just beyond the reef line, nor of those species found in aqua-green water beyond the reef line, or the blue water of the Gulf Stream. The Gulf of Mexico is a huge body of water and its fishable waters from Keys ports are, generally, near the western Lower Keys and Key West. Gulf of Mexico waters north of Cape Sable are not normally a day trip and as such are not covered in this book.

NOTE: Offshore captains in the Keys travel considerable distances to find fish and heed no stop sign or line we may have arbitrarily defined as beginning and ending their pursuits.

JANUARY

Prime for sailfish in Upper Keys. Seatrout in the Gulf of Mexico along with Spanish mackerel. King Mackerel and blackfin tuna. Jack crevalle and cero mackerel inside reef edges. Barracuda throughout Keys (flats). Ladyfish in Florida Bay backcountry. Cobia around wrecks and flats near mangrove (best Lower Keys). Wahoo, sharks, redfish, and snappers. Snook (closed season).

FEBRUARY

Prime for sailfish in the Upper Keys to Marathon, or beyond, if weather is cooperative. African pompano on wrecks with Key West being best. Bonefish Upper Keys mudding in deeper water. Barracuda throughout Keys. Permit in the Lower Keys, Key West and the Marquesas Keys. Wahoo, mackerels (king, Spanish and cero), blackfin tuna, little tunny, cobia, redfish, snook and seatrout. Sharks more prevalent. Tarpon could show up.

MARCH - TARPON RUN

Prime time for permit in the Lower Keys, Key West and the Marquesas Keys. Some mackerels (king, Spanish and cero). Sailfish start working down towards Lower Keys. Dolphin could turn on. Big schools of jack crevalle down the reef line. Cobia, African pompano, wahoo, blackfin tuna, little tunny, ladyfish, sharks, seatrout, snook and redfish. Mutton, although rare, could show on the flats. Always mangrove snappers. Big tarpon show up at Government Cut.

APRIL - TARPON RUN

Big tarpon everywhere if you know where to look. Bonefish in Biscayne Bay and Upper Keys. Sailfish Lower Keys and Key West. Cobia, wahoo, jack crevalle, ladyfish, little tunny, dolphin, permit, blackfin tuna, sharks, redfish and snook. Mutton, although rare, could show on the flats. Always mangrove snappers. NOTE: White marlin, although their stocks are greatly diminished worldwide, could show April through August.

MAY - TARPON RUN

Tarpon are prime time this month. Bonefish and permit are also prime. Sailfish Lower Keys and Key West best. Blue marlin. Plenty of dolphin, wahoo, little tunny, blackfin tuna, sharks and snook. Mutton and mangrove snappers.

JUNE - TARPON RUN

Lots of bonefish, early morning and late in day. Tarpon in channels at dawn and dusk, as well as backcountry. Blue marlin, blackfin tuna, and dolphin. Permit at one point will begin leaving to spawn June/July, but when they return they are hungry. Snook season closed (June, July and August).

JULY AND AUGUST

Oddly, one of the best times to fish the Keys. Just about everything possible to catch is here: Dolphin, blue marlin, little tunny, tuna, tarpon, bonefish and permit. Mutton and mangrove snappers on the flats.
These two months are our favorite.

TIDBITS

Phil Caputo, Pulitzer Prize winner and Key West resident, described fishermen, marlin fishermen in particular, in terms of having a dementia he calls "The Ahab Complex" in his 1988 essay by the same name. " . . . *an obsession to pursue and conquer a monster of the depths regardless of the consequences to one's bank account, career and family life.*"

Caputo won his Pulitzer Prize for investigative reporting on Chicago's corrupt political system. He also wrote the definitive book on the Viet Nam War, *A Rumor Of War.*

SEPTEMBER

Blue marlin, skipjack tuna, little tunny, snook, redfish, big tarpon start returning, permit, seatrout, tripletail (Florida Bay) and bonefish.

OCTOBER - BONES AND REDS

King mackerel, skipjack tuna, ladyfish, snook, redfish, seatrout, tarpon, tripletail (Florida Bay) and bonefish. Mutton and mangrove snappers on the flats.

NOVEMBER

Juvenile sailfish may show, barracuda, ladyfish, sharks, mackerels, snook, redfish and seatrout. Bonefish and permit.

DECEMBER

Sailfish arrive, juveniles first, cobia, barracuda, ladyfish, sharks, African pompano, blackfin tuna, mackerels (cero and kings), snook (15th starts closed season), redfish and seatrout.

NOTE: Permit are far more plentiful in the Lower Keys, Key West and the Marquesas Keys, as are bonefish in the Upper Keys and Middle Keys. The Lower Keys, Key West and the Marquesas Keys are considered by 'permitarians' to be mecca. The world's largest bonefish belong to the Upper Keys with Islamorada always setting records, and usually it's in October.

MORE CALENDAR NOTES

Cobia are distributed throughout the Keys in the winter months, but stay a part of the scene in the Lower Keys and especially Key West year round. Tarpon are residents of the Keys throughout the year, and are seen and caught in every month, but the spring is prime. The spring tarpon run brings the triple-digit fish. The spring run can start as early as January and last, sometimes, into July. By June many tarpon have already migrated up the Atlantic and west coasts of Florida.

A net ban and slowly improving upstream water hydraulics in the Everglades has improved the distribution and populations of seatrout, snook and redfish. Seatrout are now being taken in historic habitats that had been void of them for many years. Also, redfish are showing up all the way down into the Lower Keys, and snook seem to be where they were not just a few years ago. Dolphin are possible to find in any month. The yellowfin tuna is highly migratory and its visits to the Keys are never a calendar sure bet, but it's bankable that they will come. When they do show, it's usually in the spring for a few days or a week, and again in the early Dcember to January. Occasionally, black drum can be found in the northwest corner of Florida Bay during the winter months. You'll know they are there as their croaking can be heard for some distance.

THE TERM OUTFITTER

Well-meaning motel, hotel and resort staff will often tell their guests that they can put them in touch with expert fly-fishing guides or offshore captains. They mean no harm and only want to serve. Too often, however, they provide uninformed and, thus, disappointing referrals. Generally, well-intentioned staff personnel do not have a clue about who in their area is, in fact, an expert fly-fishing guide or offshore captain. Some motels, hotels and resorts have referral arrangements with guides and offshore captains, but not too often a reference point from which to judge credentials. There are a few exceptions.

Here's a sound piece of advice for having a good fly-fishing experience in the Keys, and you can take it to the bank. Make all arrangements for an outing through a legitimate outfitter, qualified fly shop or marina (see below). The entities we have listed have the preferred list of guides and offshore captains, all of whom have an earned reputation. You can totally rely on them. You can, of course, get lucky with your own search, but there is no need to roll the dice, and it won't save you a dime. If you do randomly select a guide or offshore captain, and there's no good reason to do so, you should always ask for several references, and are well advised to follow through by calling those references. Paradoxically, there are many expert fly-fishing guides and offshore captains in the Keys that are not attached to an outfitter, fly shop, marina, hotel or any other establishment that could possibly offer a referral. These guides and offshore captains, however, have an earned, stand-alone reputation and their bookings reflect that.

THE VERY BEST ADVICE

Below, you'll find a brief review of the best outfitters and fly shops. They all have proven track records, and make a living from satisfying their clients. All of their histories and reputations have been earned. For many years they have proven reliable at having highly skilled fly-fishing professionals available for you to book, and they know which guides and offshore captains have personalities that can stand up for a day, a week or a longer engagement. Remember, a date alone on the water in a small boat with someone out on work release, or an attitude, may not be what you want.

BUD N' MARY'S

Bud N' Mary's (Offshore Fly Fishing), Richard Stanczyk, P. O. Box 628, MM 79.8 (oceanside), Islamorada, FL 33306. 305-664-2461, FX 305-664-5592 or toll free 800-742-7945.

Do not expect to walk into Bud n' Mary's Marina and find anything you'll need for a fly-fishing outing. This operation is strictly a charter-boat marina. What separates it from most others is that they have the best offshore fly fishing captains in the Upper Keys. Skip Nielsen, before he retired, kept his boat here. Owner Richard Stanczyk is also a remarkable offshore fly-fisherman, as is his teenage son, Nick. NOTE: Nick recently caught a near-world-record bull dolphin on his own hand-tied fly in a tournament held in Ft. Lauderdale (see flies).

SEA BOOTS OUTFITTERS & CHARTERS

Sea Boots Outfitters & Charters, Captain Jim Sharpe, MM 30 Bayside, 29975 US I, Box 430652, Big Pine Key, FL

33043-0652. Toll free 800-238-1746. Shop telephone (ask for Christina) 305-745-1530 or FX 305-872-0780. Email: seaboots5@aol.com or get them online, www.seaboots.com. NOTE: Website has photo gallery and you can shop on-line.

Captain Jim Sharpe and his wife, Barbara, own Sea Boots and their daughter, Christina, runs it. It is probably the best-stocked fly-tier's shop in the Keys. Expert and many-times-published tier, Captain Lenny Moffo, is Sea Boots' consultant. Sea Boots is also a full-service fly shop, flies to reels and everything in between. Captain Jim Sharpe is an offshore fly-fishing expert. He wrote the definitive book on dolphin, *Dolphin: The Perfect Gamefish*, which also includes how to go about catching all the major offshore game fish in the Keys. Jim has also written many articles, regularly consults with fishery researchers, hosts a lot of in-the-news personalities from around the world, and is very involved in the Lower Keys and Key West offshore tournament scene. When you are in the Lower Keys you could not be in better hands than in Sea Boots.' They have a handle on absolutely everything going on in their neck of the Keys. The Lower Keys are the least-fished waters in the Keys, and most of the backcountry is in the Great Heron National Wildlife Refuge, so there are no interruptions from those horrid personal watercraft. Anyone wishing to take on this enormous piece of healthy fishing real estate can rely on a check-in at Sea Boots. You can book Captain Lenny Moffo or Captain Tim Carlile through Sea Boots Outfitters & Charters.

THE FLORIDA KEYS OUTFITTERS

The Florida Keys Outfitters, Sandy Moret, P.O.B 603, Islamorada, FL 33036. Telephone: 305-664-5423 or FX 305-664-5501. Email Sue (suefko@bellsouth.net) or Sandy (flkeyout@bellsouth.net). Online at flakeysoutfitters.com

Sandy Moret's fly shop is dedicated to fly-fishing and acknowledged by all as the premier technical fly shop in the Florida Keys. Sandy has been at the business of fly-fishing the Keys for more than two decades and this is reflected in the whole of the shop, a no-nonsense place all about fly-fishing. The shop's staff plain-talks on every part of the subject of fly-fishing: flies, rods, reels, line, and rigging, as well as the seasons, even the upcoming tides fishing possibilities. The shop is 'behold' stocked. They also have every qualified and relevant book, rod, reel, line and accouterments thereof, as well as all your practical clothing needs. Sue Moret, Sandy's wife, is very active in the business, and she is also an expert fly-fisherman. You can also book Drew Moret or Dustin Huff (Marathon), through The Florida Keys Outfitters.

WORLD WIDE SPORTSMAN

World Wide Sportsman, George Hommell, Jr. and Doug Berry, 81576 Overseas Highway, Islamorada, FL 33036. Telephone 305-664-4615 or toll free 800-327-2880 and FX: 305-517-2618. Online at www.worldwidesportsman.com.

World Wide Sportsman (WWS) is a signature tour stop kind of place and it's another of Johnny Morris' mega outdoor store successes. It is a huge and classy retail store that is dedicated, solely, to the outdoor experience. It has just about everything you would expect and more, but is not, of course, 100% devoted to fly-fishing. The staff assigned to the fly-fishing section is, however, clued in about things fly-fishing in the Keys. You will find them to always be extremely helpful and very reliable. Their offerings in fly-fishing equipment are excellent.

Two of the best captains to have ever cast a line in the Keys waters are now executives at WWS, Captain George Hommell, Jr. (President George Bush's former personal guide) and Captain Doug Berry. Doug captained the first offshore charter boat in the Florida Keys regularly equipped with fly-fishing gear. Doug also ushered in a now-standard practice of tagging billfish.

The WWS's second floor houses the Keys' largest travel agency. They can book you into and out of the Keys, including accommodations, or to any premier fishing or hunting lodge, anyplace in the world.

NOTE: World Wide Sportsman (2nd floor) is also where you'll find the very popular Zane Grey Bar. The landmark Islamorada Fish Company is on the WWS grounds. There you can order one of the best fish sandwiches in the Keys and enjoy eating it while overlooking Florida Bay backcountry.

THE SALTWATER ANGLER

Dave Maynard, a long-time friend and client of Jeff's, bought The Saltwater Angler. Although Jeff is now only a consultant, Curtis White and Ken Ivey have made the transition seamless. Flyfishing is still spoken well. The Saltwater Angler, Key West Hilton Resort & Marina, 243 Front Street, Key West, FL 33040. Telephone 305 294 3248 or FX 305 296 7272. Online at www.saltwaterangler.com.

Former owner, Jeffrey Cardenas is the quintessential gentleman and renaissance man. He guided in Key West, professionally, for over 25 years and holds innumerable tournament titles. He also wrote *Marquesa: A Time And Place With Fish*, a stand-alone literary achievement, and his new book, *Sea Level: Adventures Of A Saltwater Angler*, is another gem. While his store is clearly set-up to meet the Key West cruise ships at wharf side, the fly-shop section is a store within a store. It has an enormous selection of everything one would need for any kind of saltwater fly-fishing outing. The Saltwater Angler can also put anyone in touch with the very best fly-fishing guides or offshore captains familiar with Key West, backcountry or Marquesa fisheries. In Key West, it's still The Saltwater Angler. You can also book Captain Tom Rowland or Captain Bob Trosset through The Saltwater Angler.

THE FLORIDA KEYS FLY FISHING SCHOOL

It is not our intention to be less than democratic in the presentation of services available in the Florida Keys to the saltwater fly-fishing visitor, but it would be a disservice not to put Sandy Moret's Florida Keys Fly Fishing School, into some perspective. Without editorial hesitation, Sandy's school is far-and-away the best saltwater fly-casting/fishing school in the world. Many, many agree with us.

Over the years, Sandy Moret's school has had more than casual mentions in the *Robb Report, Men's Journal, Polo Magazine, Travel South, Boating For Women, Power MotorYacht, Saltwater Sportsman* and there have never been shortages of positive comments in the South Florida newspapers. More importantly, however, are its graduates opinions: "Two Thumbs Up."

Featured instructors are: Sandy Moret himself (winner of numerous fishing tournament titles), Steve Rajeff, 37 casting titles to his name (try 306 feet with a two-handed rod and 248 feet with a single-handed rod), Rick Ruoff, Orvis-endorsed guide and Ph.D. marine biologist, and Steve Huff (guided to more world records and major tournament wins combined than any guide in history). Steve is considered by his guide peers to be the most accomplished fisherman to have ever cast a line in the Keys. Also teaching in the school are: Chico Fernandez (published several fly-tying, fly-casting, destination fishing videos, and has written expansively on the subject of fish catching), Flip Pallot, whom most of you will recognize as having been the regular host on "Walkers Cay Chronicles" (ESPN Saturday morning), Craig Brewer, past Commodore of The Florida Guides Association, and Tim Klein, who is considered the most talented fly-casting instructor in the world, as well as holder of several tournament titles.

One of the best values of the entire experience, aside from walking away a lot smarter about fishing salt water and being more comfortable with rod and reel than when you arrived, is enjoying the easy balance with which these professionals carry themselves amongst academy participants. Participants are at instant ease among celebrities; never intimidated. The instructors are, of course, impressive, but they are more tuned to the participants' gains than their own stature. It seems to be a Keys

---

TIDBITS
Tarpon

The estimated survival rate for a hooked, caught and released tarpon is 96%. A permit ($50) is required for anyone who wants to kill a tarpon. Today, however, taxidermists can reproduce a perfect mount by simply providing a girth and length measurement. These mounts are far more realistic than the old skin mounts ever were, and they last forever.

Please practice catch and release.

---

thing, being natural, and everyone who comes here finds it refreshing. Everyone knows, right away, that these guys are all comfortable with themselves, love what they do for a living, and find great pleasure in sharing what they know. The whole experience makes for a quite a memorable learning experience, especially if you decide to stay at Cheeca Lodge. See above, Florida Keys Fly Fishing Outfitters, for contact information about the school.

ALL THE REST

In addition to the aforementioned, there are many marinas and stores throughout the Keys that purport to be in the business of satisfying a fly-fisherman's needs, but none are, as of this writing. Some establishments embrace fishing directly or indirectly, such as bait shops. These shops will have some conventional tackle, but seldom any fly-fishing equipment. There are also other shops that could have anything from used fishing equipment to books about the subject of fishing. All delights for those who have time to rummage.

Captain Duane Baker takes Captain Keith Abbott out for a shot at some bonefish.
A chilly winter day (83 degrees). Upper Keys 1998.

PHOTO PROVIDED COURTESY OF VAN RENZBERG

CHAPTER VI

FLY PATTERNS THAT CATCH FISH IN THE FLORIDA KEYS

Captain Lenny Moffo And Others Share Their Choices.

Most of the fly patterns shown below were originally tied, and photographed, by Captain Lenny Moffo. The name assigned to each pattern was selected by Captain Lenny Moffo, and many are very near cousins of more recognizable patterns that have already been named. It is, however, always the prerogative of a professional tier to name his work. For a wider choice of patterns, refer back to each species.

NOTE: Almost all fly patterns are simply modifications, or hybrids, of former patterns, tied anew to meet the peculiarities of local conditions. There are, of course, exceptions, but not too many. Each of the following fly patterns are proven fish-catchers, but they are not the only patterns that work well in the Keys. Always defer to your guide or captain's selections.

Several pattern illustrations were drawn from Captain Moffo's photos (watercolor and pencil) by Floridian, and regionally well-known artist, Frank Zorman.

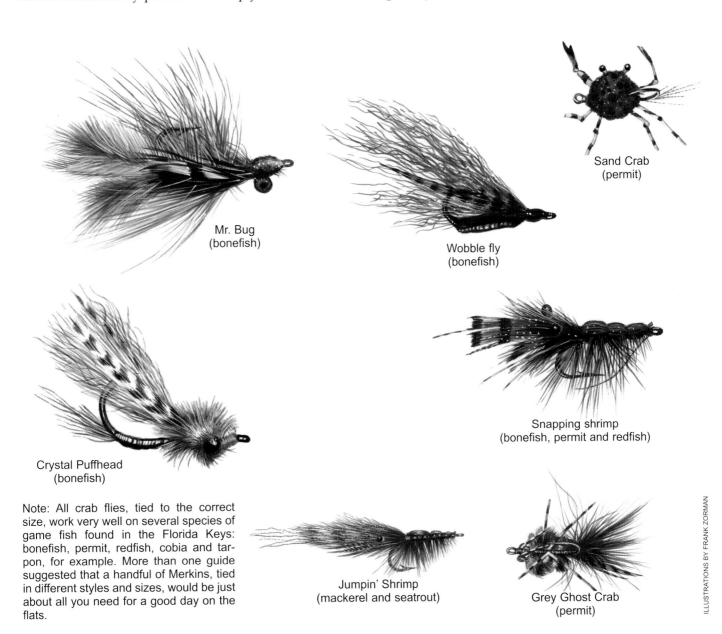

Mr. Bug
(bonefish)

Wobble fly
(bonefish)

Sand Crab
(permit)

Crystal Puffhead
(bonefish)

Snapping shrimp
(bonefish, permit and redfish)

Note: All crab flies, tied to the correct size, work very well on several species of game fish found in the Florida Keys: bonefish, permit, redfish, cobia and tarpon, for example. More than one guide suggested that a handful of Merkins, tied in different styles and sizes, would be just about all you need for a good day on the flats.

Jumpin' Shrimp
(mackerel and seatrout)

Grey Ghost Crab
(permit)

ILLUSTRATIONS BY FRANK ZORMAN

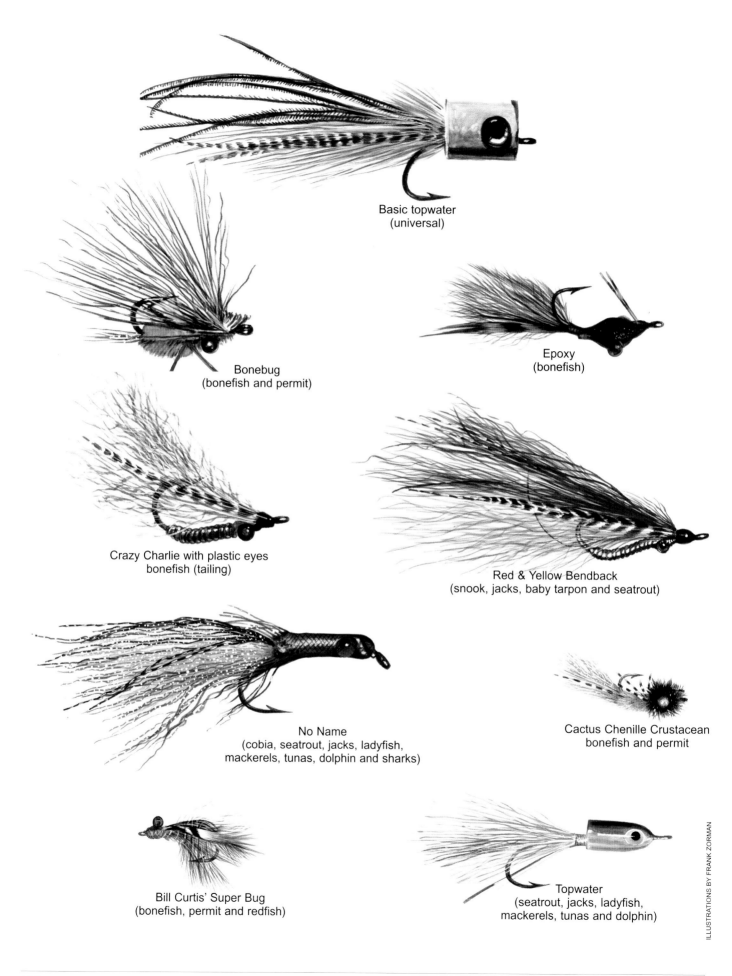

Basic topwater
(universal)

Bonebug
(bonefish and permit)

Epoxy
(bonefish)

Crazy Charlie with plastic eyes
bonefish (tailing)

Red & Yellow Bendback
(snook, jacks, baby tarpon and seatrout)

No Name
(cobia, seatrout, jacks, ladyfish,
mackerels, tunas, dolphin and sharks)

Cactus Chenille Crustacean
bonefish and permit

Bill Curtis' Super Bug
(bonefish, permit and redfish)

Topwater
(seatrout, jacks, ladyfish,
mackerels, tunas and dolphin)

ILLUSTRATIONS BY FRANK ZORMAN

Tube Fly
(billfish and offshore)

Black Death
(tarpon)

Cochran's Black Fly
(tarpon)

Feathered Sea Pup
(tarpon)

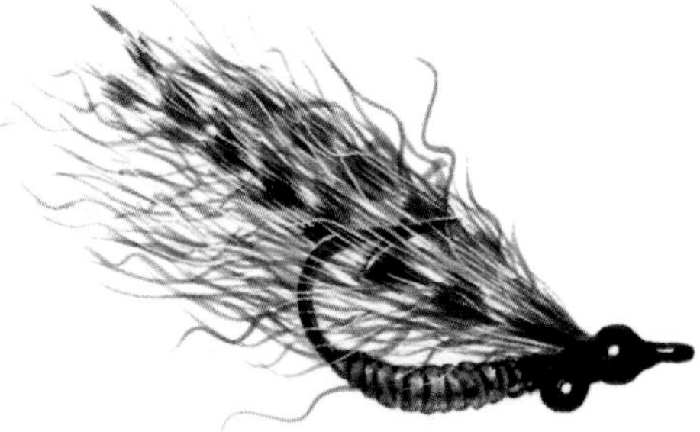

Epoxy Bone-Crab
(bonefish)

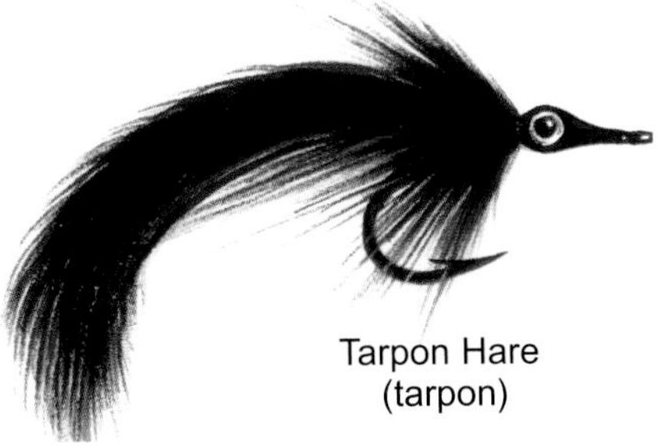

Tarpon Hare
(tarpon)

Lenny's Tarpon Toy
(tarpon)

Paolo Worm
(tarpon)

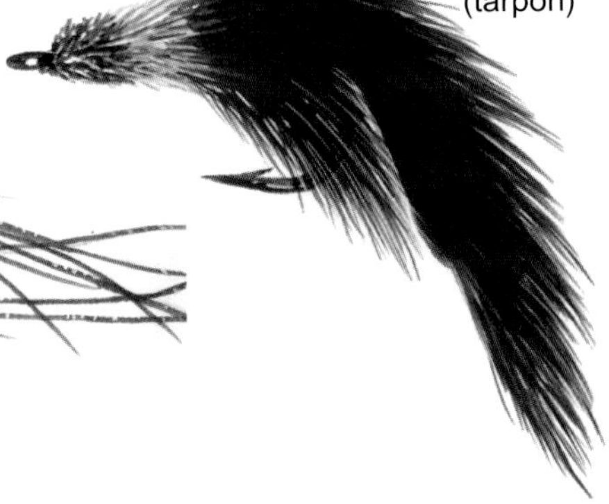

Nick Stanczyk's Bull Dolphin Teaser
(dolphin, tunas and mackerels)

FLY PATTERNS THAT CATCH FISH IN THE FLORIDA KEYS

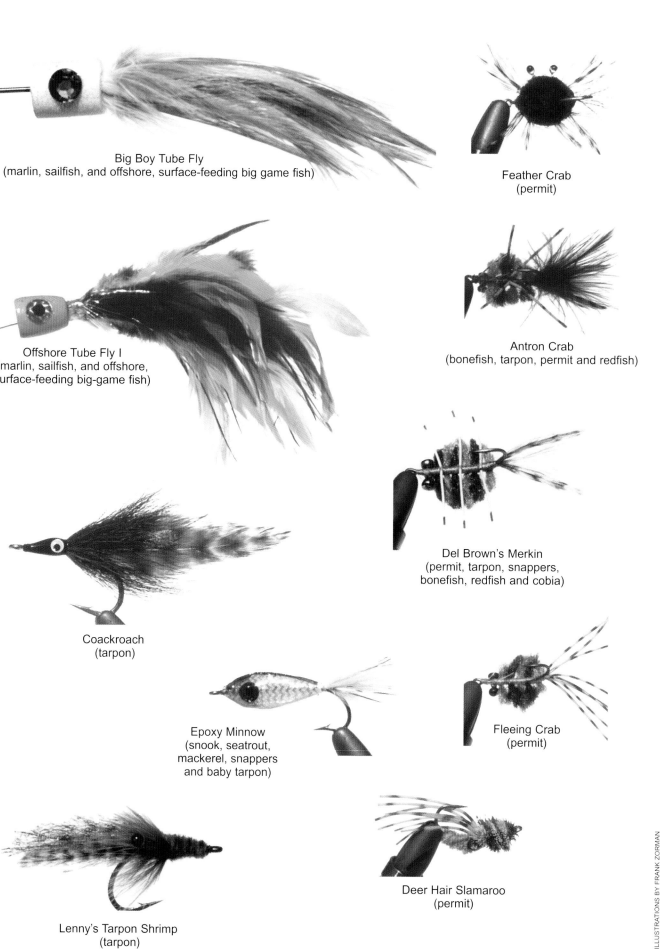

Big Boy Tube Fly
(marlin, sailfish, and offshore, surface-feeding big game fish)

Feather Crab
(permit)

Offshore Tube Fly I
(marlin, sailfish, and offshore,
surface-feeding big-game fish)

Antron Crab
(bonefish, tarpon, permit and redfish)

Del Brown's Merkin
(permit, tarpon, snappers,
bonefish, redfish and cobia)

Coackroach
(tarpon)

Epoxy Minnow
(snook, seatrout,
mackerel, snappers
and baby tarpon)

Fleeing Crab
(permit)

Deer Hair Slamaroo
(permit)

Lenny's Tarpon Shrimp
(tarpon)

ILLUSTRATIONS BY FRANK ZORMAN

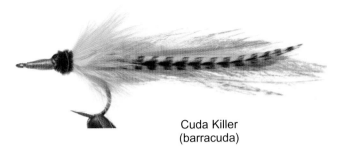

Cuda Scotta
(barracuda)

Cuda Killer
(barracuda)

Topwater Tiger
(barracuda, seatrout, jacks and bluefish)

Deer Hair Chugger
(barracuda, seatrout, jacks
and bluefish)

Sweet Meat Bait
(chartreuse or orange/baracuda, snook, seatrout, jacks,
cobia tunas, snappers, sharks, tripletail and little tunny)

Sweet Meat Bait
(chartreuse and white)

No Name Streamer
(doll eyes/snook, seatrout, mackerels, jacks, cobia, dolphin, tunas, ladyfish, sharks and little tunny)

No Name Streamer
(bead eyes/snook, seatrout, mackerels, jacks, cobia, dolphin,
tunas, ladyfish, sharks and little tunny)

Jail Bait Pinfish
(snook, seatrout, mackerels,
cobia and baby tarpon)

Reverse Epoxy
(bonefish)

Lenny's Crab-Shrimp
(tarpon)

Crystal Head Streamer
(snook, seatrout, mackerel, jacks, cobia, dolphin, ladyfish,
sharks and little tunny)

Bob Clouser-like Minnow
(Works on just about any game fish. Its uni-
versality similar to Lefty Kreh's
Deceiver. Both can be tied in an infinite
number of colors and sizes)

Chartreuse Bend Back
(seatrout, snook, jacks and baby tarpon)

Bendback Jail Bait
(snook, seatrout, jacks, redfish,
baby tarpon and mackerel)

Tan Puffhead
(bonefish)

Yellow Dude
(tarpon)

Epoxy Bone-Crab
(bonefish)

Grey Ghost Crab
(permit)

Crazy Charlie
(bonefish)

Utility Minnow
(cobia, snook and baby tarpon)

Gold Wobble
(redfish)

Sea Pup/bunny strip
(tarpon)

Classic Tarpon
(tarpon)

Tarpon-Tarpon
(tarpon)

Tarpon Hare/natural brown & yellow
(tarpon)

Clouser Minnow
(universal)

Pinfish Bendback

Cuda Killa

Chapter VII

Practical Information

LAST CAST

In the Florida Keys there are many, many accommodations, restaurants and attractions that a visitor could find, respectively suitable to his pocketbook, interest or intellectual curiosity. The few restaurants, accommodations and non-fishing day attractions we review were all discovered by coincidence, word-of-mouth or by the familiarity that comes from living in the Keys and traversing the Over-the-Sea Highway for over 5 years. Additionally, our reviews are purposely limited to those establishments and places that we've experienced more than once and, usually, many times. A partial exception, Little Palm Island Resort and Spa, which was simply beyond our lodging budget. We did, however, eat there and visit more than once. We are confident that all of our selections are excellent choices, and more importantly, they will be just as noteworthy when you get there.

We would like to make it perfectly clear, again, that there are many, many more fine options for dining and lodging in the Keys than we present here, and that almost any budget can be met in the Keys.

THREE KEYS TRAVEL BOOKS WORTH OWNING

Key West & The Florida Keys by June Keith
Keith has been a part- and full-time resident of the Keys for the past 25 years. She is also a columnist for the *Miami Herald*, as well as the author of *Postcards From Paradise* and *Romancing Key West*. She delivers readers to the Keys with humour and a candidness about its persona that makes a visitor at once familiar. Keith works her way into all corners of the Keys history. Everything she speaks to has simmered to perfection.

The Florida Keys by Joy Williams
Joy Williams treats the reader to a history of the Keys that flows. It is the work of a good observer/writer/researcher coming from the perspective of an outsider looking in. She stitches in her opinions about everything she observes and pulls no punches. Ms. Williams did not intend for her book to be anything other than a current day walk through the Keys, a look at the oddities and historical events with the added charm of anecdotes as mile markers.

The Insiders' Guide To The Florida Keys & Key West by Victoria Shearer & Janet Ware
This third book is pure thoroughbred guide book. It leaves nothing out and delivers thumbnails that we have all become familiar with in guide books. It is not, however, fair to classify *The Insiders' Guide To The Florida Keys & Key West* in the same genre as a Fodor's-like guide book. It is far more, covering the Keys knowledgeably, and

almost inch by inch. It is always current (revised editions). It does not, however, distinguish itself in any way by evaluating, or in the slightest way grading, any service other than suggesting prices. Unfortunately, a reader would have a hard time distinguishing a biker motel from a Four Seasons Resort Hotel, except for the delineation it chooses to define value ($$$) and, perhaps, number of services offered. The tone of the copy describing anything and everything that a visitor could sleep in, eat at or find in the Keys is unrealistically bubbly, and that is the only similarity this book has with generic guide books. It is, however, easily the best ready reference guide book about the Keys.

POTPOURRI

• The humidity in the Keys is much, much less than on the mainland (FL), especially, in the summer.
• Key West is the only true "frost free" coordinate in the U. S.
• It is the Gulf Stream that most influences the temperature in the Keys, not their southern location.
• There are far more writers in the Keys than you could possibly imagine.
• 18-weight fly rods are gaining in popularity.
• Jeffrey Cardenas' book, *Marquesa: A Time & Place With Fish* is destined to become a classic.
• The Looe Key dive is sensational.
• Key West is totally different than the rest of the Keys.
• The Upper Keys and Middle Keys are totally different from the Lower Keys.
• The only crocodiles in the Americas are in the Keys.
• The only alligators in the Keys (2) live in the Blue Hole on Big Pine Key.
• Every guide in the Florida Keys despises jet skis.
• Most guides and offshore captains are not against the Tortugas 2000 Proposal.
• Captain Paul Dixon says; "It's how you wiggle the worm, not the worm, that makes the difference."
• All the top guides and offshore captains in the Keys practice catch and release.
• If you'd like to see 300-pound tarpon, go to Bud n' Mary's when the charter boats come in. When the mates clean fish and discard the innards of the day's catches, the water boils with humongous tarpon.
• Jim Sharpe's book, *Dolphin: The Perfect Gamefish*, is one of the best offshore fishing books ever written.
• In the Keys, there are more quality fly-fishing guides and offshore captains than anywhere in the world.
• The largest bonefish in the world are found in the Keys.
• The Lower Keys and Key West are the best permit-fishing destinations in the world.

- The largest permit ever caught on a fly rod was caught in the Keys.
- Every IGFA fly-rod record for permit comes from Keys waters.
- Many of today's saltwater light-tackle fishing techniques came from Keys guides.
- Many of the tried-and-true saltwater fly patterns, used throughout the world today, had their origins in the Keys.
- The Lower Keys are the least fished waters in the Keys.
- Book Sandy Moret's Florida Keys Fly Fishing School early.
- 1,058,000 visitors fished the Keys in 1996.
- The amount of taxpayers' money spent on recreational fishing in the last 100 years: $0.
- A square grouper is now the name of a fish sandwich in Key West, but was the code word in the '70's and 80's for bails of smokable hemp air-dropped into the backcountry mangroves of the Keys.
- 40% of all of Keys residents are directly or indirectly employed in outdoor activities businesses.
- Summer (July, August and September) are fabulous times to fish the Florida Keys. Almost everything that swims in Keys waters is a possibility in those months.

ARRIVING IN THE KEYS

MIAMI, YOUR MOST LOGICAL POINT OF DISEMBARKATION

Miami, dubbed by radio, TV, magazine and newspaper pundits from across the nation as a corrupt Banana Republic is, clearly, out of order. It is not a Republic. The city of Miami, in spite of itself, is still a remarkable place. A place that calls for a layover for those who like their days in the sun, nightlife bold, bawdy, and decidedly Latin flavored. Miami is also the business hub for almost all commerce with South America and the principal U. S. airport connection for just about everything south of the border.

Unfortunately, Miami (Dade County) has earned much of its national image. Miami seems to enjoy its political and moral dis-connect with Florida and the rest of the country. Its estrangement not at all due, in full measure, to its relatively new cultural distinction. Miami's politicians, police, lawyers and judges have been being indicted, going to jail, and getting reelected for over a century.

Carl Hiaasen's book, *Sick Puppy*, delivers a telling portrait of Miami's politicians. One of his principal characters is a high-powered lobbyist, Palmer Stoat. Stoat refuses a call from a Miami commissioner. *"Stoat had a firm rule against speaking directly with Miami commissioners—those who weren't already under indictment were under investigation, and all telephone lines into City Hall had long ago been tapped."*

Both Miami and Dade County, as fiduciaries of the people's tax monies, have proved to be so financially inept that the State of Florida has threatened to step in and take over fiscal matters more than once. The beat goes on, and the world loves to come to Miami.

MIAMI AIRPORT

Arriving in Miami via air can end up a challenge once on the ground. The Miami Airport is still under construction, and has been since the Pleistocene Epoch. It is not a people friendly or luggage-moving airport. The discombobulating bottleneck-layout of the airport, established by the original planners, remains intact.

RENTAL CARS IN MIAMI

Miami is popular 365 days a year. Make car reservations a priority. All the major national car rental agencies can be found at the Miami Airport. Never wing it by trying to get a car without a reservation. Try to get your rental car from an agency located at the airport, not off-site. Returning your car off-site can be a traffic nightmare.

GETTING OUT OF THE MIAMI AIRPORT HEADING TO THE KEYS

From the main airport rental lot, choose LeJune road (NW 42nd Avenue) and look for signs to 836 West. Everything starts out with good signage. An 836 W directive, however, does come up fast so stay in the right lane. Warning: As you approach the ramp to 836 W, do not take the frontage road exit. It comes before the actual 836 W exit and tricks even inattentive home-boys. Route 836 West will intersect with the Florida Turnpike Extension in about 20 minutes (7, or so, miles) in normal traffic conditions. Remember to stay alert and expect little driving courtesy from others while in Dade County/Miami. Note: Never, ever return the favor of finger signals or protest in any way if you are cut-off. Many Miami-Dade County drivers use their vehicles as an extension of an odd, but pervasive, and ever-present machismo. For those who survive making it to the turnpike (Florida Keys /Key West extension), you will end up deposited on U. S. I in Florida City, the entrance to the Keys, and a most pleasant world away.

U.S. I: THE OVERSEAS HIGHWAY

Driving entry to the Keys starts at the terminus of the Florida Turnpike at an unavoidable intersect with U.S. I

TIDBITS

1 Fathom = 6 Feet
1 Knot = 6,086 Feet
3 Knots = 1 League
1 Kilo = 2.205 Pounds.
1 Centimeter = .394 Inches or .0328 Feet
1 Liter = .264 Gallons
1 Kilometer = .621 Miles
60 Seconds (") = 1 Minute (')
60 Minutes = 1 Degree

U.S. I immediately gives way to the historic Overseas Highway that ends in Key West. No alternate routes are possible, nor could you make a route mistake. It's the only road into the Keys. The exception, selecting Card Sound Road (905A) just as you begin (Florida City). The choice is very well marked with overhead signage. Card Sound Road is a narrow, and dangerous, 2 lane toll road ($1) designed to deliver the more affluent to North Key Largo, principally the Ocean Reef Club, or the exceptionally elite Key Largo Anglers Club (see History Chapter). Reentry to the Overseas Highway from Card Sound Road is a right turn on 905 (the only choice and no mistake possible as 905A ends). Route 905 will take you into Key Largo proper and put you back on the Overseas Highway. You will have lost no time at all by choosing the Card Sound Road. Actually, it is a better option, especially late at night.

As you descend the Keys, or ascend them, you will notice small green signs with white numbers on posts at the right shoulder of the road. They indicate your exact position on the Keys. Every establishment refers to its address by using the (MM) mile marker system. Adding bayside/gulfside, or oceanside, and 10th (MM 00.0) makes finding anything in the Keys a snap. MMs are a left-over from the Florida East Coast Railroad Extension, built by Henry Flagler (see History Chapter).

GETTING TO THE KEYS FROM FT. LAUDERDALE

Ft. Lauderdale's airport is the antithesis of Miami's, an efficient people mover. Everyone is a little more relaxed here. Versace, however, never made it big in Ft. Lauderdale. Polyester leisure suits are still in vogue. Also, there's plenty of gaudy jewelry, scary face lifts and heavy New Yawka accents. Baggage claim is a snap and car rental access is right behind baggage claim. Advance car rental reservations are necessary year round.

Ft Lauderdale's airport could not be easier to negotiate. Leaving from the car rental exit, select a well-marked 595 West. Take 595 West to the Florida Turnpike (6 minutes). You could choose to continue on 595 West (best bet) to its terminus, and take 75 south (Miami). The latter route avoids the many tolls of the turnpike and it is also faster. Your only remaining choice, with the latter route, is to select the Key West Extension (Turnpike) turnoff. NOTE: There is only one sign alerting you of the Keys option, and the turnoff comes up very, very quickly (about 15 miles south of 595). If you're in the speed lane on 75 south, crossing over to make the right turn-off to the Keys extension is difficult at least, and life threatening

for sure. If all goes right you will end up on U.S. I in Florida City in about an hour and fifteen minutes.

CHAMBERS OF COMMERCE

Key Largo's Chamber of Commerce introduces the entire Keys (Upper Keys, Middle Keys, Lower Keys and Key West). It is housed in a modern building found bayside, MM 106, just as you enter Key Largo proper. The staff efficiently administers to the millions who enter. Any question gets answered by a friendly bunch, and they all have good knowledge of what's going on in all of the Keys, A to Z. Pamphlets by the thousands introduce visitors to everything from veterinarians, gay B&B's, party boats, RV camps and everything in between. All of the Keys Chambers of Commerce have knowledgeable and resourceful staffs. On-line websites carry much of the need-to-know information for general travellers. Never expect a Chamber of Commerce employee to grade services or facilities for you. They do not, and will not.

Key Largo Chamber of Commerce
10600 Overseas Highway @ MM #106 Bayside
Key Largo, FL 33037
305-451-1414 or 800-822-1088
www.floridakeys (good for entire Keys)
or www.keylargo.org
Islamorada Chamber of Commerce
Islamorada @ MM 82.5 Bayside
P.O.B. 915, Islamorada, FL 33306
305-664-4503/Fax: -4289/800-322-5397
www.islamoradachamber.com
Marathon Chamber of Commerce
Marathon @ MM 53.5 Bayside
305-743-5417/Fax: 289-0183
800-262-7284
www.floridakeysmarathon.com
Big Pine Key Chamber of Commerce
Big Pine Key @ MM 31 Oceanside
P.O.B. 430511. Big Pine Key, FL 33304
305-872-2411/Fax: -0752/800-872-3722
www.lowerkeyschamber.com
Key West Chamber of Commerce
Mallory Square, Key West, FL 33040
305-294-2587/800-648-6269
www.fla-keys.com

FLORIDA KEYS FISHING TOURNAMENTS, INC.

There are more than 50 fishing tournaments held each year in the Florida Keys, according to the official Florida Keys Fishing Tournaments, Inc. brochure. Every month of the year is accounted for. You can almost choose any quarry, cost of participation ($50 to $500 per angler), charity benefited, type of tackle (offshore, inshore, flats or backcountry) and even the celebrities you prefer rubbing elbows with: President George Bush, NFL, MLB, NBA legends, as well as top entertainment personalities, artists and writers.

NOTE: Billfish and flats tournaments are all catch and release. Prizes range from cash to art to trophies, but all include the satisfaction of just fishing. Some are fly-fishing dedicated. Several are for women only, and some for kids only. Tournament locations run the length of the Keys, Key Largo to Key West. All in all, the Keys host more fishing tournaments than any place in the world.

ORGANIZATIONS

We introduce The International Game Fish Association (IGFA), The Billfish Foundation TBF), and The Bonefish & Tarpon Unlimited (BTU) because they advance the cause of protecting, understanding and perpetuating the world's fisheries. They step up to the plate where we, as individuals, cannot: the back rooms of state and federal commissions on fisheries, the state and federal halls of congress where bills are introduced, connect with the media in all its forms, and associate throughout the world with organizations, associations, commissions and governments whose policies and actions affect the future of the world's fisheries. For over a decade, these organizations have been fighting our battles. They deserve our allegiance. Supporting them pays off, and not just in the long run for our children and grandchildren, but for the influence they put forth in their research, data, and informative nature of their publications. Supporting them means, in everyday terms, your being on top of what is going on in the world as it relates to your sportfishing future, below and above the water line. The publications that these organizations distribute to its members alone are worth the price of admission.

INTERNATIONAL GAME FISH ASSOCIATION

The IGFA was founded in 1939, and it has had a strong relationship with worldwide sport fishing ever since. The past and present Boards of Trustees, representatives and members, established the IGFA as the world's authority on international angling rules, and for the compilation of world gamefish records.

Members of the IGFA's Hall of Fame include: Zane Grey, Curt Gowdy, Ted Williams and many other luminaries. Today, the IGFA's membership exceeds 25,000. Its official representatives and members are from over 100 countries, all walks of life and all corners of the globe. In recent years, the IGFA has become globally outspoken on matters of concern to all of us: the health of fisheries and the preservation of fish stocks. Its clout in these matters has made inroads, and its voice has carried across continents. The IGFA now enjoys even more international recognition than ever, and it has a much broader demographic base of appeal because of its activism.

The IGFA is headquartered, literally, minutes away from the Ft. Lauderdale International Airport. In 1998, it completed one of sport's most intelligent museums, The International Game Fish Association Hall Of Fame Museum. Sixty thousand amazing square feet. A museum

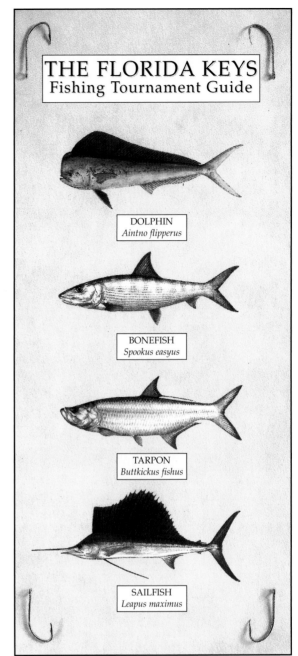

THE FLORIDA KEYS
Fishing Tournament Guide

DOLPHIN
Aintno flipperus

BONEFISH
Spookus easyus

TARPON
Buttkickus fishus

SAILFISH
Leapus maximus

Florida Keys Fishing Tournaments, Inc.

Florida Keys Fishing Tournaments, Inc.
P.O.B. 420358
Summerland Key, FL 33042

www.fla-keys.com

that is guaranteed to keep the attention of fishermen and non-fishermen, young and old. It is open to the public 7 days a week. The admission fee is modest. Members get in free. This museum's educational value and ability to hold anyone's interest goes beyond telling. There's more to the museum than the name alone implies. A marina displays modern-day fishing craft, Zane Grey's boat (*Avalon*), and a replica of Ernest Hemingway's boat (*Pilar*). Also, there's a Tackle Gallery, a Legacy Gallery (interactive), Discovery Room (youngsters), Catch

Gallery (virtual reality), Places Gallery (world destinations), Fish Gallery (ID) and a rotating art gallery with fine art from Don Ray, Guy Harvey and others. There's a perfect four-acre replication of wetlands, which serves as a working conservation lab. Additionally, there are classes on just about anything related to the fishing and the environment. There are fishing instruction for kids, a touch tank, day camps and a whole host of other interrelated activities.

Members get to enjoy access to the E.K. Harry Library, which houses over 15,000 books, 2,000 articles, periodicals, scientific papers, rare photographs and over 1,500 films. In addition, a staff biologist maintains up-to-the-minute relations with scientific bodies from around the world and gladly answers members' questions. Members also get to enjoy a 6-times-a-year newsletter and an annual copy of "World Record Game Fishes." The latter a 350-page publication, which alone is worth more than the membership fee.

NOTE: Gail Morchow, librarian, is extremely helpful and knowledgeable about the library's contents. Glenda Kelley, fish biologist, is a walking encyclopedia of the world's briny creatures. She is also an accomplished fisherman (world-record holder) and member of the historic Islamorada Fishing Club.

Another bonus, within walking distance of the museum, is Johnny Morris' mega retail store, Outdoor World. It also has many programs, fly tying and fly casting, for example. NOTE: Legendary Keys and Everglades guide, Captain Bill Curtis, is a part-time employee at Outdoor World. When you stop in, say hello to him. NOTE: Directions to the IGFA's Hall of Fame Museum from Ft. Lauderdale International Airport: Take 595 West. In just a few miles take 95 south. Stay on the 95 south entry road (you do not get on 95). Get off on the first road to your right, Exit 26, Griffin Road (West). Make a right on Griffin Road (west), get in extreme left lane and turn left at the first red light (Anglers Avenue). Go to the first red light (few hundred yards) and turn left into Sportsman's Park and follow the signs. Time lapse and distance from Ft. Lauderdale International Airport about 8 minutes and 5 miles, respectively. For more information: International Game Fish Association, 300 Gulf Stream Way, Dania, FL 33304. 954-927-2628 or Fax 954-924-4299. www.igfa.org

TBF

There are many associations, organizations and foundations we fishermen of the salt could belong to, but one deserves special consideration: The Billfish Foundation. Its track record is impressive. The reason we should all consider supporting the TBF runs to our most selfish side, they provide the best short- and long-term ROI.

To begin with, TBF is pro-sport fishing. They are present at all the big billfish tournaments held throughout the world. They come to educate and promote their highly successful tagging program (over 90,000 tagged billfish). Why the TBF is so vital to all of us is that its mandate speaks the language of facts, hard core evidence about the state of billfish throughout the world, and it delivers their message, and all of ours, in the world's corridors of influence.

In the age of supposition, sensationalism, hyperbole and downright guessing, the TBF's charter strategies have marched on the sure footing of research: economic studies, stock assessments, genetic studies and comprehensive analysis. While the picture of the world's fisheries that host the highly migratory species of billfish is not good (white marlin at 15% of historic population and blue marlin at 40%), it would be a lot worse if it were not for TBF. Since 1987, TBF has been funding science. In and of itself, a brilliant strategy that has produced in its wake irrefutable data that has changed more than one ersatz government strategy, reigned in some of the commercial fishing industry's free-wheeling over-exploitative practices, and helped educate sport fishermen around the world to the folly of killing a billfish just for the boast of it, the latter a long-held belief of the Keys captains.

TBF now has a well-placed foothold where it counts the most—government agencies, backroom fisheries committees, and the scientific community as a whole. TBF has come of age as its data is now considered authoritative. Any conflicting data has to stand the scrutiny of being measured against the real McCoy, TBF's. For more information: The

Billfish Foundation, POB 8787, Ft. Lauderdale, FL 33310-5311. 954-938-0150 or Fax 954-938-5311. Email: billfish@bell-south.net or website www.billfish.org

BONEFISH & TARPON UNLIMITED

Bonefish & Tarpon Unlimited is a relatively new organization that supports projects and research to help understand, nurture, and enhance a healthy bonefish and tarpon population. Fashioned after Trout Unlimited, this tax deductible, non-profit organization has, literally, a membership that reads like a who's who of sport fishing. Memberships are available to all comers. You can join by sending $50 or more to: Bonefish & Tarpon Unlimited, 24 Dockside Lane, PMB 83, Key Largo, FL 33037. 305-367-3416 or FX: 305-367-3546

NOTEWORTHY PUBLICATIONS

The Redbone Journal is a full-fledged quarterly color magazine that enjoys a large subscriber base for a good reason. The articles are always well written, diverse in subject matter and there are always anecdotal stories about celebrities who partake in the Mercury/Redbone tournaments. The art coverage is probably the best you'll see anywhere. *The Redbone Journal* provides, like no other Keys-based publication, full flavor of the fishing scene in the Keys, and a real connection to the guides. NOTE: Both the Redbone/Mercury Series Tournaments, and *The Redbone Journal* are tax deductible costs, benefitting the Cystic Fibrosis Foundation.

To subscribe to The Redbone Journal: 200 Industrial Road, P. O. Box 273, Islamorada, FL 33306 (305-664-2002) or FX: 305-664-9036. Email: redboneinc@aol.com

The following publications provide coverage on Florida Keys fishing:

Saltwater Fly Fishing
Terry Gibson, Editor
Editorial Offices
160 Benmont Ave.
Bennington, VT 05201
www.flyfishingmagazines.com
Fly Fishing In Saltwater
David Ritchie, Editor
www.flyfishingsalt.com
Sport Fishing
www.sportfishingmag.com
Doug Olander, Editor In Chief
World Publications
460 North Orlando Avenue, Suite 200
Winter Park, FL 32789
Florida Sportsman
Karl Wickstrom, Editor
www.floridasportsman.com
P.O.B. 420235
Palm Coast, FL 32142-0235
800-274-6386

Fishing the Florida Keys
MM 48.6 Oceanside
Marathon, FL 33050
www.keynoter.com
305-743-5551
Saltwater Sportsman
C. M. "Rip" Cunningham
263 Summer St.
Boston, MA 12210
www.saltwatersportsman.com
Fishing Lines
Division of Marine Fisheries
620 South Meridian Street
Tallahassee, FL 32399-1600
www.state.fl.us/fwc/marine

The following newspapers have outdoor editors, columnists or writers that regularly cover fishing in the Keys. For visitors, the best way to get up-to-date information will be online.

The Key West Citizen
www.keysnews.com
A Cooke Communications publication. It is in print every day but Saturday. Tom Walker has a column on the subject of sport fishing. He's knowledgeable and connects with the right people for up-to-date information.
The Miami Herald
Susancocking @ www.herald.com
Sue Cocking has been covering sport fishing for the *Herald* since 1993. She is a rarity in her field. She was a professional guide, owns IGFA fly-fishing records, has several tournament titles to her name, and can speak to the broader issues facing sport fishing. Cocking is often in the Keys, fishing with the top guides and offshore captains.
Sun Sentinel
Steve Waters @ www.sunsentinel.com
Steve's column is widely read and covers everything fishy from Key West to Palm Beach, sail fishing to bass tournaments and everything briny in between. A reliable source for Keys fishing.
Tampa Tribune
Frank Sargeant @ www.tampatribune.com
Frank has written many books on the subject of fishing. He capably speaks on every aspect of fishing.

GASTRONOMY AND THE KEYS

NOTE: The Upper Keys are quite different from the Lower Keys, and Key West. Key West, itself, is an improbable outpost at the end of the road, and a world apart.

The Florida Keys claim an estimated 240 places to eat. Key West owns about 155 of them. The ambience and table fare throughout the Keys and Key West ranges from an old shack finger-food to resort extravaganza, and as you might expect, some shacks serve delicious food and some resorts only recently-thawed panache *au gratin*. Fish and shellfish can be counted on to be fresh anywhere in the Keys. In the Keys you can also enjoy a world of cosmopolitan flavors. No one could ever depart the Keys without having had spectacular gastronomical indulgences, and it would not require a great search or long trek to find culinary treats to satisfy even curmudgeonly palates.

Restaurants worldwide are notorious for being subject to great swings of reliability and terminating business without notice. The Upper, Middle and Lower Keys dining businesses are from that same genetic issue. Key West restaurants, however, are as capricious in this respect as the predictability of a hurricane path. Therefore, we suggest you reconnoiter on your own when you arrive. Also, when making your dining reservations anywhere in the Keys, we suggest you double-check whether credit cards are accepted.

Left: Michael Lerner, International Game Fish Association founder. **Middle**: Key West resident Ernest Hemingway. **Right**: Helen Lerner, a formidable angler in her own right, and so noted in the book, *Reel Women*, by Lyla Foggia. Hemingway and the Lerners were lifelong friends. Photo taken in Bimini 1934.

COURTESY OF INTERNATIONAL GAME FISH ASSOCIATION, E. K. HARRY LIBRARY OF FISHES

STAYING IN THE KEYS

In the Florida Keys, a visitor could stay in a two-bit room, trailer, motel, hotel, B&B, inn, guest cottage, house, palazzo, resort, boat, RV park or camp out. One could also find fast food, pizza joints, take outs, grocery stores, convenience stores, low-end eateries, or moderate to expensive places to refuel. There are no shortages of places to secure stimulating beverages in the Keys.

Our review of Keys accommodations are decidedly safe bets. We limit our reviews to those accommodations that we've experienced and thoroughly enjoyed. They all have a history of performing as advertised.
NOTE: Monroe County has a whopping tax that will add almost 12% to your accommodations bill.

UPPER KEYS: CHEECA LODGE

Cheeca Lodge is, literally, minutes away from Florida Keys Outfitters, World Wide Sportsman, and Bud n' Mary's Marina. Sandy Moret's Florida Keys Fly Fishing School is held at Cheeca. Cheeca Lodge should be your headquarters when you are in or near the Upper Keys. At Cheeca you can bring your fishing buddies, clients, staff, family and mother-in-law. Everyone will be happy, rain or shine.

The lodge itself is woven into the fabric of the Keys history. It is also very much a part of Upper Keys fishing and fly-fishing scene, past and present. Currently, there are several fishing tournaments headquartered at Cheeca (Mercury Cheeca/Redbone Celebrity Tournament, and two President George Bush Tournaments).

Cheeca Lodge's history began as Olney Inn in 1946. Its next owners, Carl and Che-Che Twitchell, rebuilt the inn in the 1950's and called it Cheeca. Their names, of course, mixing to come up with Chee-ca. The Twitchell's had in mind a semi-private resort that was dedicated to serving the socially elite of the day. In 1970, Coca-Cola bottler, Carl Navarre (an avid fly-fisherman), bought Cheeca Lodge, expanded it, improved it and advanced its current open-to-the-public persona. Cheeca has changed hands a few more times since Navarre sold it, and it has undergone more than one multi-million-dollar facelift. It is now a Rockresorts property (2001). Through it all, Cheeca has maintained its old-fashioned charm and old-shoe feel. NOTE: Captain George Hommell, Jr., a legendary fishing guide in the Keys, has managed Cheeca Lodge more than once.

Today, Cheeca Lodge sits amid 27 purposefully planted, and manicured acres on 1,100 feet of Atlantic Ocean beachfront flats. It has three pools, several hot tubs, six lighted Lay-Kold tennis courts (all weather and well maintained), golf course (9 hole par 3 designed by Jack Nicklaus), 525-foot long pier and a world-class 5,000-square-foot spa, *Avanyu*. The latter a professionally staffed, state-of-the-art European-style spa and ultimate exercise facility. Cheeca also offers their guests professionally guided dive excursions to the world's third largest reef tract, chartered sailing and guided eco-tours. For those who need a little space and a pleasant stretch of the legs there's a mile-long trail winding through the property, dotted with signage identifying 26 uniquely different trees. A real bonus for families with youngsters is that Cheeca Lodge offers several day programs for the wee ones. Other amenities are what you would expect from a quality resort: video center, boutique, sports shop, sundries, concierge, business services and meeting rooms. Cheeca has 203 rooms in the three-story main lodge, and independent cottages scattered around the grounds. You can't find a bad room.

The ambience at Cheeca Lodge is all Keys, upscale, and it starts with a Key Largo limestone entrance and ends with a staff that measurably adds to the whole experience. Water, fishing and someone having paid attention to details is immediately apparent when you enter. Lending to that feel is the newly named bar, Curt Gowdy Light Tackle Lounge, right across from check-in. The lounge has an unmistakable club feel. Any bar stool or table offers a grand and panoramic view of the Atlantic. The pictures that adorn the walls of the bar add a hallowed museum-like quality. On any Wednesday evening you can stop in for a 2-for-1 drink special and listen to a live broadcast of Captain Gary Ellis' radio talk show. Gary always has interesting fishing-captain guests, and no one seems bothered by chit-chat coming from the busy bar. Cheeca Lodge, by the way, does not serve thimble-size drinks, nor are they high priced, so typical these days of resorts and hotels. You can get quite expansive on just two.

The main restaurant, Atlantic's Edge, has a setting that is all Keys. Every table providing a view of the Atlantic Ocean flats that extend to the limits of the horizon. We've eaten dinner there innumerable times, tried everything on the menu, and have yet to walk away without mentioning how good our meals were. Atlantic's Edge is always written up in the

Art by Klaus Schuler.

major travel magazines as one of the best restaurants in South Florida. Make the Atlantic's Edge a priority stop for dinner, even if you're not a resort guest. If you're not up to the complete dining experience of the Atlantic's Edge, then try casual dining at the Ocean Terrace Grill, but you might be sharing space with cranky kids. You could, instead, opt to dine in the Curt Gowdy Light Tackle Lounge. For sport fishermen of any discipline, Cheeca Lodge is ground zero in the Upper Keys. You'll want for nothing, and it will not break the bank.

NOTE: The Pioneer Cemetery is a Historical Association of Southern Florida historic site. It is found near the beach (white picket fence) on Cheeca's property. Public access is granted.

Cheeca Lodge, MM 82 Oceanside, Islamorada, FL. 800-541-3491 or local 305-664-4651/Fax 305-664-2893. Online at www.cheeca.com or email: information@cheeca.com.

THINGS TO DO IN THE UPPER KEYS

NOTE: For those of you who are history buffs you can contact the Historical Preservation Society of the Upper Keys, POB 2200, Key Largo, FL 33037. You can also e-mail jerry@keyshistory.org or go to www.keyshistory.org. Jerry

Right: Awards night, Cheeca Lodge 1997. Floridian Andy Mill with President George W. Bush.

Below: Two legends, Captain George Hommell, Jr. (middle) and Mr. President (right), heading out to the flats for bonefish. Man on the left, unidentified, is assumed to be a Secret Service Agent.

Wilkinson, President of the society, is helpful, knowledgeable and can direct you to all available historical resources. In addition, you should secure any book that was written by John Viele (*The Florida Keys*, *The Florida Keys* Vol. 2 , and *The Florida Keys* Vol. 3). Also, the main library in Key West is a treasure trove of historical information. Ask for Tom Hambright (Mary Hill Russell Branch).

KEY LARGO HAMMOCKS STATE BOTANICAL SITE

The Key Largo Hammocks Botanical Site is 2,700 acres of very rare hardwood hammock forest (largest in the U.S.). Most of the West Indian hardwoods found in the Keys were timbered out centuries ago. The only other remaining hardwood hammock in the Keys is on Lignum Vitae Key. Hardwoods do, however, exist throughout the Keys, but not in numbers that would qualify them as hammocks/forests (Windley Key, for example). Many of the over 200 species of fauna and flora, found only in the Florida Keys, are in the Key Largo Hammocks Botanical Site.

The Key Largo Hammocks Botanical Site was salvaged by the State of Florida just before it was doomed to the developer's bulldozers. The development, called Port Bougainvillaea, was to be on the grandiose scale of the

Ocean Reef Club, and just as environmentally disastrous. Remnants of the Port Bougainvillaea project are still quite visible. The site has walking trails, and an elevated boardwalk delivers visitors deep into the hammocks' varied landscapes. Visitors get to see the overstory, midstory and understory of a classic hardwood hammock, an always bustling aviary, seasons of flowering plants and trees, and, occasionally, indigenous fauna. You can take a self-guided tour with the aid of a pamphlet that is available as you enter. Park Ranger tours are scheduled (Wednesdays and Saturdays, usually), but you'll have to call the number below for updates.

NOTE: You get to the site, if you are coming from the mainland, by taking Card Sound Road (905A) to its terminus. Turn right (905 heading towards Key Largo). The site will come up on your left, oceanside. Look for a tired, but

Master of ceremonies, Curt Gowdy, and the Commander-in-Chief preside over the evening's awards.

Dusk, December 1999, Captain Andrew Derr and Captain Darren Wilcox, heard them tailing on their way back to Key Largo from respective guide trips. "What the heck. Let's try a blind cast or two."

typical entrance that is reserved for gated communities. The signage for the Key Largo Hammocks Botanical Site is modest so you'll have to pay attention. If you're heading back to the mainland, then turn off the Overseas Highway when the option for 905 (Ocean Reef Club) sign appears in Key Largo. Key Largo Hammocks State Botanical Site, Rte. 905, Key Largo, FL. 305 451 1202 (ranger station @ Pennekamp Park) or www.dep.state.fl.us/parks.

WINDLEY KEY FOSSIL REEF STATE GEOLOGICAL SITE

Windley Key and Key Largo Hammocks State Botanical Site are two of the best-kept secrets in the Upper Keys. Windley Key's three bayside quarries have the remains of once-huge deposits of fossilized rock. The walls of the quarry reveal thousands of once-symbiotic animals that made up the heartbeat of a long-ago vibrant, but now dead, ancient reef.

At 17 feet above sea level, Windley Key is one of the highest points above sea level on the entire Keys. Windley Key's vast deposits of fossilized coral were extensively mined during the building of the Over-the-Sea railroad. Originally, Windley Key was two islands, named the Umbrella Keys, but like so many small islands in the Keys, Flagler's engineers ordered them filled in to hasten railroad construction. After the railroad was completed, several companies continued to mine the rock for decorative building facings. NOTE: It is difficult to arrange for a guided tour, but it's worth the effort to try. Windley Key Fossil Reef State Geological Site, MM 85.5 Bayside, Windley Key. 305-664-2540. NOTE: There are a few rare hardwoods growing above the quarry walls. See the history chapter for more on Windley Key.

INDIAN KEY

See history chapter for more on Indian Key. MM 77.5 Oceanside, Indian Key. 305-664-2540

LIGNUM VITAE KEY

See history chapter for more on Lignum Vitae Key. MM 77.5 Bayside, Lignum Vitae Key. 305-664-2540
NOTE: There are several other family-oriented attractions in the Upper Keys: Florida Keys Wild Bird Center, Theater of the Sea, Dolphin Plus, Hurricane Monument and several smaller historical sites.

MIDDLE KEYS: HAWK'S CAY RESORT, DUCK ISLAND

Hawk's Cay Resort is decidedly family oriented, and its five restaurants all have a theme and price points designed to cover any wallet. We found their daily buffet offerings to be excellent. This resort has what most Keys resorts do not, land, which provides for long walks and a lot of facilities. If your kids are bored at Hawk's Cay Resort, you are the proud parents of slugs. If you can't find anything to do at Hawk's Cay Resort, you didn't check in at Hawk's Cay Resort. There are simply more things to do than are reportable. One of the best is their Dolphin Discovery, where in-water encounters with dolphins follows a classroom introduction. Leave a half day open for this most memorable experience. Also, Hawk's Cay has real Har-Tru (clay) tennis courts, and one of their pros can give you a workout, or find you a game with one of the many resident members living in this Duck Key resort. The fitness center is very much up to speed, as is its staff. There are several facilities that are set aside for adults only, so you can almost child-proof yourself if you want. NOTE: Hawk's Cay also has a Fly Fishing Academy. We signed up for it three times, but classes were always cancelled due to a lack of participants.

When we come to fish with Captain Dustin Huff, Marathon, we have always opted for Hawk's Cay's

Captain Andrew Derr(left), Captain Paul Dixon (taking photo), and fellow guide Captain "Spot" Killen (right), out for an offshore spin, New Year's Day 2000, North Key Largo. The day, and year, start off on the right foot.

townhouse-villa rental units. The villas are all well furnished and have modern everything. This option always gives us the opportunity to start the day's coffee when we want, snack from our own 'frig' and do our own laundry. Hawk's Cay Resort, MM61 Oceanside, Duck Key, FL 33050. 888-814-9154 or 305-743-7000. www.hawkscay.com

THINGS TO DO IN THE MIDDLE KEYS

When you drive through Marathon you somehow get the feeling, for a mile or two when you are in the heart of it, that you might have left the Keys, but that you're not quite on the mainland either. Then you realize that central Marathon lacks a "Keys" personality. Marathon, for example, recently went through an exercise that typified its lack of self confidence. Several of the local powers tried to get a name change. Marathon wanted itself to be a bonafide "Key," and capitalize on an association with the Florida Keys. Monroe County gave its blessing, as did the tourist board, but as you know, the word "Key" has not found its way into a name for Marathon. Vaca Key, its real name, just had no flare or romance to it. Vaca means cow in Spanish, and that handle doesn't quite get it done. Oh well, it's still a great place to fish and visit.

DOLPHIN RESEARCH CENTER

The Dolphin Research Center is a very worthwhile stop. Leave a half day, or more, if you want to interact with the dolphins. It's beyond fascinating, professionally presented and memorable to say the least. You can even take an accredited course (college level), Dolphin Lab, which lasts a week. If your family is in tow make this a priority stop, and choose the full menu. The kids will be talking about their Dolphin Research Center experience for many years to come. Dolphin Research Center, MM59 Bayside, Grassy Key, FL. 305-289-1121 or 305-289-0002 (reservations) and www.dolphins.org.

Sunset and the flats. One more cast, a real possibility with Captain Dustin Huff, Marathon.

PHOTO COURTESY OF HAWK'S CAY RESORT

PIGEON KEY NATIONAL HISTORIC SITE

See history chapter for more on Pigeon Key. Pigeon Key National Historic Site, Old Seven Mile Bridge, Bayside, Pigeon Key, FL. 305-289-0025 or 305-743-5999 and www.pigeonkey.org.

CRANE POINT

Crane Point is a small but interesting museum with an adjoining children's museum. A real potpourri of trails, artifacts, birds, fish, tours, audio, native growths and more. Just about everything you could have seen or can see in the Florida Keys is accounted for at Crane Point. A very worthwhile stop. Crane Point, MM 50.5 Bayside, Marathon, FL. 305-743-9100.

LOWER KEYS: LITTLE PALM ISLAND RESORT AND SPA

You get to Little Palm Island Resort and Spa by launch. The launch leaves on the half hour and returns on the hour. The trip takes about 20 minutes or so. You know your in for something special right away. The launch, a replica of a classy 1930's Chris-Craft, is named the *Truman*. President Harry was a previous guest when it was Munson Island (see history chapter). You will have to have a reason for going to Little Palm Island Resort and Spa: drinks, brunch, lunch, dinner or, excuse us, resort guest.

NOTE: You are not allowed to wander the grounds if you are a non-guest.

If $2,000 a day doesn't scare you off (about $600 a night off-season), then you've found Nirvana, and it's here on Little Palm Island. Nothing in the Keys, or Florida for that matter, speaks to elegant quite like this little 5-acre island. It is simply beyond beyond. Name a celebrity, or in-the-news personality, and they've been here. Obviously, only the well-heeled get to sleep here. We did not. Little Palm Island Resort and Spa is on just about every top ten-list of special places to stay, worldwide. The restaurant, alone, always gets international mention.

There are no children under 16 allowed. At $2,000 a day one does not expect to deal with full diapers. There are only 15 guest bungalows. Each thatched hut-bungalow has two suites, one up and the other down. Each suite is exquisitely appointed. Motifs are British colonial, Polynesian or Indonesian; no fakery and nothing looks wanna-be. Telephones, of any kind, are *verboten*. There is, however, one community telephone. It's off by itself in an old outhouse. There are no TVs or radios, but you do get a newspaper, free. There is also a stately library that houses over 600 books (superb selection). If you prefer more vertically oriented events, then there's plenty to do: sail, dive, swim, eco-tour or

TIDBITS

Marathon
In the 1700's, real estate between Knights Key and Duck Key was called, Cayos de Vaccas by Spanish cartographers.

Little Palm Island Resort and Spa from the air. Little Palm Island Resort has its own seaplane. You can arrange exploring visits to isolated islands in the Keys. See history chapter for more on Munson Island, its prior name.

snorkel. Captain Jim Sharpe, if you made prior arrangements, will come and get you for each day's offshore fishing. Sea Boots (Big Pine) could also arrange to send Captain Lenny Moffo or Captain Tim Carlile out to get you for each day's backcountry fishing.

Off season, we like to have Sunday brunch there. The food is excellent, as you would expect. It's pretty much a day commitment and well worth the not-too-unreasonable, off-season, price tag. The whole experience of being taken out by launch adds to the specialness of being committed to opulence. Before you get to the resort you can't help but reinvent yourself. Little Palm Island Resort and Spa, by launch at MM28.5 Oceanside, Little Torch Key, FL. 800-343-8567 or 305-872-2524 and www.littlepalmisland.com.

LOWER KEYS - SUGAR LOAF LODGE - A SPECIAL MENTION

No public accommodation is more tethered to the history, or fishing the Keys, than Miriam & Lloyd Good's Sugar Loaf Lodge. Its 400 acres are the original sites of the Chase sponge-farming scheme and Perky's fishing camp/bat-tower venture (see history chapter for more on both). The remnants of each entrepreneurial effort is still in evidence. Perky's Bat Tower contribution is still standing strong.

The lodge itself has a 1970's motel veneer, not unlike hundreds you'll see up and down the Overseas Highway,

but never judge this accommodation by its cover. Big mistake. Everything the lodge offers its guests is just why you come to the Keys. Local flavor, laid-back, backcountry mangrove flats vistas from every room, fishing, diving, pool, comfort and a real insider connection with all things Keys. The lodge has remained faithful to the property's long history of being associated with fishing by maintaining its original funky marina. Several fishing guides, including legend, and many times tournament champion, Captain Tim Carlile (see profile), keep their flats boat there.

After a day fishing for permit, sharks, cobia, bonefish, mangrove snapper and tarpon, or whatever Tim puts you on, you'll welcome a stop for a cold one. You find that delight at the always breeze-cooled, open-air Tiki Bar nestled between buildings on the lodge grounds. No bar in the Keys offers up more character than the Tiki. Here there are true renegades of thought. They come from miles away, or just down the road, to percolate up their thoughts on all manner of subjects, but always accounts of engagements with fish and nature. The collection includes: local writers, a guru yoga instructor, a historian, artists, business owners, guides, mechanics, fishermen, clerks, an engineer, a lawyer, a publisher and lodge guests. Lloyd Good, himself, serves as mediator. At the Tiki Bar your participation is almost unavoidable because this delightfully engaging collection of Lower Keys personalities welcomes it. Hemingway and Joe Russell, we're sure, would forego Sloppy Joe's for Sugar Loaf's Tiki Bar if they were alive today.

Sugar Loaf's restaurant has not been a secret for 30 years. It's well worth a timed stop for dinner, even if you are not able to be a lodge guest. During the season make a reservation. The fish, lobster (in season) and shrimp dishes are beyond fresh, they were swimming only hours before.

If you need to pick up some grocery or notion items in the morning there's a general store on the lodge property. Make it a priority to investigate. The store is also Sugarloaf Key's post office and, most curiously, a tire repair shop. Step inside and you can blink yourself right into a 1940's Bogart movie. Speaking of which, the films, *True Lies* (Arnold Schwarzenegger) and *Drop Zone* (Wesley Snipes) had many scenes shot on Sugar Loaf Lodge's airport. Its air strip was also used to shoot the opening scenes of the James Bond movie, *License To Kill*. A sign with the name chosen for the airport by the films writers, Cray Cay, still hangs on the outside of the airport office. Incidentally, the airport is operational, and here's where you sky dive when you're in the Keys.

The number of returning guests each year to Sugar Loaf Lodge produce the best reference; many weeks are sold out. Miriam & Lloyd Good are very much a part of the lodge's specialness, and are just about the nicest and most interesting people you'll ever meet in the Keys, or anywhere in the world.

Amenities: two tennis courts (hard and not lighted), 3,000-foot paved air strip, skydiving, Perky's Bat Tower and other historical on-property sites, miniature golf, restaurant and indoor bar, outdoor Tiki Bar, entertainment on weekends and dancing. The marina accommodates small boats, has ice, also bait and fishing guides. Don't forget the frozen-in-time general store where you can also get gas.

NOTE: If you stay at Sugar Loaf Lodge you can be in Key West at Jeffrey Cardenas' Saltwater Angler in about 25 minutes, or at the Sharpe's Sea Boots in Big Pine Key in about 20 minutes. Also, if you're up to it, the Looe Key Reef, maybe the best dive spot in the Keys, is just minutes down the road. The Good's can put you in touch with the dive shops. Also, Little Palm Island is just down the road. Sugar Loaf Lodge, MM 17 Bayside (P.O. Box 148), Sugarloaf Key, FL 333044. 800-553-6097 or 305-745-3211.

THINGS TO DO IN THE LOWER KEYS

Once you cross the Seven Mile Bridge you're in the Lower Keys, and the real estate is decidedly different, so are the people and so is the flora and the fauna. People who live in the Lower Keys consider the Upper Keys to be mainland Florida, and themselves the real Conchs. The Lower Keys are less inhabited and less fished. Everyone tending to be more pioneer in thought and less estranged from the strange, but paradoxically, more opinionated. It's old-time Keys here in every way. Characters abound. The National Key Deer Refuge, Looe Key National Marine Sanctuary, and the Great White Heron Wildlife Refuge are all part of the Lower Keys. All of the latter, spectacular encouragements for enjoying being alone with nature.

NATIONAL KEY DEER REFUGE, AND WATSON TRAIL

NOTE: See the history chapter for more on the National Key Deer Refuge, Mr. Watson and Watson Trail.

PHOTO BY MALTZ

Top: Sugar Loaf Lodge from the air, looking north-north-west, towards the backcountry and Gulf of Mexico.

Left: Lloyd and Miriam Good, Sugar Loaf Lodge's owners, at the always conversation rich and congenial Tiki Bar.

Do not speed in Big Pine Key. Protecting the heritage of the key deer is taken seriously by law-enforcement personnel. Road kill accounts for most of the deaths of these smaller-than-a-great-Dane deer.

The Watson Trail is 2/3 of a mile long, and well marked. The trail winds its way through pinelands where the key deer are found. These diminutive creatures are not found anywhere else in the world. They are cousins of the whitetailed deer, trapped here during the Wisconsin glacial period, when the waters receded. Their now-toy-size stature is all part of a Darwinian evolution due to sparseness and a limited variety of food. You find Watson Trail 1.3 miles north of the intersection of Key Deer and Watson boulevards. You'll probably see deer on the drive in, and none while walking. There is also the Manillo Trail which winds through wetlands and rocklands. Here you will see at least evidence of deer much more easily. National Key Deer Refuge and Watson Trail, MM30.5 Bayside, Key Deer Blvd., Big Pine, FL. 305-872-2239

SIDEBAR: No Name Pub, it's everything the Keys once were noted for, a total do-drop-out place. A tough place to find. When you're in Big Pine, turn onto Watson Blvd. At the light (MM30), bear right onto Wilder Road. At stop sign, turn right and go over bridge. The pub will come up on your left, without familiar neon signage. Enter, and you are in the yester-world of the Keys. Beer comes in bottles, there is very good pizza, a jukebox, dollar bills (more than you can imagine) adorn the walls, and each has a hand written message. At the No Name Pub, no grip on the day is required.

THE BLUE HOLE

You find the Blue Hole 1.25 miles north of the intersection of Key Deer and Watson boulevards. The Blue Hole has 2 alligators as residents, and if you're lucky, you'll see one or both. The water hole always has ducks in it and wading birds around it, which leads one to believe that's what the gators dine on. These two alligators are the only known to be living in the Keys. The Blue Hole, MM30.5 Bayside, Key Deer Blvd., Big Pine, FL. 305-872-2239

KEY WEST: MANY CHOICES

In Key West there are several excellent hotels and resorts, and there are so many B&B's or guest houses that you could stay at a new one every night for a month and never come near exhausting the possibilities. There are also many motels, almost all are run-of-the-mill. If Key West is your fishing destination, then you will be a lot happier if you choose to be within walking distance of Old Town (historic area). The Saltwater Angler is also right there in "Old Town." Parking in Key West (Old Town) is torture if you're

Key deer, smaller than a great dane. Please do not feed the deer.

not a hotel/resort guest there. If you stay outside of the Old Town area make taxis your mode of transportation. Most of what you'll find to do in Key West (dine, shop or attractions) will be in or very near Old Town.

KEY WEST AND FOOD

Key West is separate from the rest of the Keys, and culinary distinction is very much a part of that. For over 500 years, Key West has been a melting pot of herbs, spices, oils and food-preparation techniques. All brought to it by a world of influences and, today, that simmering pours out as one of the world's most brilliant smorgasbord of flavors. Although possessing a cuisine of its own, an influence of Bahamian Conch, African and Cuban, it is the wider international inheritance that provides the gustatory smack. Few cities in the world can boast of such flavorful variety, and none so small as Key West. Its always having 150 or so restaurants on tap is a tribute to Key West's dedication to food and its success as one of the world's great gastronomical meccas. If you stay in Key West proper (Old Town area), you will have the luxury of not having to get in your car to restaurant shop; always a positive in the old city. Also, you get the chance to walk and sample the whole Key West scene, as well as preview sidewalk-displayed menus. Several excellent restaurants are outside Old Town. We strongly suggest you travel intra-Key West by taxi.

Dinner in Key West is an affair. Reservations are always in order. To get the full effect of Key West, reserve some time for sunset at Mallory Square. There's a sunset ritual that includes a drum roll and applause. It's something you should not leave without trying, at least you can say you did it. Hors d' oeuvres, a margarita and sunset in Key West could not help but start any evening off on the right foot. If you can throw in a hand rolled, locally-made Cuban cigar, you're there. There is nothing like these combinations at sunset to help expand the day's fishing memories.

Note: Duval Street is pronounced Do Vall. A 'Conch' is someone who can trace ancestry to Bahamian roots. Bahamians came to the Keys, lived off harvesting and eating conch meat, which makes it all logical. Nowadays, having been born in the Keys qualifies one as a Conch.

KEY WEST BARS AND NIGHTLIFE

Everybody drinks a lot here. Key West is a hard-hitter's town. Hemingway, and the publicity he attracted, made famous the residents' already in-place predilection for it, and his. Bars occupy a lot of square footage in Key West. Nightlife in Key West is an all-day thing. The crowd that makes it happen, aside from the imported tourist variety, move from one watering hole to the next during the day and, magically, replacements fill their departed stools. Obviously, there are shifts, subscriptions or an insider's coupon system. Breakfast kicks off serious cocktail hour, and it rolls into night without too much tribute, except for the sunset ritual at Mallory Square. Bar life is a seriously-taken vocation for some. Professional Key West drinkers are friendly, engaging and practiced at delivering their tall tales to the willing ear of any out-for-the-day, carousing tourist. These dedicated men and women add to the party atmosphere that holds sway here 365 days a year, stopping only for Category 3 hurricanes, maybe. Serious nightlife entertainment has a paradoxical shortfall in Key West unless you can catch Jimmy Buffett singing for his dinner at Louie's Backyard, but that's unlikely as he now lives in a *palazzo* on the mainland. There are, of course, several roadside military-base beer halls with pool tables, stale popcorn, lard sandwiches, and terribly uninteresting fist fights. All produced and directed by 130-pound teenagers unable to properly digest beer and defend democracy at the same time. Then there are the usual Caribbean stabs at steel drums and Reggae. Rounding it all out are a few piano bars. Actually, the latter format has some rather decent examples. Serious daily entertainment is just not part of the charm equation in Key West. There are, however, several gay review places that are entertaining in very small doses. There are also several DJ dance and disco places that are encouraging for single meat hunters. In addition, there are a smattering of decent jazz happening places. There just seems to be too much good fishing, diving, boating, sightseeing, food and a far too serious a carousing schedule to be had here for anyone to be bothered with serious entertainment, or so it seems.

Legitimate theater during the season is, however, excellent, and events that are literary in direction are world class. Also, the list of past and present authors of note, those that now live in Key West, previously lived there, now winter, or did winter there, is staggering. Key West, for pure quality of writers, is the equal of New York and LA. Key West's total population is miniscule in comparison to either of the latter.

> ### TIDBITS
>
> A WORD OF CAUTION
>
> All good nautical navigation charts have marked indicators predicting current speed, tide depth of water, show channels, buoy markers and where inlets and outlets are found. These maps also inform you of bottom depth at low tide. However, never bet on any nautical map in the Keys backcounty as tide entrapment is an unhappy affair. When night falls, the wee mosquitoes arrive to dine, and even an old salty-dog can be brought to tears.

NOTE: You might want to recheck your schedule if you are planning a fly-fishing trip to Key West during college spring-break time. The place hums 24 hours a day when thousands of 19-year-old college kids converge on it to show off non-silicone enhanced shapes, act on libidos, put their organs in gear and try out intoxication. Key West gets taxed physically, and its service personnel can get grumpy by the whole of it. Anyone out of the testosterone loop might want to avoid it.

KEY WEST: INNS, B&BS AND GUEST HOUSES

We barely touch on all the accommodation possibilities in Key West. One thing, however, is certain here: You can find what you like based on your needs. We suggest you contact the Key West Chamber of Commerce, Mallory Square, Key West, FL 33040. 305-294-2587 or 800-648-6269 and www.fla-keys.com or use the guide book. *The Insiders' Guide to the Florida Keys & Key West* (be sure you have a current edition).

THE BANYAN RESORT

The Banyan Resort is a time share of the most unusual kind, with some units also condos. There are 38 units in 8 Victorian-period houses. Each with independent architectural character. One house was a cigar factory, and five of the houses are on the national registry of historic homes. Very expensive, but decidedly a fabulous stay. Every unit has a kitchen, private bath and patio. The rates are governed by the size of the unit you occupy. You cannot do much better if you've got the bucks. The banyan trees on the property are quite magical. The Banyan Resort, 323 Whitehead St. Key West, FL. 305-296-7786 or 800-853-9937 and www.banyanresort.com.

CENTER COURT HISTORIC INN & COTTAGES

Owner and proprietor Naomi Van Steelandt proudly presides over her award-winning restorations of a main building and several cigar-maker cottages. This property is a perfect Key West headquarters. The property is tucked away on a lane just one block off Duval Street, but it's miles away in feel. Center Court Historic Inn & Cottages, 916 Center St., Key West, FL. 305-296-9292 or 800-797-8787 and www.centercourtkw.com.

THE GARDENS HOTEL

Bill and Corina Hettinger fully restored this 1870's property, which opened for business in 1993. There are 17 units, two of which are suites. It is not an inexpensive stay. It is, however, beautiful and comfortable. The Gardens is listed on the National Register of Historic Places, and also listed as a member of the Small Luxury Hotels of the World. A stay here will not be regretted. The Gardens Hotel, 526 Angela St., Key West, FL. 305-294-2661 or 800-526-2664 and www.gardenshotel.com.

KEY WEST RESORTS: PIER HOUSE RESORT & CARIBBEAN SPA

The Pier House is everything a grand hotel should be.

Gulfside adds to the charm. The Pier House is always busy and its guest list is rich with celebrities: John Travolta, Liz Taylor, Truman Capote, Tennessee Williams, Margaux Hemingway and Jimmy Buffet, to name a few. At the Pier House, there are plenty of bars to enjoy after being pampered at the full-service spa, or working out at the state-of-the-art fitness center. The Chart Room, our favorite, is classy and expensive, but a terrific spot for cocktails, nibbles and watching the wanna-bes perform. There's always a talkative and, most of the time, interesting crowd. June Keith, in her book, *Key West and the Florida Keys* (1997), said, ". . . Pier House has attracted the fat Miami cigar smoking nouveau rich." Well, June, they're still there: fifties, fat, gold everything, talk to the entire room on their cell phones and dress, head to toe, in passe designer black. Pier House Resort & Caribbean Spa, 1 Duval St. 305-296-4600 or 800-327-8340 and www.pierhouse.com.

WYNDHAM CASA MARINA RESORT AND BEACH HOUSE

This hotel is Henry Flagler's 1918 flagship endeavor to bring tourists to Key West. It is also a historic landmark. A Gatsby kind of place that was, from the get-go, suited for the rich and famous: Astors, Vanderbilts, Al Jolson, Lou Gehrig, President Harry S. Truman, Gregory Peck and many more like them signing the guest register. It was the place to stay, and still is. The elegant yesteryear ambience of the whole place is still intact, giving your stay its old Key West feel. You can even play tennis on lighted courts. If it's a grand Key West stand you wish to make, then you've arrived on memory lane. Wyndham Casa Marina Resort and Beach House, 1500 Reynolds Street, Key West, FL. 305-296-3535 or 800-626-0777. NOTE: There are many more nice places to stay in Key West. We suggest you contact the Key West Chamber of Commerce, Mallory Square, Key West, FL 33040. 305-294-2587 or 800-648-6269 and www.fla-keys.com

THINGS TO DO IN KEY WEST

Key West is another world. Almost every sight and sound unfamiliar. The people that make it tick, other than the tourists, are themselves unfamiliar, even in the way they look, think and breathe. Everyone we've ever met who lived there and then moved away says the exact same thing, "It's not the same anymore." Oddly, that's what Hemingway said in 1939. What's true then is that Key West is constantly reinventing itself, just as it always has.

MONROE COUNTY LIBRARY

Knowing that every writer who lives in Key West enters its doors makes this a hollowed place. Tom Hambright, a walking encyclopedia of historical facts on the Keys, Monroe County and Key West, heads up the extensive local history section. The local history section has a very large collection of books, rare photos and documents. The library is a Florida Keys researcher's dream come true, and Tom couldn't be more helpful. Monroe County Library, Mary Hill Russell Branch, 700 Fleming St., Key West, FL. 305-292-3595.

AUDUBON HOUSE & TROPICAL GARDENS

John James Audubon never set foot in the Audubon House. He was in Key West 12 years before the wrecker, Captain John Geiger, built the house. Nonetheless, Audubon was a good friend of the Geigers. Eighteen of Audubon's original lithographs are on display, which were all drawn while he was in the Keys. The earphone tour is more about Geiger. The marvelous gardens are worth the admission fee: under $10. Audubon House, 205 Whitehead St., Key West, FL. 305 294 2116 or www.audubonhouse.com.

KEY WEST SHIPWRECK HISTOREUM

Wrecker, Captain Watlington's mansion, is billed as the oldest house in Key West (1835). It stayed in his family for 135 years until it was donated to the state in 1974. The museum is a walk back in time to the wrecking hay days of Key West. Plenty of photos and items confiscated from ship wrecks produce a true look at history. Key West Shipwreck Historeum, 1 Whitehead St, Key West, FL. 305-292-8990 or www.historictours.com.

HEMINGWAY HOUSE AND MUSEUM

Wrecker Asa Tift built the original version of this house back in 1851, but Pauline, Hemingway's wife, extensively remodeled it. The pool, which she had put in, was the first in Key West. From the pool house, which Pauline also masterminded, Ernest Hemingway wrote: *For Whom the Bell Tolls, Death in the Afternoon, The Green Hills of Africa*, and *To Have and Have Not*. Hemingway lived in the house from 1931 to 1939. The tour is worth the price of admission, and if you love cats you are in cat heaven. Hemingway House and Museum, 907 Whitehead St., Key West, FL. 305-294-1575 or www.hemingwayhome.com.

KEY WEST LIGHTHOUSE MUSEUM

The Lighthouse sits right across the street in front of the Hemingway House and provides a nice bird's-eye view of Key West from 90 feet up. There are 88 steps to climb. Admission fee. Key West Lighthouse Museum, 938 Whitehead St. Key West, FL. 305-294-0012 or www.kwahs@aol.com.

MEL FISHER MARITIME HERITAGE SOCIETY AND MUSEUM

Most know the story of salvage diver Mel Fisher who, on July 20th of 1985, found the mother-lode of all sunken treasure. He recovered over $400,000,000 worth of gold and silver from the *Nuestra Senora de Atocha*. The Spanish ship went down loaded with its spoils from the New World while on its way back to Spain. Don't miss this stop, its extraordinary. Admission fee. Mel Fisher Maritime Museum, 200 Greene St., Key West, FL. 305-294-2633.

KEY WEST CITY CEMETERY

Strange place, but so is Key West. The tombstones help the legend along. The makers and shakers are there, and so are the notorious, along with the flakes. You can take a self-guided tour with the help of a pamphlet. The pamphlet you'll need is distributed at the library or at the Chamber of Commerce. You can also take a guided tour, which is worth scheduling. No charge. Don't forget to ask about Elena Hoyos and Count von Cosel. Wow! Key West City Cemetery, Frances and Olive Sts. and Windsor Lane, Key West, FL. 305-292-8177 and for tour information 305-294-8380.

FLAGLER STATION OVER-SEA RAILWAY HISTOREUM

A must stop for history buffs. Memorabilia and artifacts galore, and a film, *The Day the Train Arrived*. The museum provides an insightful look at one our nations engineering marvels. A feat, in scale, equal to the Panama Canal. Flagler Station Over-Sea Railway Historeum, 901 Caroline St, Key West, FL. 305-295-3562 or www.historictours.com

DRY TORTUGAS NATIONAL PARK

Do not miss any window of opportunity in your schedule to take in the Dry Tortugas, which is only accessed by boat or plane. Opt for a plane. The Tortugas, named by Ponce de Leon for its multitude of turtles (tortugas), is where you'll find another screwed-up government project. Fort Jefferson never fired a shot and began sinking the day construction started. The fort was not built on coral rock, but sand. Fort Jefferson was never finished, but hundreds of workers lost their lives to diseases. It housed only Civil War deserters, a few bad boys and a doctor who set an assassin's broken leg. You can camp out there (Garden Key), no thanks. For sanctioned and insured services to the Dry Tortugas use the phone number below or online at www.nps.gov/drto. Dry Tortugas National Park, National Park Service, Key West, FL. 305-242-7700 or 800-368-4753.

NOTE: There are many, many more interesting places to visit in Key West, such as: Curry Mansion, East Martello Museum, Robert Frost Cottage, and The Key West Museum of Art and History. There are plenty of walking tours. Also, Harry Truman's White House Museum, which is flawlessly restored to its 1948 state. President Truman spent 175 days here, and Presidents Eisenhower and Kennedy also visited. For more about Key West, you can contact the Key West Chamber of Commerce, Mallory Square, Key West, FL 33040. 305 294 2587 or 800 -648-6269 and www.fla-keys. com. Or use the guide book, *The Insiders' Guide To The Florida Keys & Key West.*

Diane Rome Peebles
Spiny Lobster

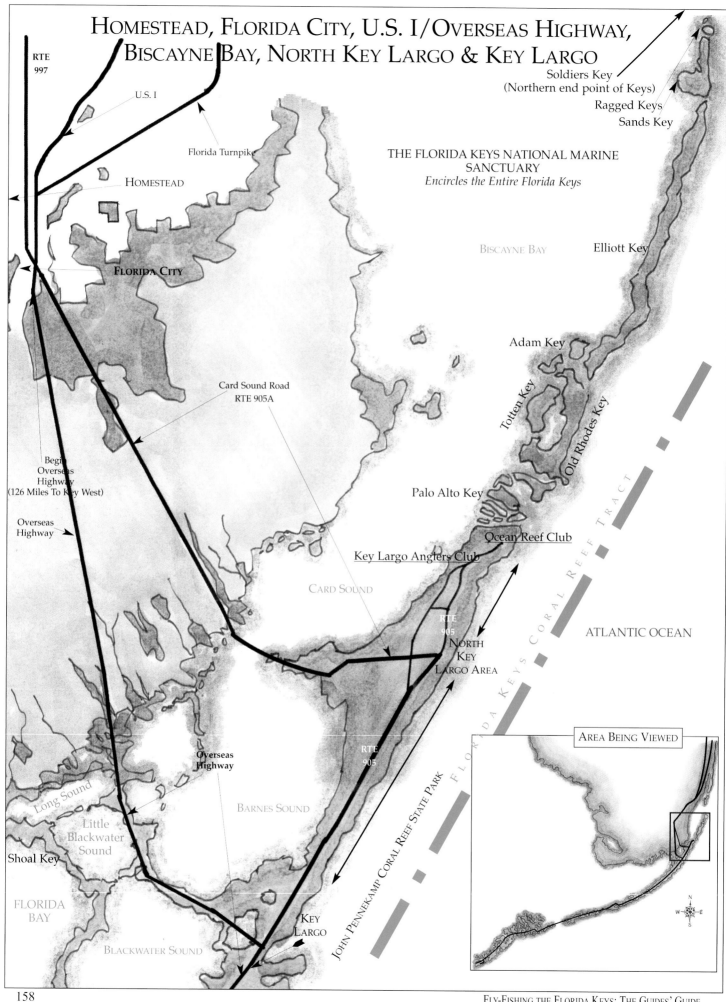

HOMESTEAD, FLORIDA CITY, U.S. I/OVERSEAS HIGHWAY, BISCAYNE BAY, NORTH KEY LARGO & KEY LARGO

RTE 997

U.S. I

Florida Turnpike

HOMESTEAD

FLORIDA CITY

THE FLORIDA KEYS NATIONAL MARINE SANCTUARY
Encircles the Entire Florida Keys

Soldiers Key
(Northern end point of Keys)
Ragged Keys
Sands Key

BISCAYNE BAY

Elliott Key

Adam Key

Card Sound Road
RTE 905A

Totten Key

Old Rhodes Key

Begin Overseas Highway
(126 Miles To Key West)

Overseas Highway

Palo Alto Key

Ocean Reef Club

Key Largo Anglers Club

CARD SOUND

RTE 905

NORTH KEY LARGO AREA

ATLANTIC OCEAN

FLORIDA KEYS CORAL REEF TRACT

Long Sound

Overseas Highway

BARNES SOUND

Little Blackwater Sound

Shoal Key

FLORIDA BAY

JOHN PENNEKAMP CORAL REEF STATE PARK

AREA BEING VIEWED

Key Largo

BLACKWATER SOUND

N
W E
S

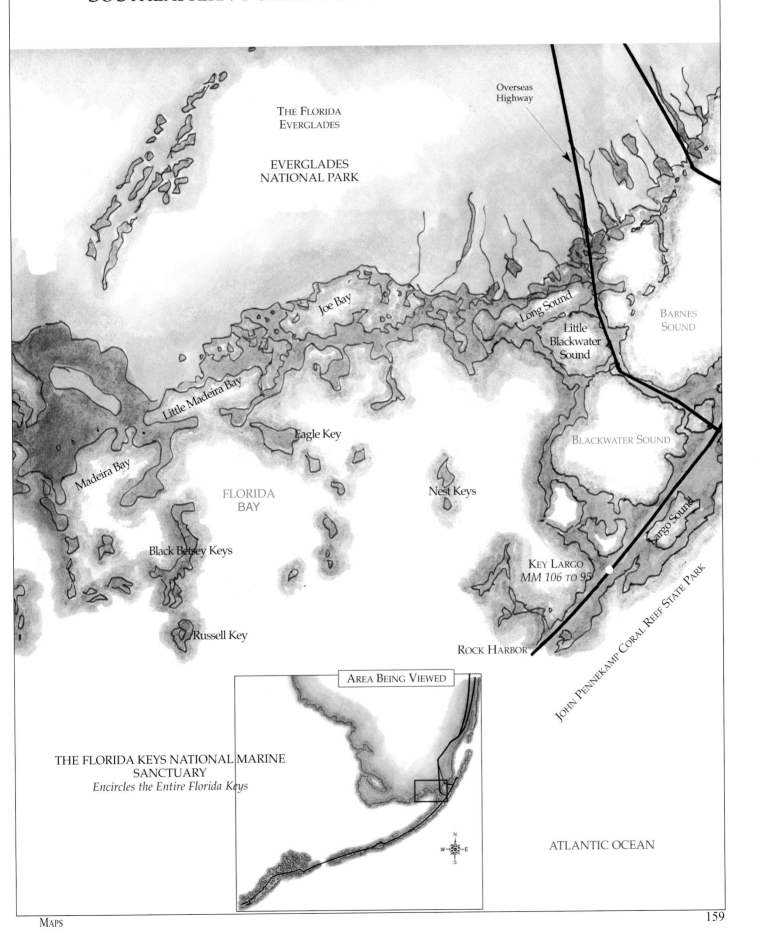

FLORIDA BAY, KEY LARGO TO ROCK HARBOR AND SOUTHEASTERN PORTION OF THE FLORIDA EVERGLADES

Overseas
Highway

THE FLORIDA
EVERGLADES

EVERGLADES
NATIONAL PARK

Joe Bay

Long Sound

BARNES
SOUND

Little
Blackwater
Sound

Little Madeira Bay

Eagle Key

BLACKWATER SOUND

Madeira Bay

Nest Keys

FLORIDA
BAY

Largo Sound

Black Betsey Keys

KEY LARGO
MM 106 TO 95

JOHN PENNEKAMP CORAL REEF STATE PARK

Russell Key

ROCK HARBOR

AREA BEING VIEWED

THE FLORIDA KEYS NATIONAL MARINE
SANCTUARY
Encircles the Entire Florida Keys

N
W E
S

ATLANTIC OCEAN

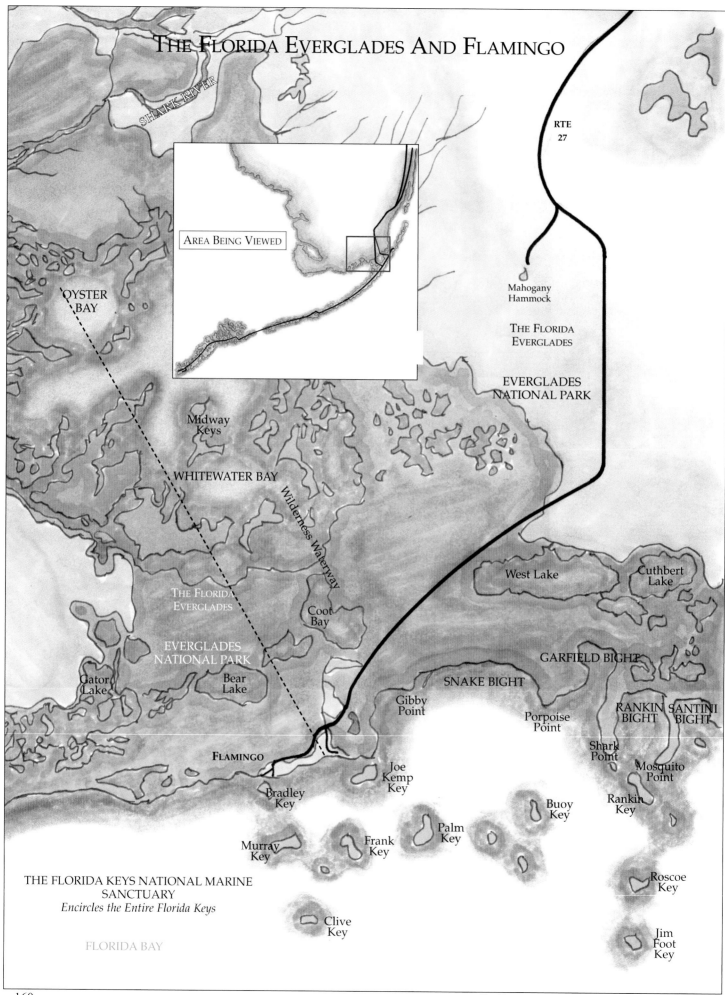

The Florida Everglades And Flamingo

SHARK RIVER

AREA BEING VIEWED

RTE 27

OYSTER BAY

Mahogany Hammock

The Florida Everglades

EVERGLADES NATIONAL PARK

Midway Keys

WHITEWATER BAY

Wilderness Waterway

West Lake

Cuthbert Lake

The Florida Everglades

Coot Bay

EVERGLADES NATIONAL PARK

GARFIELD BIGHT

Gator Lake

Bear Lake

SNAKE BIGHT

RANKIN BIGHT

SANTINI BIGHT

Gibby Point

Porpoise Point

Shark Point

Mosquito Point

FLAMINGO

Joe Kemp Key

Bradley Key

Buoy Key

Rankin Key

Murray Key

Frank Key

Palm Key

THE FLORIDA KEYS NATIONAL MARINE SANCTUARY
Encircles the Entire Florida Keys

Roscoe Key

Clive Key

Jim Foot Key

FLORIDA BAY

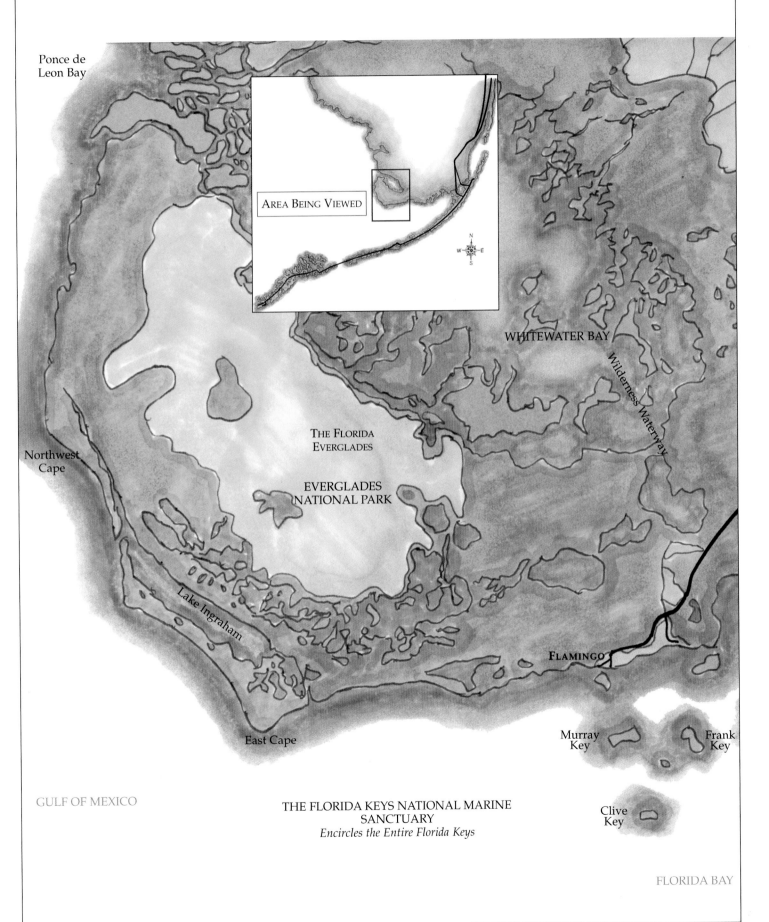

THE FLORIDA EVERGLADES TO CAPE SABLE

Ponce de
Leon Bay

AREA BEING VIEWED

N
W · E
S

WHITEWATER BAY

Wilderness Waterway

THE FLORIDA
EVERGLADES

EVERGLADES
NATIONAL PARK

Northwest
Cape

Lake Ingraham

FLAMINGO

East Cape

Murray
Key

Frank
Key

GULF OF MEXICO

THE FLORIDA KEYS NATIONAL MARINE
SANCTUARY
Encircles the Entire Florida Keys

Clive
Key

FLORIDA BAY

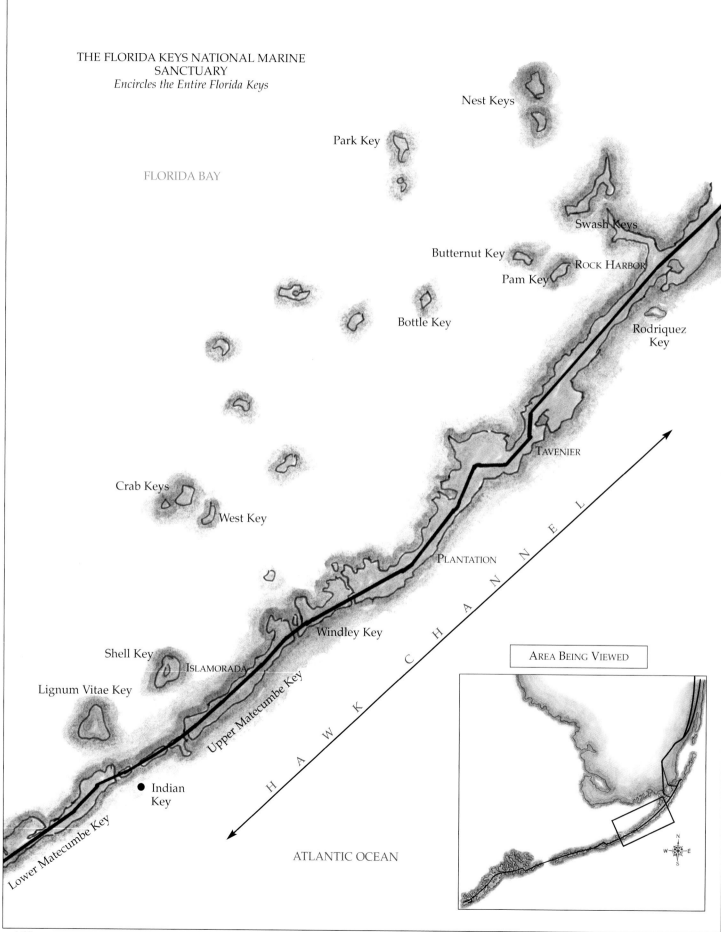

Rock Harbor To Lower Matecumbe

THE FLORIDA KEYS NATIONAL MARINE
SANCTUARY
Encircles the Entire Florida Keys

FLORIDA BAY

Nest Keys

Park Key

Swash Keys

Butternut Key

Rock Harbor

Pam Key

Bottle Key

Rodriquez
Key

Tavenier

Crab Keys

West Key

Plantation

Windley Key

Shell Key

Islamorada

Upper Matecumbe Key

Lignum Vitae Key

HAWK CHANNEL

Indian
Key

Lower Matecumbe Key

ATLANTIC OCEAN

AREA BEING VIEWED

N
W · E
S

CRAIG KEY TO MARATHON

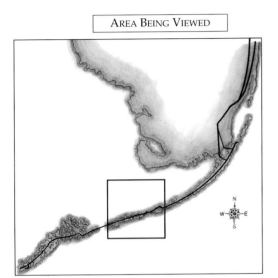

Barnes Key

Upper Arsnicker Key

Lower Arsnicker Key

Craig Key

FLORIDA BAY

THE FLORIDA KEYS NATIONAL MARINE
SANCTUARY
Encircles the Entire Florida Keys

Craig Key

LAYTON

Long Key Viaduct

Long Key
(State Recreation Area)

Grassy Key

Duck Key

Crawl Key

Vaca Key

Marathon Shores

Key Colony Beach

H A W K   C H A N N E L

MARATHON

Boat Key

ATLANTIC OCEAN

Seven Mile Bridge To Cudjoe Key

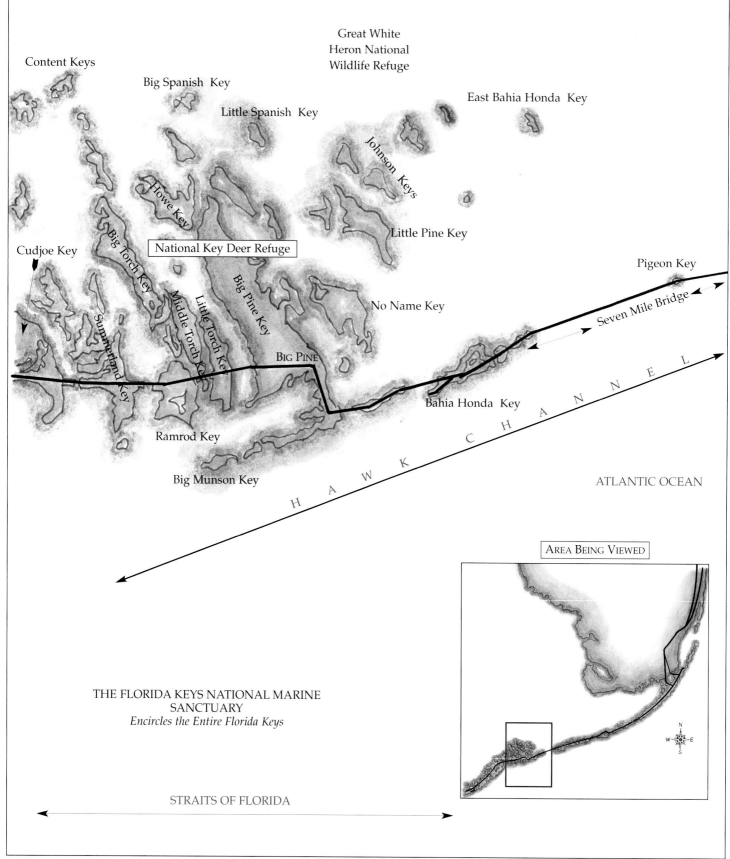

Great White
Heron National
Wildlife Refuge

Content Keys

Big Spanish Key

Little Spanish Key

East Bahia Honda Key

Johnson Keys

Howe Key

Little Pine Key

National Key Deer Refuge

Cudjoe Key

Big Torch Key

Big Pine Key

Pigeon Key

Middle Torch Key

Little Torch Key

No Name Key

Seven Mile Bridge

Summerland Key

Big Pine

Ramrod Key

Bahia Honda Key

H A W K   C H A N N E L

Big Munson Key

ATLANTIC OCEAN

Area Being Viewed

N
W   E
S

THE FLORIDA KEYS NATIONAL MARINE
SANCTUARY
Encircles the Entire Florida Keys

STRAITS OF FLORIDA

CUDJOE KEY TO KEY WEST

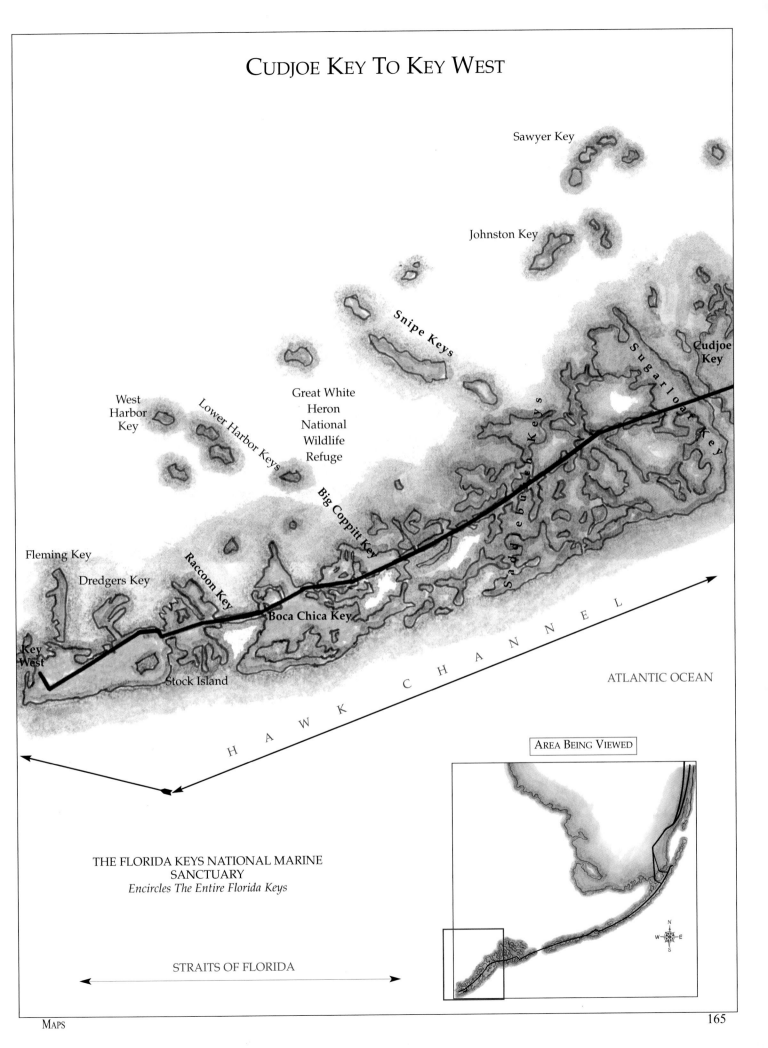

Sawyer Key

Johnston Key

Snipe Keys

Cudjoe Key

Sugarloaf Key

West Harbor Key

Lower Harbor Keys

Great White Heron National Wildlife Refuge

Saddlebunch Keys

Big Coppitt Key

Fleming Key

Raccoon Key

Dredgers Key

Boca Chica Key

Key West

Stock Island

HAWK CHANNEL

ATLANTIC OCEAN

AREA BEING VIEWED

N
W E
S

THE FLORIDA KEYS NATIONAL MARINE SANCTUARY
Encircles The Entire Florida Keys

STRAITS OF FLORIDA

Marquesas Keys And The Dry Tortugas

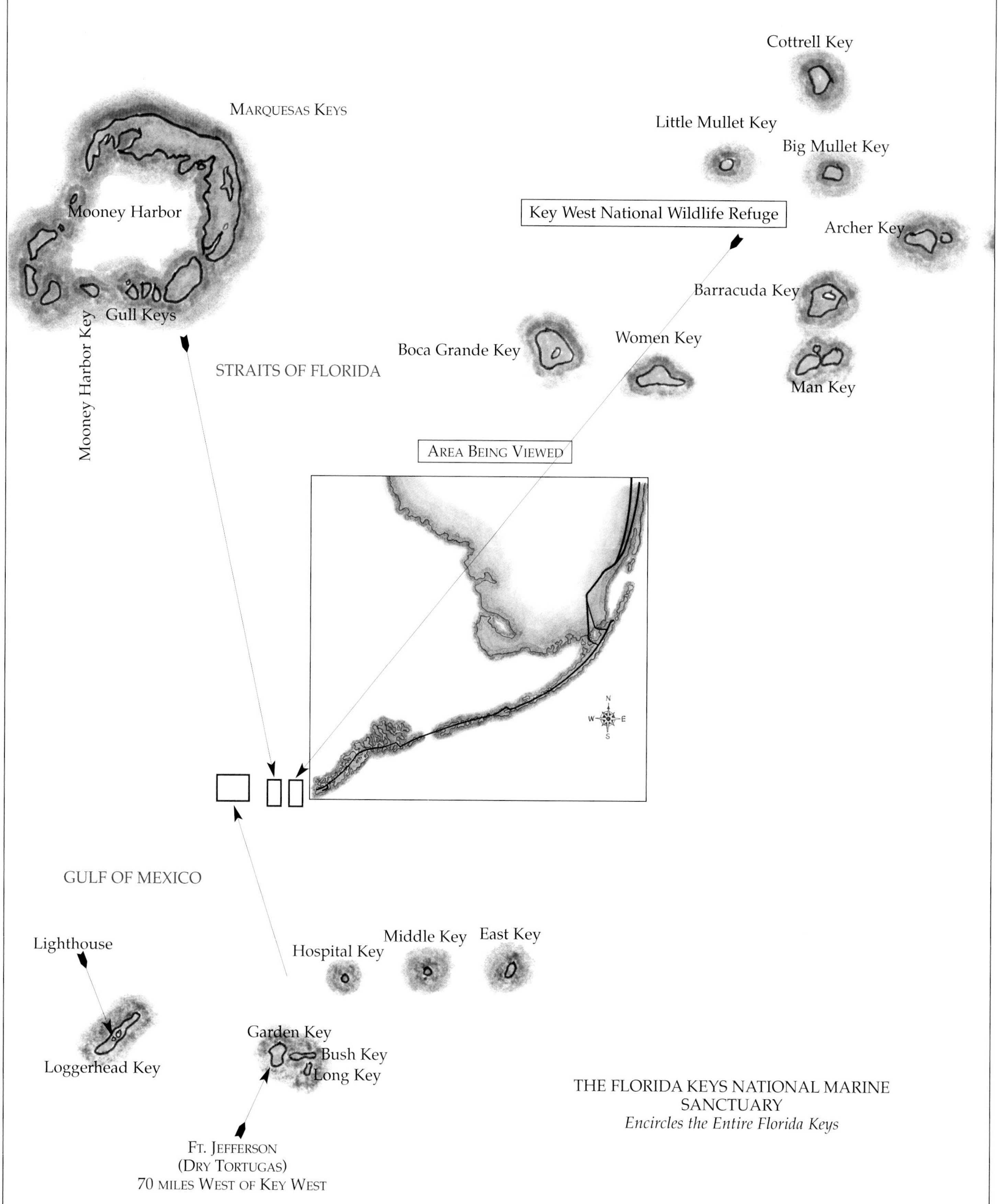

Cottrell Key

Little Mullet Key

Big Mullet Key

Marquesas Keys

Key West National Wildlife Refuge

Archer Key

Mooney Harbor

Barracuda Key

Gull Keys

Straits Of Florida

Boca Grande Key

Women Key

Man Key

Mooney Harbor Key

Area Being Viewed

Gulf Of Mexico

Lighthouse

Middle Key

East Key

Hospital Key

Loggerhead Key

Garden Key

Bush Key

Long Key

THE FLORIDA KEYS NATIONAL MARINE
SANCTUARY
Encircles the Entire Florida Keys

Ft. Jefferson
(Dry Tortugas)
70 miles West of Key West

Key West, Marquesas & Dry Tortugas

DRY TORTUGAS
West of the Marquesa Keys (44 miles)

(70 miles from Key West)

Key West National
Wildlife Refuge

Key West

Overseas Highway (U.S. I)
Ends @ MM 0

MARQUESA KEYS
Just west of Key West
(26 miles from Key West)

MAP ILLUSTRATIONS COURTESY OF
FRANK ZORMAN
Maps Not To Scale

BIBLIOGRAPHY

BOOKS

—*Fish Florida: Saltwater/Better Than Luck-The Fool Proof Guide to Florida Saltwater Fishing*
by Boris Arnov

—*Fly Fishing for Dummies*
by Peter Kaminsky. 1998

—*Fly-Fishing for Bonefish*
by Chico Fernandez, Aaron J. Adams. 2004

—*Practical Fishing Knots*
by Mark Sosin, Lefty Kreh. 1991

—*The Longest Silence: A Life in Fishing*
by Thomas McGuane. 1999

—*Fly Fishing for Bonefish, Permit, and Tarpon*
by Lefty Kreh. 2002

—*Fly Fishing in Saltwater*
by Lefty Kreh. 2003

—*Fly Fishing for Bonefish*
by Dick Brown. 2003

—*Fly Fishing: Saltwater Basics*
by C. Boyd Pfeiffer, Dave Hall. 1999

—*Saltwater Fly Fishing*
by Jack Samson. 1991

—*Saltwater Fly Patterns*
by Lefty Kreh. 1995

—*The Fisherman's Ocean*
by David A. Ross. 2000

—*Bluewater Fly Fishing*
by Trey Combs

—*Inshore Fly Fishing*
by Lou Tabory. 1992

—*Saltwater Fly-Casting Techniques: How to Cast Effectively for the Biggest Fish and Under the Most Demanding Situations*
by Lefty Kreh. 2002

—*Pop Fleyes: Bob Popovic's Approach to Saltwater Fly Design*
by Ed Jaworowski, et al. 2001

—*West of Key West*
by John N. Cole, et al. 1996

—*Lou Tabory's Guide to Saltwater Baits and Their Imitations: An All Color Guide*
by Lou Tabory

—*Billfish on a Fly*
by Jack Samson. 1995

—*Sea Level: Adventures of a Saltwater Angler*
by Jeffrey Cardenas, Jimmy Buffett. 2002

—*Tarpon on Fly*
by Donald Larmouth. 2002

—*Permit on a Fly*
by Jack Samson. 1996

VIDEOS

—*Borski Ties Flies*

—*Lefy Kreh on Fly Casting*

—*Captain Lenny Moffo's Fly Tying Series (6)*